HAMMOND

THE WORLD ALMANAC

BOOK OF THE UNITED STATES

HAMMOND WORLD ATLAS CORPORATION

Chairman Andreas Langenscheidt

President Marc Jennings

VP of Cartography Vera Lorenz

Director Database Resources Theophrastos E. Giouvanos

Cartography Walter H. Jones Jr., Sharon Lightner, Harry E. Morin,
James Padykula, Thomas R. Rubino, Thomas J. Scheffer

Senior Editor Lori Baird

Designer Marian Purcell

Produced for Hammond World Atlas Corporation by

HYLAS PUBLISHING

129 MAIN STREET

IRVINGTON, NY 10533

WWW.HYLASPUBLISHING.COM

HYLAS PUBLISHING

Publisher Sean Moore

Publishing Director Karen Prince

Editorial Director Aaron R. Murray

Art Director Brian MacMullen

Contributing Writer Stuart A.P. Murray

Senior Editor Susan Meigs

Assistant Editor Amber Rose

Contributing Editor Suzanne Lander

Designers Brian MacMullen, Terry Egusa, Erica Lubowicki

Production Lee Bartow, Ken Crossland, Eunho Lee

Photo Researcher Ben DeWalt

Editorial Assistants Andy Lawler, Matthew Gross,
Rachel Greene, Gabrielle Kappes

ISBN-13: 978-084-370968-1

HAMMOND

THE WORLD ALMANAC

BOOK OF THE UNITED STATES

THE DEFINITIVE GUIDE TO THE
50 STATES IN FACTS, PHOTOS & MAPS

CONTENTS

Left: New Hampshire's White Mountains
Title page: A soybean field in Iowa

INTRODUCTION

North America extends from Canada's Arctic regions in the north to the tropical southern border of Mexico. The United States of America occupies the center of the North American landmass as well as the extreme northwest (Alaska) and a Pacific Ocean archipelago (Hawaii).

The 48 contiguous states reach from the North Pacific Ocean in the West to the North Atlantic in the East. The Canadian province of British Columbia is between the contiguous states and Alaska, while Hawaii is 2,000 miles southwest of California.

Founded by the uniting of the 13 colonies that threw off British rule in 1776, the United States grew westward, adding territories and eventually admitting them as states. By both purchase and conquest, territory was acquired from France, Mexico, Spain, and Russia. In addition to the 50 states, there is one federal district, Washington, D.C., and there are 14 territories in the Caribbean and Pacific.

The United States, at 3.7 million square miles, is the world's fourth largest country in total area, behind Russia, Canada, and China. With 302 million people, it is third in population, after China (1.32 billion) and India (1.13 billion).

Topography of the United States

The continental United States is composed of several main topographic regions. In the far West, the Coastal Mountains run north–south, parallel with the Pacific Coast; to their east is the basin and range region of semi-arid and arid plateaus and mountain ranges. Further eastward are the Western Highlands, which run from Alaska to Mexico and include the Rocky Mountains.

STATE GROUPINGS

In this atlas, states are described and grouped in various ways. States are sometimes identified by the natural features they share—lakes, plains, river systems, and mountains—such as the Mountain States, Plains States, and Great Lakes States; the southern Tidewater States, for instance, all have major waterways that are affected by tides.

States are also grouped by geographic region: the Northeast, Southeast, Midwest, Southwest, and Northwest. These can, in turn, again be subdivided. For example, the Northeast includes the states of New England (Maine, New Hampshire, Vermont, Massachusetts, Connecticut, and Rhode Island), the Mid-Atlantic States (New York, New Jersey, and Pennsylvania), and two Tidewater States (Delaware and Maryland). States in the Southeast may also be Tidewater States or South Atlantic States.

States can also be designated by their major crops, such as wheat or cotton, or by the products most important to their economy, such as oil. Many Midwestern states, for example, are also grouped as Grain States; Oklahoma, a Plains State, is also defined, along with Texas, Arkansas, and Louisiana, as an Oil State.

The Grand Canyon, in northwest Arizona, was carved by the Colorado River over millennia. One of America's oldest parks, Grand Canyon National Park hosts nearly 5 million visitors a year.

To the east of the Rockies is the vast central plain, extending from Canada to Texas, known as the Great Plains. The Mississippi–Missouri River system, the world's fourth largest, flows southward, draining the plains and much of the Rocky Mountain range. Above the plains and rivers of America's heartland are the five Great Lakes, the world's largest group of freshwater lakes. These inland seas drain eastward to the Atlantic through the Saint Lawrence River.

East of the Mississippi, the main topographical feature is the Eastern Highlands, which includes the Canadian Shield, an enormous plateau that stretches from the extreme northeast to Minnesota. The Appalachian Mountains are part of these highlands, running southward from eastern Canada, parallel with the Atlantic coastline, to a terminus in Georgia. East of the Appalachians is the Coastal Plain, a lowland region that is narrow in the North, widens in the South, and reaches to the Gulf of Mexico.

Cities and Population Centers

The United States ranks 172nd in the world in population density, at 80 people per square mile. Density varies greatly from state to state, with the majority of the population grouped in five main zones: the urban corridor from Boston to New York, Philadelphia, and Washington, D.C.; the states south of the Great Lakes, from western New York to Wisconsin, including Cleveland, Pittsburgh, Chicago, and Milwaukee; California's Pacific coast and southern Arizona; the metro areas of Texas, and the cities of the Florida peninsula.

The Census Bureau classifies the largest concentrations of urban populations as Metropolitan Statistical Areas (MSAs) in the United States, which can include neighboring communities across a national border. There are 50 MSAs with populations above a million. The New York–New Jersey MSA is the largest, with more than 18 million people.

The highest peak in the Blue Ridge Mountains, Grandfather Mountain boasts America's highest footbridge, at a mile above sea level, as well as a nature preserve.

GRANDFATHER MOUNTAIN
NORTH CAROLINA
ELEVATION – 5964
HIGHEST MOUNTAIN
IN THE BLUE RIDGE

MAP OF THE 50 STATES

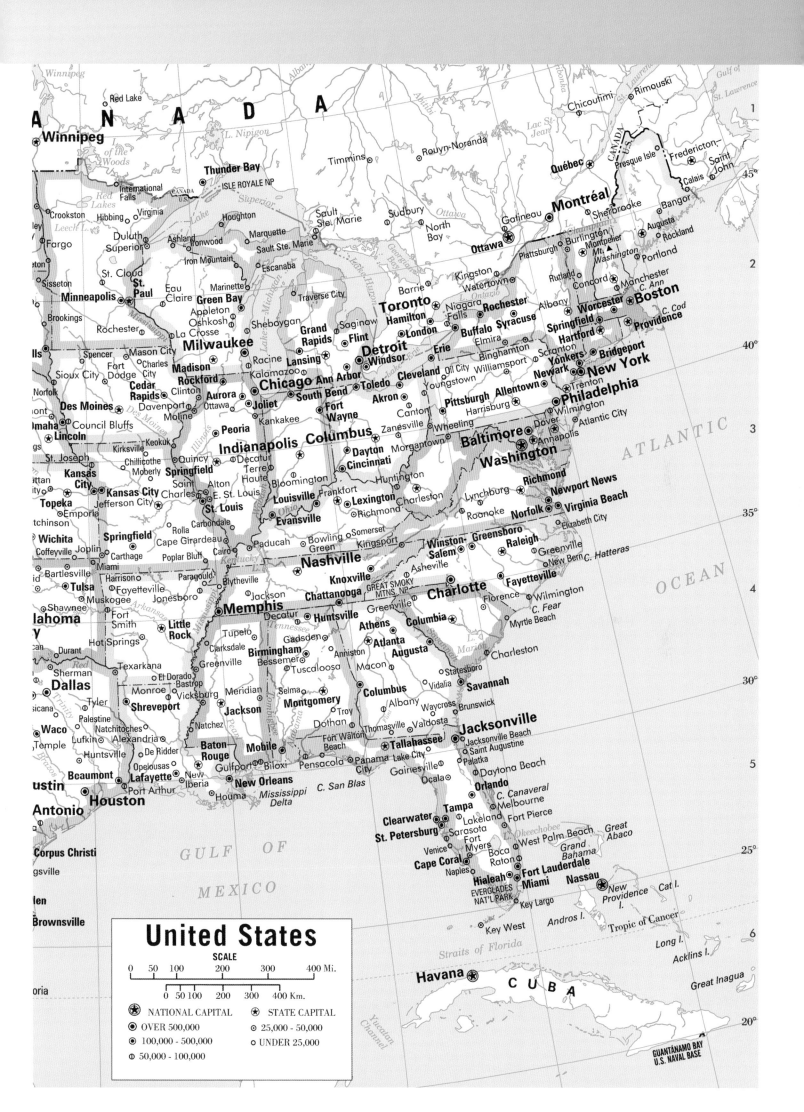

United States

SCALE

0   50   100   200   300   400 Mi.

0   50 100   200   300   400 Km.

⊛ NATIONAL CAPITAL   ⊛ STATE CAPITAL

◉ OVER 500,000   ⊙ 25,000 - 50,000

◉ 100,000 - 500,000   ○ UNDER 25,000

⊕ 50,000 - 100,000

TOPOGRAPHIC MAP

PACIFIC
OCEAN

Victoria
Mt. Baker ▲
Seattle ◉
Seattle

Spokane ◉

Mt. Rainier ▲
Portland ◉
Mt. St. Helens ▲
Salem ✦
Columbia
Eugene ◉
Mt. Hood ▲

St. Joe

Salmon

Salmon River Mts.

Boise ✦
Snake
Borah Pk. ▲

Bitterroot Range

Rocky

S. Saskatchewan
Qu'Appelle
Regina ✦

Milk

Missouri

Ft. Peck L.

Yellowstone

Granite Pk. ▲
Tongue
Powder

Mountains

Gannett Pk. ▲

Bighorn Mts.

Black Hills
Harney Pk. ▲

L. Manitoba
Wi◉

Bismarck
Missouri
L. Oahe
James
Si◉

Mt. Shasta ▲
Goose L.
Santa Rosa Range
Humboldt
Great Salt Lake
Bear L.

Laramie Mts.
Medicine Bow Mts.
Cheyenne ◉
North Platte
Niobrara

Sand Hills

Omaha
L◉

Lassen Pk. ▲
Pyramid L.
Sierra
Reno ✦
Carson City ✦
Sacramento ✦
L. Tahoe

San Francisco

San Jose

Coast
Ranges

Nevada

Reese
Great Basin

Salt Lake City ◉
Provo ◉
Wasatch Ra.

Green
Colorado
Mt. Elbert ▲
Denver ✦
Pikes Pk. ▲
Colorado Springs

S. Platte
Smoky Hill
Arkansas
Republican

Wich◉

Mt. Whitney ▲
Las Vegas ✦
L. Mead
Colorado
L. Powell
Carrizo Mts.

Cinarron

Los Angeles
Mojave Desert
Colorado
Humphreys Pk. ▲
Plateau
Painted Desert
Wheeler Pk. ▲
Rio Grande
Santa Fe
N. Canadian
Canadian

Oklahoma City ◉

San Diego
Tijuana ◉
Salton Sea
Phoenix ✦
Gila

Albuquerque ◉

Sacramento Mts.

Llano Estacado

L. T◉

PACIFIC

OCEAN

Baja California

Gulf of California

El Paso ◉
Guadalupe Pk. ▲
Pecos
Rio Grande
Davis Mts.
Stockton
Edwards Plateau
Colorado
Brazos

Fort Worth ◉
D◉

Austin ◉

San Antonio ◉

Sierra Madre Occidental
Conchos

Rio Grande

Gulf Coast

Chukchi Sea
Brooks Ra.
Yukon

St. Lawrence I.

BERING
SEA

Nunivak I.

Kuskokwim
Yukon
Tanana
Mt. McKinley ▲
Alaska Range
Anchorage ◉

Bristol Bay

Aleutian Is.
Kodiak I.
Gulf of Alaska

PACIFIC
OCEAN

0   200 MI
0   200 KM

Kauai
Niihau
Oahu
Molokai
Honolulu ✦
Lanai
Kahoolawe
Maui
Mauna Kea ▲
Hilo ◉

PACIFIC
OCEAN

Mauna Loa ▲
Hawaii

0   100 MI
0   100 KM

Sierra Madre Oriental

Winnipeg

L. of the Woods

L. Nipigon

Abitibi

Lac St-Jean

Laurentian Mts.

Québec

Montréal

Ottawa

L. Champlain

Mt. Washington

Gulf of Maine

Red Lakes

Leech L.

Mesabi Ra.

Lake Superior

Ottawa

Georgian Bay

Lake Huron

Minneapolis

St. Paul

Wisconsin

L. Ontario

Albany

Hudson

Boston

Providence

Mississippi

Lake Michigan

Toronto

Buffalo

Hartford

Sioux Falls

Milwaukee

Madison

Lansing

Detroit

Lake Erie

Allegheny

New York

Long I.

Cedar Rapids

Chicago

Cleveland

Trenton

Philadelphia

Des Moines

Des Moines

Illinois

ATLANTIC

Omaha

Lincoln

Indianapolis

Columbus

Ohio

Appalachian Mts.

Washington

Topeka

Springfield

Wabash

James

Richmond

Allegheny Mts.

Neosho

St. Louis

Ohio

Charleston

Norfolk

L. of the Ozarks

Roanoke

OCEAN

Wichita

Kentucky L.

Nashville

Blue Ridge

Raleigh

Piedmont

Ozark

Ozark Plateau

Knoxville

Tulsa

Ozark Mts.

Arkansas

Columbia

Coastal Plain

Little Rock

Memphis

Tennessee

Atlanta

Savannah

Eufaula L.

Ouachita Mts.

L. Texoma

Mississippi

Birmingham

Montgomery

Augusta

L. Marion

Red

Alabama

Flint

Dallas

Trinity

Jackson

Pearl

Tombigbee

Jacksonville

Tallahassee

Red

Baton Rouge

Mobile

Brazos

New Orleans

Orlando

Coastal Plain

Mississippi Delta

Florida Pen.

Houston

Tampa

L. Okeechobee

Grand Bahama

Great Abaco

Bahamas

GULF OF

Miami

New Providence I.

Cat I.

MEXICO

Florida Keys

Andros I.

Tropic of Cancer

Long I.

Straits of Florida

Cuba

Acklins I.

Havanah

Guantanamo

United States

SCALE

0   50   100   200   300   400 Mi.

0 50 100   200   300   400 Km.

✪ NATIONAL CAPITAL   ✶ STATE CAPITAL

◉ OVER 500,000   ⊙ 25,000 - 50,000

◉ 100,000 - 500,000   ○ UNDER 25,000

Φ 50,000 - 100,000

NATIONAL PARKS

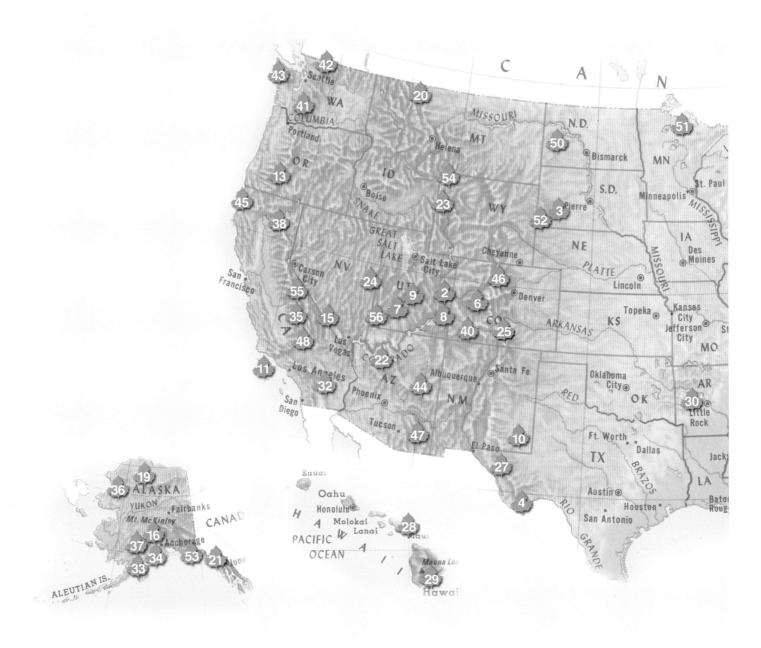

The National Park Service now administers over 84 million acres of federal land. Dates when sites were authorized for protection by Congress or by presidential proclamation are given in parentheses, followed by dates (if later) that they received their current designation or were transferred to the National Park Service.

1 ACADIA, ME
(1916/1929). 47,390 acres. Includes Mount Desert Island, half of Isle au Haut, Schoodic Peninsula on mainland.

2 ARCHES, UT
(1929/1971). 76,519 acres. Contains giant red sandstone arches and other products of erosion.

3 BADLANDS, SD
(1929/1978). 242,756 acres. Reformations and native prairie. Animal fossils 23–37 million years old.

4 BIG BEND, TX
(1935). 801,163 acres. Rio Grande, Chisos Mts.

5 BISCAYNE, FL (1968/1980). 172,971 acres. Aquatic park encompassing chain of islands south of Miami.

6 BLACK CANYON OF THE GUNNISON, CO
(1933/1999). 30,750 acres. Has a canyon 2,900 ft deep and 40 ft wide at its narrowest part.

7 BRYCE CANYON, UT
(1923/1928). 35,835 acres. Spectacularly colorful and unusual display of erosion effects.

8 CANYONLANDS, UT
(1964). 337,598 acres. At junction of Colorado and Green rivers; extensive evidence of prehistoric Indians.

9 CAPITOL REEF, UT
(1937/1971). 241,904 acres. A 70-mi uplift of sandstone cliffs dissected by high-walled gorges.

10 CARLSBAD CAVERNS, NM
(1923/1930). 46,766 acres. Largest known caverns; not yet fully explored.

11 CHANNEL ISLANDS, CA
(1938/1980). 249,561 acres. Sea lion breeding place, nesting sea birds, unique plants.

12 CONGAREE, SC
(1974/2003). 21,888 acres. Floodplain with largest region of old growth on North American continent.

13 CRATER LAKE, OR
(1902). 183,224 acres. Extraordinary blue lake in the crater of Mt. Mazama, a volcano that erupted about 7,700 years ago; deepest U.S. lake.

14 CUYAHOGA VALLEY, OH
(1974/2000). 32,861 acres. Rural landscape along Ohio and Erie Canal system between Akron and Cleveland.

15 DEATH VALLEY, CA–NV
(1933/1994). 3,372,402 acres. Large desert area. Includes the lowest point in the Western Hemisphere.

16 DENALI, AK
(1917/1980). 4,740,912 acres. Formerly Mt. McKinley National Park. Contains highest mountain in U.S.; wildlife.

17 DRY TORTUGAS, FL
(1935/1992). 64,701 acres. Formerly Fort Jefferson National Monument.

thermal waters from the park's 47 hot springs (waters used for bathing only).

31 ISLE ROYALE, MI
(1931). 571,790 acres. Largest island in Lake Superior, noted for its wilderness and wildlife.

32 JOSHUA TREE, CA
(1936/1994). 789,866 acres. Desert region of Joshua trees; other plant and animal life.

33 KATMAI, AK
(1918/1980). 3,674,530 acres. "Valley of Ten Thousand Smokes," scene of 1912 volcanic eruption.

34 KENAI FJORDS, AK
(1978/1980). 669,983 acres. Abundant marine mammals, birdlife; Harding Icefield, one of four major icecaps in the United States.

35 KINGS CANYON, CA
(1890/1940). 461,901 acres. Mountain wilderness, dominated by Kings River Canyons and High Sierra; contains giant sequoias.

36 KOBUK VALLEY, AK
(1978/1980). 1,750,717 acres. Contains geological and recreational sites. Limited federal facilities.

37 LAKE CLARK, AK
(1978/1980). 2,619,733 acres. Across Cook Inlet from Anchorage. A scenic wilderness rich in fish and wildlife. Limited federal facilities.

38 LASSEN VOLCANIC, CA
(1907/1916). 106,372 acres. Contains Lassen Peak, recently active volcano, and other volcanic phenomena.

39 MAMMOTH CAVE, KY
(1926/1941). 52,830 acres. 144 mi of surveyed underground passages, beautiful natural formations, river 300 ft below surface.

40 MESA VERDE, CO
(1906). 52,122 acres. Most notable and best preserved prehistoric cliff dwellings in the United States.

41 MOUNT RAINIER, WA
(1899). 235,625 acres. Greatest single-peak glacial system in the United States.

42 NORTH CASCADES, WA
(1968). 504,781 acres. Spectacular mountainous region with glaciers, lakes.

43 OLYMPIC, WA
(1909/1938). 922,651 acres. Mountain wilderness with finest remnant of Pacific Northwest rain forest, active glaciers, Pacific shoreline, rare elk.

44 PETRIFIED FOREST, AZ
(1906/1962). 221,540 acres. Extensive petrified wood and Indian artifacts; contains part of Painted Desert.

45 REDWOOD, CA
(1968). 112,512 acres. 40 mi of Pacific coastline, groves of ancient redwoods, and world's tallest trees.

46 ROCKY MOUNTAIN, CO
(1915). 265,828 acre. On the Continental Divide; includes peaks over 14,000 ft.

47 SAGUARO, AZ
(1933/1994). 91,440 acres. Part of the Sonoran Desert; includes the giant Saguaro cacti, unique to the region.

48 SEQUOIA, CA
(1890). 404,051 acres. Groves of giant sequoias, with world's largest tree; Mt. Whitney, highest mountain in conterminous U.S.

49 SHENANDOAH, VA
(1926). 199,074 acres. Portion of the Blue Ridge Mts.; overlooks Shenandoah Valley; Skyline Drive.

50 THEODORE ROOSEVELT, ND
(1947/1978). 70,447 acres. Contains part of Roosevelt's ranch and scenic badlands.

51 VOYAGEURS, MN
(1971). 218,200 acres. Abundant lakes, forests, wildlife, canoeing, boating.

52 WIND CAVE, SD
(1903). 28,295 acres. Limestone caverns in Black Hills; extensive wildlife includes a herd of bison.

53 WRANGELL-ST. ELIAS, AK
(1978/1980). 8,323,148 acres. Largest area in park system, most peaks over 16,000 ft, abundant wildlife; day's drive east of Anchorage. Limited federal facilities.

54 YELLOWSTONE, ID-MT-WY
(1872). 2,219,791 acres. World's first national park. World's greatest geyser area has about 10,000 geysers and hot springs; spectacular falls and impressive canyons of the Yellowstone River; grizzly bear, moose, and bison.

55 YOSEMITE, CA
(1890). 761,266 acres. Yosemite Valley, with the nation's highest waterfall, grove of sequoias, mountains.

56 ZION, UT
(1909/1919). 146,598 acres. Unusual shapes and landscapes resulting from erosion and faulting; evidence of past volcanic activity; Zion Canyon has sheer walls ranging up to 2,640 ft.

18 EVERGLADES, FL
(1934). 1,508,539 acres. Largest remaining subtropical wilderness in continental U.S.

19 GATES OF THE ARCTIC, AK
(1978/1984). 7,523,898 acres. Vast wilderness in north central region. Limited federal facilities.

20 GLACIER, MT
(1910). 1,013,572 acres. Superb Rocky Mt. scenery, glaciers and glacial lakes.

21 GLACIER BAY, AK
(1925/1986). 3,224,840 acres. Great tidewater glaciers that move down mountainsides and break up into the sea; much wildlife.

22 GRAND CANYON, AZ
(1893/1919). 1,217,403 acres. Most spectacular part of Colorado River's greatest canyon.

23 GRAND TETON, WY
(1929). 309,995 acres. Most impressive part of the Teton Mts.; winter feeding ground of largest American elk herd.

24 GREAT BASIN, NV
(1922/1986). 77,180 acres. Includes Wheeler Park, Lexington Arch, and Lehman Caves.

25 GREAT SAND DUNES, CO
(1932/2000). 85,000 acres. Largest sand dunes and some of the oldest archeological remains in North America.

26 GREAT SMOKY MTS., NC-TN
(1926/1934). 522,199 acres. Largest Eastern mountain range; magnificent forests.

27 GUADALUPE MTS., TX
(1966). 86,416 acres. Extensive Permian limestone fossil reef; vast earth fault.

28 HALEAKALA, HI
(1916/1960). 29,111 acres. Dormant volcano on Maui with large colorful craters.

29 HAWAII VOLCANOES, HI
(1916/1961). 323,431 acres. Contains Kilauea and Mauna Loa, active volcanoes.

30 HOT SPRINGS, AR
(1832/1921). 5,550 acres. Bathhouses furnished with

HISTORIC SITES AND BATTLEFIELDS

HISTORICAL PARKS

ADAMS, MA
(1946/1998). 24 acres. Home of Pres. John Adams and John Quincy Adams.

APPOMATTOX COURT HOUSE, VA (1930/1954). 1,774 acres. Where Lee surrendered to Grant.

BOSTON, MA
(1974). 43 acres. Includes Faneuil Hall, Old North Church, Bunker Hill, and Paul Revere House.

CANE RIVER CREOLE (and heritage area), **LA**
(1994). 207 acres. Preserves Creole culture that developed along Cane River.

CEDAR CREEK AND BELLE GROVE, VA
(2002). 3,593 acres. Civil War battle site and an antebellum plantation in the Shenandoah Valley.

CHACO CULTURE, NM
(1907/1980). 33,960 acres. Ruins of prehistoric pueblos.

CHESAPEAKE AND OHIO CANAL, MD-DC-WV
(1938/1971). 19,586 acres. 184-mile historic canal.

COLONIAL, VA
(1930/1936). 8,677 acres. Jamestown, site of first successful English colony;

Yorktown, site of Cornwallis's surrender to Washington; Colonial Parkway.

CUMBERLAND GAP, KY-TN-VA
(1940). 20,512 acres. Mountain pass of the Wilderness Road, which carried the first great migration of pioneers into America's interior.

DAYTON AVIATION HERITAGE, OH
(1992). 86 acres. Commemorates the area's aviation heritage.

GEORGE ROGERS CLARK, VINCENNES, IN
(1966). 26 acres. Commemorates American defeat of British in West during Revolution.

HARPERS FERRY, MD-VA-WV
(1944/1963). 3,646 acres. Site of John Brown's 1859 raid on the Army arsenal.

HOPEWELL CULTURE, OH
(1923/1992). 1,170 acres. Formerly Mound City Group National Monument.

INDEPENDENCE, PA
(1948). 44 acres. Sites associated with the American Revolution and the founding of the U.S. Includes Independence Hall.

JEAN LAFFITE (and preserve), **LA**
(1907/1978). 20,005 acres. Includes Chalmette, site of 1815 Battle of New Orleans; French Quarter.

KALAUPAPA, HI
(1980). 10,779 acres. Molokai's former leper colony site and other historic areas.

KALOKO-HONOKOHAU, HI
(1978). 1,161 acres. Preserves the native culture of Hawaii.

KEWEENAW, MI
(1992). 1,869 acres. Site of first significant copper mine in U.S.

KLONDIKE GOLD RUSH, AK-WA
(1976). 13,192 acres. Alaskan Trails in 1898 Gold Rush. Museum in Seattle.

LEWIS AND CLARK, OR-WA
(1958/2004). 1,415 acres. Lewis and Clark encampment, 1805–06.

LOWELL, MA
(1978). 141 acres. Textile mills, canal, and 19th-century structures.

LYNDON B. JOHNSON, TX
(1969/1980). 1,570 acres. President's birthplace, boyhood home, and ranch.

MARSH-BILLINGS-ROCKEFELLER, VT
(1992). 643 acres. Boyhood home of conservationist George Perkins Marsh.

MINUTE MAN, MA
(1959). 961 acres. Where the Minute Men battled the British, Apr. 19, 1775. Also contains Hawthorne's home.

MORRISTOWN, NJ
(1933). 1,711 acres. Sites of important military encampments during the American Revolution; Washington's headquarters, 1777, 1779–80.

NATCHEZ, MS
(1988). 105 acres. Mansions, townhouses, and villas related to history of Natchez.

NEW BEDFORD WHALING, MA
(1996). 34 acres. Preserves structures and relics associated with the city's 19th-century whaling industry.

NEW ORLEANS JAZZ, LA
(1994). 5 acres. Preserves and interprets jazz as it has evolved in New Orleans.

NEZ PERCE, ID
(1965). 2,494 acres. Illustrates the history and culture of the Nez Perce Indian country (38 separate sites).

PECOS, NM
(1965/1990). 6,670 acres. Ruins of ancient Pueblo of Pecos, archeological sites, and two Spanish colonial missions from the 17th and 18th centuries.

PU'UHONUA O HONAUNAU, HI
(1955/1978). 420 acres. Until 1819, a sanctuary for Hawaiians vanquished in battle or guilty of commiting crimes or breaking taboos.

ROSIE THE RIVETER WWII HOME FRONT, CA
(2000). 145 acres. Site of a shipyard that employed thousands of women in WWII.

SAN ANTONIO MISSIONS, TX
(1978). 826 acres. Four of finest Spanish missions in U.S., 18th-century irrigation system.

SAN FRANCISCO MARITIME, CA
(1988). 50 acres. Historic artifacts, photographs, and vessels related to the development of the Pacific Coast.

SAN JUAN ISLAND, WA
(1966). 1,752 acres. Commemorates peaceful relations between the U.S., Canada, and Britain since the 1872 boundary disputes.

SARATOGA, NY
(1938). 3,394 acres. Scene of a 1777 battle that was a turning point in the American Revolution.

SITKA, AK
(1910/1972). 112 acres. Scene of last major resistance of the Tlingit Indians to the Russians, 1804.

The Liberty Bell, Philadelphia, Pennsylvania

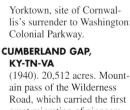

Sited at the confluence of the Shenandoah and Potomac rivers, Harpers Ferry was a crucial strategic location in the Civil War, during which it changed hands eight times.

TUMACACORI, AZ
(1908/1990). 360 acres. Spanish mission building near site first visited by Father Kino in 1691.

VALLEY FORGE, PA
(1976). 3,466 acres. Continental Army campsite in 1777–78 winter.

WOMEN'S RIGHTS, NY
(1980). 7 acres. Seneca Falls site where Lucretia Mott, Elizabeth Cady Stanton organized movement in 1848.

BATTLEFIELDS

ANTIETAM, MD
(1890/1978). 3,255 acres. Battle here ended first Confederate invasion of North, Sept. 17, 1862.

BIG HOLE, MT
(1910/1963). 1,011 acres. Site of major battle with Nez Perce Indians, Aug. 9–10, 1877.

COWPENS, SC
(1929/1972). 842 acres. American Revolution battlefield, Jan. 17, 1781.

FORT DONELSON, TN-KY
(1928/1985). 552 acres. Site of first major Union victory, Feb. 14–16, 1862.

FORT NECESSITY, PA
(1931/1961). 903 acres. Site of first battle of French and Indian War, July 3, 1754.

MONOCACY, MD
(1934/1976). 1,647 acres. Site of Civil War battle in defense of Washington, DC, July 9, 1864.

MOORES CREEK, NC
(1926/1980). 88 acres. 1776 battle between Patriots and Loyalists commemorated here.

PETERSBURG, VA
(1926/1962). 2,739 acres. Scene of 10-month Union campaigns, 1864–65.

STONES RIVER, TN
(1927/1960). 709 acres. Scene of battle that began federal offensive to trisect the Confederacy, Dec. 31, 1862 to Jan. 2, 1863.

TUPELO, MS
(1929/1961). 1 acre. Site of crucial battle over Sherman's supply line, July 14-15, 1865.

WILSON'S CREEK, MO
(1960/1970). 2,365 acres. Scene of Civil War battle for control of Missouri, Aug. 10, 1861.

BATTLEFIELD PARKS AND SITES

KENNESAW MOUNTAIN, GA
(1917/1935). 2,888 acres. Site of two major battles of Atlanta campaign in Civil War.

MANASSAS, VA
(1940). 5,073 acres. Scene of two battles in Civil War, 1861 and 1862.

RICHMOND, VA
(1936). 7,127 acres. Site of battles defending Confederate capital.

BRICES CROSS ROADS, MS
(1929). 1 acre. Civil War battlefield.

MILITARY PARKS

CHICKAMAUGA AND CHATTANOOGA, GA-TN
(1890). 9,036 acres. Site of major Confederate victory, 1863.

FREDERICKSBURG AND SPOTSYLVANIA COUNTY, VA
(1927/1933). 8,374 acres. Sites of several major Civil War battles and campaigns.

GETTYSBURG, PA
(1895/1933). 5,990 acres. Site of decisive Confederate defeat in North, July 1863, and of Gettysburg Address.

GUILFORD COURTHOUSE, NC
(1917/1933). 230 acres. American Revolution battle site.

HORSESHOE BEND, AL
(1956). 2,040 acres. Where Gen. Andrew Jackson broke the power of the Upper Creek Indian Confederacy, March 27, 1814.

KINGS MOUNTAIN, SC
(1931/1933). 3,945 acres. Site of American Revolution battle, fought on Oct. 7, 1780.

PEA RIDGE, AR
(1956). 4,300 acres. Scene of Civil War battle.

SHILOH, TN
(1894/1933). 5,065 acres. Major Civil War battlesite; includes well-preserved Indian burial mounds.

VICKSBURG, MS
(1899/1933). 1,795 acres. Site where Union victory gave North control of the Mississippi and split the Confederate forces.

MEMORIALS

ARKANSAS POST, AR
(1960). 758 acres. First permanent French settlement in the lower Mississippi River valley.

ARLINGTON HOUSE, THE ROBERT E. LEE MEMORIAL, VA
(1925/ 1972). 28 acres. Lee's home overlooking the Potomac River.

CHAMIZAL, EL PASO, TX
(1966/1974). 55 acres. Commemorates 1963 settlement of 99-year border dispute with Mexico.

CORONADO, AZ
(1941/1952). 4,750 acres. Commemorates first European exploration of the Southwest.

DESOTO, FL
(1948). 27 acres. Commemorates 16th-century Spanish explorations.

FEDERAL HALL, NY
(1939/1955). 0.45 acres. First seat of U.S. government under the Constitution.

FLIGHT 93, SHANKSVILLE, PA
(2002). 2,262 acres. Commemorates the passengers and crew of Flight 93, who died thwarting a terrorist attack on Sept. 11, 2001. In planning stages; no federal facilities.

FORT CAROLINE, FL
(1950). 138 acres. Overlooks site of a French Huguenot colony.

FRANKLIN DELANO ROOSEVELT, DC
(1982). 8 acres. Statues of Pres. Roosevelt and Eleanor Roosevelt; waterfalls and gardens.

GENERAL GRANT, NY
(1958). 0.76 acres. Tomb of Grant and wife.

HAMILTON GRANGE, NY
(1962). 1 acre. Home of Alexander Hamilton.

JEFFERSON NATIONAL EXPANSION MEMORIAL, ST. LOUIS, MO
(1935). 91 acres. Commemorates westward expansion.

Gettysburg Military Park, Gettysburg, Pennsylvania.
Fought over three days in July 1863, the Battle of Gettysburg was one of the bloodiest battles in American history. The Union victory is often cited as the major turning point in the Civil War.

JOHNSTOWN FLOOD, PA
(1964). 178 acres.
Commemorates tragic flood
of 1889.

KOREAN WAR VETERANS, DC
(1986). 2 acres. Dedicated
in 1995; honors those who
served in the Korean War.

LINCOLN BOYHOOD, IN
(1962). 200 acres. Lincoln
grew up here.

LINCOLN MEMORIAL, DC
(1911/1933). 107 acres.
Marble statue of the 16th
president.

LYNDON B. JOHNSON MEMORIAL GROVE ON THE POTOMAC, DC
(1973). 17 acres. Overlooks
the Potomac River; vista of
the Capitol.

MOUNT RUSHMORE, SD
(1925). 1,278 acres. World-
famous sculpture of four
presidents.

OKLAHOMA CITY, OK
(1997). 3.3 acres.
Commemorates site of April
19, 1995, bombing which
killed 168.

PERRY'S VICTORY AND INTERNATIONAL PEACE MEMORIAL, PUT-IN-BAY, OH
(1936/1972). 25 acres.
Massive Doric column, constructed 1912–15, promotes
pursuit of peace through
disarmament.

ROGER WILLIAMS, PROVIDENCE, RI
(1965). 5 acres. Memorial to
founder of Rhode Island.

Part of Independence National Historic Park in Philadelphia, the Second Bank of the United States was discontinued by President Andrew Jackson in 1832. America did not have national oversight of banking again until the Federal Reserve was created in 1913.

THADDEUS KOSCIUSZKO, PA
(1972). 0.02 acres. Memorial
to Polish hero of Revolution.

THEODORE ROOSEVELT ISLAND, DC
(1932/1933). 89 acres. Statue
of Roosevelt in wooded
island sanctuary.

THOMAS JEFFERSON MEMORIAL, DC
(1934). 18 acres. Statue of
Jefferson in colonnaded
structure.

USS ARIZONA, HI
(1980). 11 acres.
Memorializes American
losses at Pearl Harbor.

VIETNAM VETERANS, DC
(1980). 2 acres. Memorial
to those missing or killed in
action in Vietnam War.

WASHINGTON MONUMENT, DC
(1848/1933). 106 acres.
Obelisk honoring the 1st
president.

WRIGHT BROTHERS, NC
(1927/1953). 428 acres.
Site of first powered flight.

HISTORIC SITES

ABRAHAM LINCOLN BIRTHPLACE, HODGENVILLE, KY
(1916/1959). 345 acres.
Memorial building, sinking
spring.

ALLEGHENY PORTAGE RAILROAD, PA
(1964). 1,284 acres. Linked
the Pennsylvania Canal
system and the West.

ANDERSONVILLE, ANDERSONVILLE, GA
(1970). 515 acres. Noted Civil
War prisoner-of-war camp.

ANDREW JOHNSON, GREENEVILLE, TN
(1935/1963). 17 acres. Homes
of the 17th president.

BENT'S OLD FORT, CO
(1960). 799 acres.
Reconstruction of South
Plains outpost.

BOSTON AFRICAN-AMERICAN, MA
(1980). 0.59 acres. Pre–Civil
War black history structures.

BROWN V. BOARD OF EDUCATION, KS
(1992). 2 acres.
Commemorates landmark
1954 U.S. Supreme Court
decision.

CARL SANDBURG HOME, FLAT ROCK, NC
(1968). 264 acres. Poet's
home.

CARTER G. WOODSON HOME, DC
(2006). 0.05 acres. Home
of noted African American
historian.

CHARLES PINCKNEY, SC
(1988). 28 acres. Statesman's
farm.

CLARA BARTON, MD
(1974). 9 acres. Home of
founder of the American
Red Cross.

EDGAR ALLAN POE, PA
(1978/1980). 0.52 acres.
Writer's home.

EDISON, WEST ORANGE, NJ
(1955/1962). 21 acres.
Inventor's home and
laboratory.

The now picturesque National Battlefield Park at Antietam saw one of the bloodiest days in American history. Fought on September 17, 1862, the battle cost 23,000 soldiers their lives and ended the first onslaught of the Confederacy into Union territory.

EISENHOWER, GETTYSBURG, PA
(1967). 690 acres. Home of 34th president.

ELEANOR ROOSEVELT, HYDE PARK, NY
(1977). 181 acres. The former first lady's retreat.

EUGENE O'NEILL, DANVILLE, CA
(1976). 13 acres. Playwright's home.

FIRST LADIES, CANTON, OH
(2000). 0.33 acres. Library devoted to America's first ladies.

FORD'S THEATRE, DC
(1866/1970). 0.29 acres. Restored theater where Lincoln was assassinated, house where he died, and Lincoln Museum.

FORT BOWIE, AZ
(1964). 999 acres. Site of operations against Geronimo and the Apaches.

FORT DAVIS, TX
(1961). 474 acres. Frontier outpost in West Texas.

FORT LARAMIE, WY
(1938/1960). 833 acres. Military post on Oregon Trail.

FORT LARNED, KS
(1964/1966). 718 acres. Military post on Santa Fe Trail.

FORT POINT, SAN FRANCISCO, CA
(1970). 29 acres. West Coast fortification.

FORT RALEIGH, NC
(1941). 513 acres. First attempted English settlement in North America.

FORT SCOTT, KS
(1965/1978). 17 acres. Commemorates U.S. frontier of 1840s and '50s.

FORT SMITH, AR-OK
(1961). 75 acres. Active post from 1817–90.

FORT UNION TRADING POST, MT-ND
(1966). 444 acres. Principal fur-trading post on upper Missouri, 1829–67.

FORT VANCOUVER, WA
(1948/1961). 210 acres. Headquarters for Hudson's Bay Company in 1825.

FREDERICK DOUGLASS, DC
(1962/1988). 9 acres. Home of famous abolitionist, writer, and orator.

FREDERICK LAW OLMSTED, MA
(1979). 7 acres. Home of famous city planner.

FRIENDSHIP HILL, PA
(1978). 675 acres. Home of Albert Gallatin, Jefferson's and Madison's secretary of treasury.

GOLDEN SPIKE, UT
(1957). 2,735 acres. Commemorates completion of first transcontinental railroad in 1869.

GRANT-KOHRS RANCH, MT
(1972). 1,618 acres. Ranch house and part of 19th-century ranch.

HAMPTON, MD
(1948). 62 acres. 18th-century Georgian mansion.

HARRY S. TRUMAN, MO
(1983). 7 acres. Home of Pres. Truman after 1919.

HERBERT HOOVER, WEST BRANCH, IA
(1965). 187 acres. Birthplace and boyhood home of 31st president.

HOME OF FRANKLIN D. ROOSEVELT, HYDE PARK, NY
(1944). 800 acres. FDR's birthplace and home.

HOPEWELL FURNACE, PA
(1938/1985). 848 acres. 19th-century iron-making village.

HUBBELL TRADING POST, AZ
(1965). 160 acres. Still active trading post.

JAMES A. GARFIELD, MENTOR, OH
(1980). 8 acres. Home of 20th president.

JIMMY CARTER, GA
(1987). 72 acres. Birthplace and home of 39th president.

JOHN FITZGERALD KENNEDY, BROOKLINE, MA
(1967). 0.09 acres. Birthplace of 35th president.

JOHN MUIR, MARTINEZ, CA
(1964). 345 acres. Home of early conservationist and writer.

KNIFE RIVER INDIAN VILLAGES, ND
(1974). 1,758 acres. Remnants of Hidatsa and Mandan villages.

LINCOLN HOME, SPRINGFIELD, IL
(1971). 12 acres. Lincoln's residence at the time he was elected 16th president, 1860.

LITTLE ROCK CENTRAL HIGH SCHOOL, AR
(1998). 27 acres. Commemorates 1957 desegregation during which federal troops had to be called in to protect nine black students.

LONGFELLOW, CAMBRIDGE, MA
(1972). 2 acres. Poet's home, 1837–82; Washington's headquarters during Boston siege, 1775–76.

MAGGIE L. WALKER, VA
(1978). 1 acre. Richmond home of black leader and bank president, daughter of an ex-slave.

MANZANAR, LONE PINE, CA
(1992). 814 acres. Commemorates Manzanar War Relocation Ctr., a Japanese-American internment camp during WWII.

MARTIN LUTHER KING JR., ATLANTA, GA
(1980). 39 acres. Birthplace, grave, and church of leader of Civil Rights Movement.

MARTIN VAN BUREN, NY
(1974). 40 acres. Lindenwald, home of 8th president.

MARY MCLEOD BETHUNE COUNCIL HOUSE, DC
(1982/1991). 0.07 acres. Commemorates Bethune's leadership.

MINUTEMAN MISSILE, SD
(1999). 15 acres. Missile launch facilities dating back to the Cold War era.

NICODEMUS, KS
(1996). 161 acres. Only remaining western town established by African Americans during Reconstruction.

NINETY SIX, SC
(1976). 1,022 acres. Colonial trading village.

PALO ALTO BATTLEFIELD, TX
(1978): 3,407 acres. Scene of the first battle of the Mexican War.

PENNSYLVANIA AVENUE, DC
(1965). Area between Capitol and White House, encompassing Ford's Theatre and other structures.

PUUKOHOLA HEIAU, HI
(1972). 86 acres. Ruins of temple built by King Kamehameha.

REAGAN BOYHOOD HOME, DIXON, IL
(2002). 1 acre. Childhood home of 40th president.

SAGAMORE HILL, OYSTER BAY, NY
(1962). 83 acres. Home of Theodore Roosevelt from 1885 to 1919.

SAINT-GAUDENS, CORNISH, NH
(1964). 148 acres. Home, studio, and gardens of sculptor Augustus Saint-Gaudens.

SAINT PAUL'S CHURCH, NY, NY (1943). 6 acres. Site associated with John Peter Zenger's "freedom of press" trial.

SALEM MARITIME, MA
(1938). 9 acres. Only port British never seized from the patriots. Major fishing and whaling port.

SAND CREEK MASSACRE, SAND CREEK, CO
(2000). 12,583 acres. Site where over 100 Cheyenne and Arapaho Indians were killed by U.S. soldiers in 1864.

SAUGUS IRON WORKS, MA
(1974). 9 acres. Reconstructed 17th-century colonial ironworks.

SPRINGFIELD ARMORY, MA
(1974). 55 acres. Small-arms manufacturing center.

STEAMTOWN, PA
(1986). 62 acres. Railyard, roadhouse, repair shops of former Delaware, Lackawanna & Western RR.

THEODORE ROOSEVELT BIRTHPLACE, NEW YORK, NY
(1962). 0.11 acres. Reconstructed brownstone.

THEODORE ROOSEVELT INAUGURAL, BUFFALO, NY
(1966). 1 acre. Wilcox House where Roosevelt took oath of office, 1901.

THOMAS STONE, MD
(1978). 328 acres. Home of signer of Declaration of Independence.

TUSKEGEE AIRMEN, AL
(1998). 90 acres. Airfield where pilots of all-black WWII Air Corps unit received flight training.

TUSKEGEE INSTITUTE, AL
(1974). 58 acres. College founded by Booker T. Washington.

ULYSSES S. GRANT, ST. LOUIS CO., MO
(1989). 10 acres. Home of Grant during pre–Civil War years.

VANDERBILT MANSION, HYDE PARK, NY
(1940). 212 acres. Mansion of 19th-century financier.

WASHITA BATTLEFIELD, OK
(1996). 315 acres. Scene of 1868 battle between Plains tribes and the U.S. Army.

WEIR FARM, WILTON, CT
(1990). 74 acres. Home and studio of Impressionist painter J. Alden Weir.

WHITMAN MISSION, WA
(1936/1963). 139 acres. Mission site of Marcus and Narcissa Whitman.

WILLIAM HOWARD TAFT, CINCINNATI, OH
(1969). 3 acres. Birthplace and early home of the 27th president.

Popular events at many Civil War battlefields, including Gettysburg, Shiloh, and Saltville, reenactments invite spectators to viscerally experience military history.

ALABAMA

FACTS & FIGURES

We dare defend our rights

Settled: *1702*

Origin of name: *Indian for tribal town, later a tribe (Alabamas or Alibamons) of the Creek confederacy*

Capital: *Montgomery*

Population (2005): *4,557,808 (ranked 23rd in size)*

Population density: *89.8 per sq mi*

ECONOMY

Chief industries: *Pulp and paper, chemicals, electronics, apparel, textiles, primary metals, lumber and wood products, food processing, fabricated metals, automotive tires, oil and gas exploration*

Chief manufactured goods: *Electronics, cast iron and plastic pipe, fabricated steel products, ships, paper products, chemicals, steel, mobile homes, fabrics, poultry processing, soft drinks, furniture, tires*

Chief crops: *Cotton, greenhouse and nursery, peanuts, sweet potatoes, potatoes, and other vegetables*

Chief port: *Mobile*

Commercial fishing (2004): *$37 million*

Gross state product (2005): *$149.8 billion*

Employment (May 2006): *18.5% government; 19.4% trade/transportation/utilities; 15.2% manufacturing; 10.3% education/health; 10.9% professional/business services; 8.7% leisure/hospitality; 5% finance; 5.6% construction; 5.8% other services*

Per-capita income (2005): *$29,136*

STATE FLOWER

Camellia

STATE BIRD

Yellow-shafted flicker

THE HEART OF DIXIE

Alabama, in the middle of the Deep South, is commonly called the "Heart of Dixie." It is also known as the "Yellowhammer State," after the nickname for its state bird, the yellow-shafted flicker. Although most Southern states were known for growing cotton in the 19th century, Alabama, also called the "Cotton State," produced the most. The state would be landlocked if not for 60 miles of shoreline along the Gulf of Mexico. There, many of its rivers empty into the Gulf through Mobile Bay. Alabama's climate is moderate in the interior highlands and subtropical in the Gulf Coastal Plain. Average summer temperatures are above 90° F, among the hottest in the nation. Manufacturing has overtaken agriculture as the state's leading business; Alabama is dominant in heavy industry in the South.

A Brief History

- Alabama was inhabited by the Creek, Cherokee, Chickasaw, Alabama, and Choctaw peoples when Spanish explorers arrived in the early 1500s.
- The French made the first permanent settlement at Fort Louis, 1702, and founded Mobile, 1711.
- The region was seized by United States troops, 1813.

The Selma–Montgomery march for voting rights took place in March 1965. President Johnson signed the Voting Rights Act later that year.

- Most of present-day Alabama was held by the Creeks until General Andrew Jackson defeated them, 1814, and they were removed to Oklahoma Territory.
- When Alabama became a state, 1819, black slaves made up about one-third of the population.
- The state seceded, 1861, and was readmitted, 1868.
- Birmingham, founded 1871, became a center for iron- and steelmaking.
- The Montgomery bus boycott, 1955, sparked by Rosa Parks, helped launch the Civil Rights Movement; other confrontations came at Birmingham, 1963, and Selma, 1965.
- Four-term Governor George Wallace began as a segregationist in the 1960s but later won with black support.
- Growth in the auto industry boosted the state economy at the beginning of the 21st century.

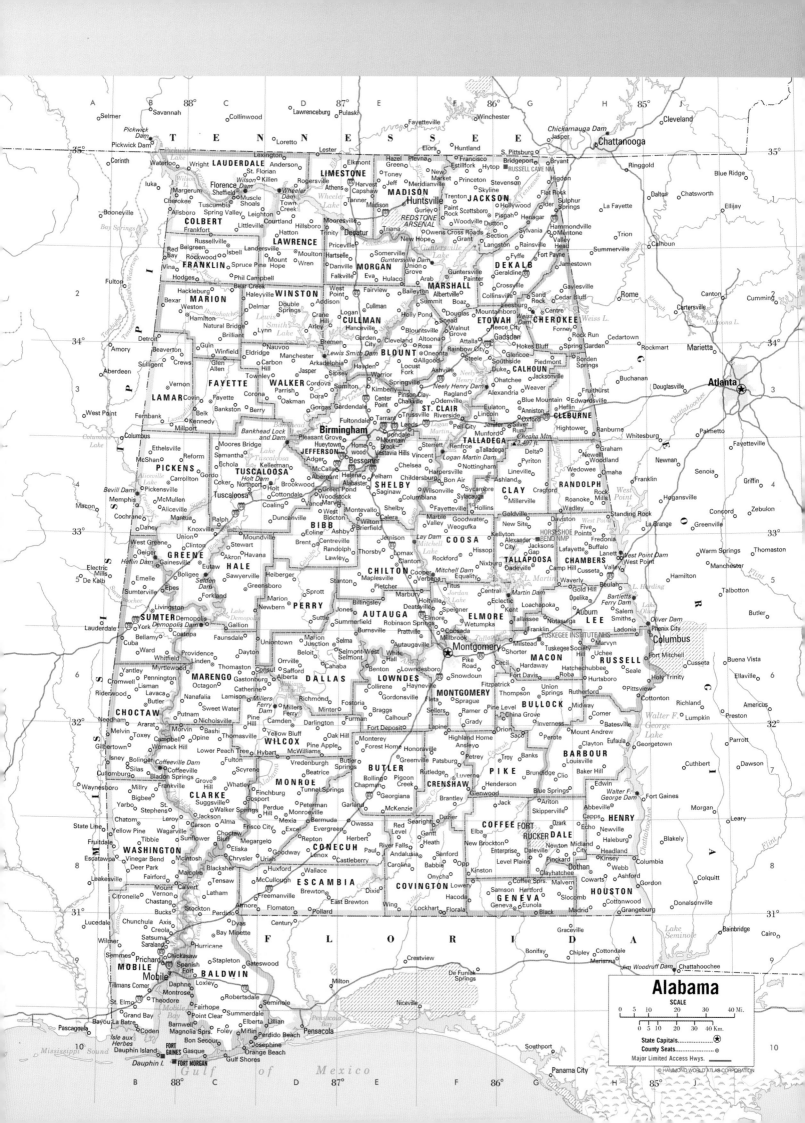

Alabama

SCALE

0 5 10   20   30   40 Mi.

0 5 10   20   30   40 Km.

State Capitals............... ★
County Seats................. ⊛
Major Limited Access Hwys.

© HAMMOND WORLD ATLAS CORPORATION

Alabama

FACTS & FIGURES

GEOGRAPHY

Total area: *52,419 sq mi (ranked 30th)*

Acres forested: *23 million*

CLIMATE

Long, hot summers; mild winters; generally abundant rainfall

STATE TREE

Southern longleaf pine

AVERAGE TEMPERATURE

CITY	JUN	DEC
Birmingham	76.4	45.6
Huntsville	76	43.1
Mobile	79.3	52.3
Montgomery	78.9	49

FAMOUS ALABAMIANS

- Hank Aaron (b. 1934), baseball player
- George Washington Carver (1864–1943), scientist
- Helen Keller (1880–1968), writer
- Harper Lee (b. 1926), novelist
- Joe Louis (1914–81), boxer
- Willie Mays (b. 1931), baseball player
- Jesse Owens (1913–80), Olympic runner
- Condoleezza Rice (b. 1954), secretary of state

Harper Lee

ATTRACTIONS

Civil Rights Memorial; First White House of the Confederacy; Alabama Shakespeare Festival, *Montgomery*

Ivy Green, Helen Keller's birthplace, *Tuscumbia*

Civil Rights Museum; statue of Vulcan, *Birmingham*

Carver Museum, *Tuskegee*

W. C. Handy Home and Museum, *Florence*

Alabama Space and Rocket Center, *Huntsville*

Moundville State Monument, *Moundville*

Pike Pioneer Museum, *Troy*

USS *Alabama* Memorial Park, *Mobile*

Russell Cave National Monument, a detailed record of human occupancy, 10,000 BCE to 1650 CE, *near Bridgeport*

TOPOGRAPHY

- Coastal plains, including Prairie Black Belt, give way to hills and broken terrain

Highest elevation:
Cheaha Mountain, 2,407 ft

Lowest elevation:
Gulf of Mexico, sea level

Cheaha Mountain

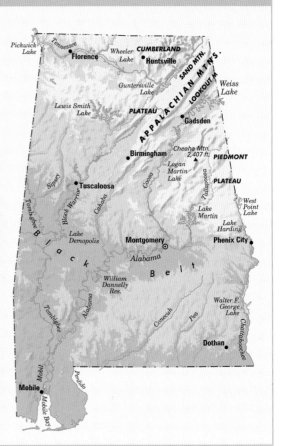

The Wheeler National Wildlife Refuge, on the Tennessee River, provides a haven for migrating birds.

Russell Cave, a national monument since 1961, was inhabited by native peoples in prehistoric times.

CAPITAL CITY: **MONTGOMERY**

Montgomery began as an Alabama River port in the early 1800s. Named state capital in 1846, Montgomery was one of the South's wealthiest cities when designated the first capital of the Confederacy in 1861. In the 1950s and 1960s, Montgomery was the scene of civil rights protests led by Dr. Martin Luther King Jr., a city resident.

With a metro population of 469,000, Montgomery is a manufacturing and cultural center. It has both a major automobile assembly plant and the Alabama Shakespeare Festival, the seventh largest in the world, with 300,000 visitors.

Area: 155.4 sq mi

Population (2005): 200,127

Population density: 1,288 per sq mi

Per-capita income: $29,699

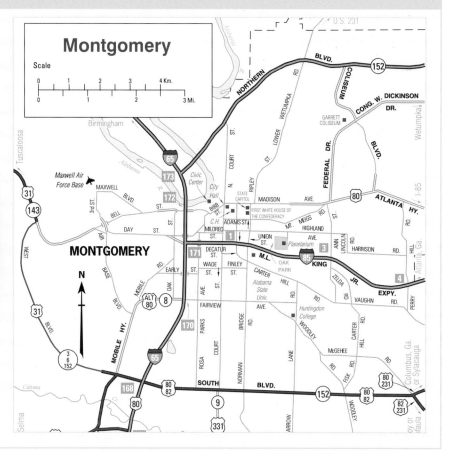

Jefferson Davis, President of the Confederate States of America, was inaugurated on the steps of the capitol building in 1861.

SPOTLIGHT CITY: **BIRMINGHAM**

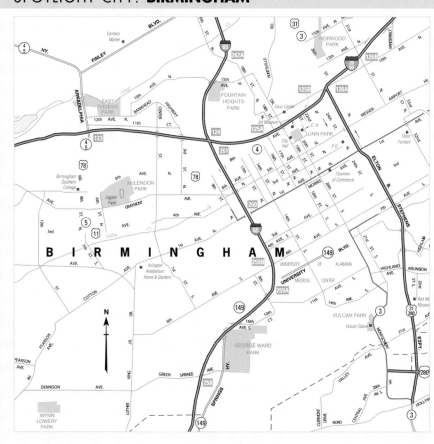

Founded in 1871, Birmingham was planned as an industrial city, situated to take advantage of the railroad and of local coal and iron deposits needed to make steel.

The city grew rapidly and became the largest in the state. Greater Birmingham has 1.18 million people—more than a quarter of Alabama's population.

During the Civil Rights Movement in the 1950s and 1960s, Birmingham was the scene of protest marches, symbolic of the nation's racial unrest, which helped lead to the national government's enforcement of racial equality under the law.

While still a major Southern manu-facturing city, Birmingham has also become an important banking and business center.

Area: 149.9 sq mi

Population (2005): 231,483

Population density: 1,544 per sq mi

Per-capita income: $33,067

Roughly a quarter of Alabama's population lives in Birmingham.

ALASKA

North to the future

Settled: *1801*

Origin of name: *Russian version of an Aleutian (Eskimo) word, alakshak, for "peninsula," "great lands," or "land that is not an island"*

Capital: *Juneau*

Population (2005): *663,661 (ranked 47th in size)*

Population density: *1.2 per sq mi*

ECONOMY

Chief industries: *Petroleum, tourism, fishing, mining, forestry, transportation, aerospace*

Chief manufactured goods: *Fish products, lumber and pulp, furs*

Chief crops: *Greenhouse products, barley, oats, hay, potatoes, lettuce, aquaculture*

Commercial fishing (2004): *$1.2 billion*

Chief ports: *Anchorage, Dutch Harbor, Kodiak, Seward, Skagway, Juneau, Sitka, Valdez, Wrangell*

Gross state product (2005): *$39.9 billion*

Employment (May 2006): *26.4% government; 20.8% trade/transportation/utilities; 3.2% manufacturing; 11.5% education/health; 7.6% professional/business services; 10.3% leisure/hospitality; 4.7% finance; 6% construction; 5.8% other services*

Per-capita income (2005): *$35,612*

STATE FLOWER

Forget-me-not

STATE BIRD

Willow ptarmigan

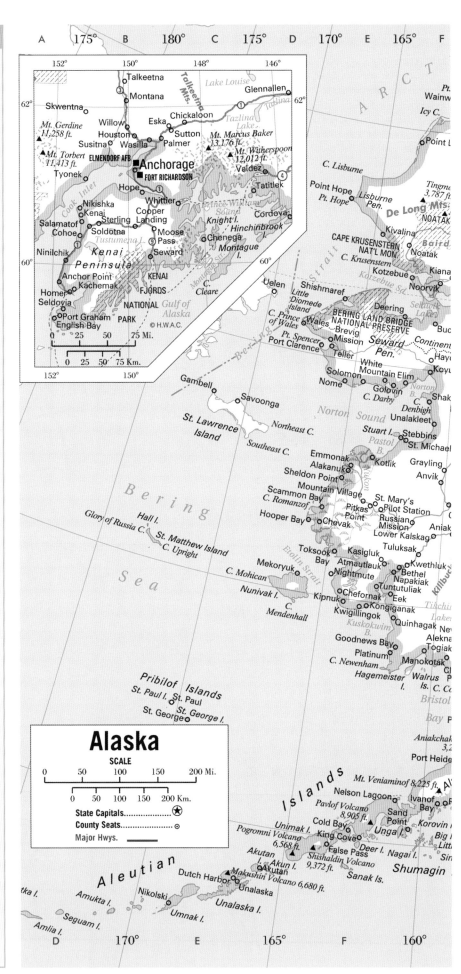

Alaska
SCALE

0   50   100   150   200 Mi.

0   50   100   150   200 Km.

State Capitals.................. ⍟
County Seats..................... ⊚
Major Hwys. ━━━━

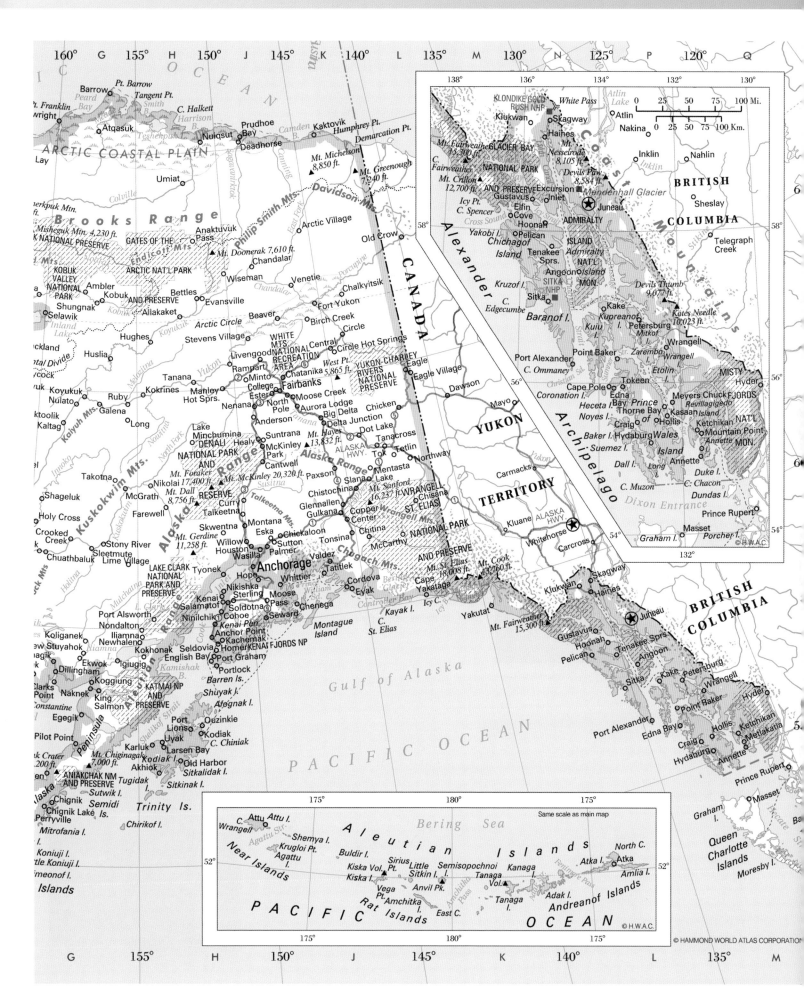

Alaska

FACTS & FIGURES

GEOGRAPHY

Total area: *663,267 sq mi (ranked 1st in size)*

Acres forested: *126.9 million*

CLIMATE

Southeast, southwest, and central regions moist and mild; far north extremely dry. Extended summer days, winter nights, throughout.

STATE TREE

Sitka spruce

AVERAGE TEMPERATURE

CITY	JUN	DEC
Anchorage	54.7	17.5
Annette	54.3	36.4
Barrow	35	-10.6
Fairbanks	59.7	-5.9
Juneau	53.9	53.9

FAMOUS ALASKANS

- Tom Bodett (b. 1955), writer
- Ernest Gruening (1887–1974), journalist, politician
- Jewel (Kilcher) (b. 1974), singer/songwriter
- Sydney Laurence (1865–1940), painter
- Libby Riddles (b. 1956), sled dog racer
- Robert W. Service (1847–1958), poet

Robert W. Service

ATTRACTIONS

Inside Passage, *Alaskan panhandle*

Portage Glacier, *Kenai peninsula*

Mendenhall Glacier, *near Juneau*

Ketchikan Totems

Glacier Bay National Park and Preserve, *Juneau*

Denali National Park, *near Healy*

Mt. McKinley, North America's highest peak

Mt. Roberts Tramway, *Juneau*

Pribilof Islands fur seal rookeries

Restored St. Michael's Russian Orthodox Cathedral, *Sitka*

THE LAST FRONTIER

Alaska, the largest state, is equal to one-fifth of the area of all the other states combined. Purchased from Russia in 1867, the territory became America's "last frontier," as an 1890s gold rush attracted thousands of prospectors and settlers. In the 20th century, "black gold"—meaning oil—and natural gas became the state's largest industries. Another nickname is "Land of the Midnight Sun," because in summertime Alaska's northern regions receive 24 hours of daylight. The topography includes the barren tundra of the Arctic slope, a dry and cold central plateau, and in the south the Alaska Range, with Mount McKinley, at 20,320 feet, the highest North American peak. Alaska's 34,000 miles of coast—the most in the nation—is part of the "ring of fire," so named for the chain of volcanoes that surround the Pacific. The largest cities, Anchorage and Juneau, the capital, are in the south, where the coastal climate is moderated by sea air.

A Brief History

- Ancestors of the Aleut and Inuit (Eskimo) probably arrived from Siberia between 10,000 and 6,000 years ago.
- Vitus Bering, a Dane sailing for Russia, was the first European to land in Alaska, 1741.
- Russians, pursuing the fur trade, established a permanent settlement on Kodiak Island, 1784.
- Secretary of State William H. Seward bought Alaska from Russia for $7.2 million in 1867, a bargain some called "Seward's Folly."
- Discovery of gold in the Klondike region of Canada's Yukon Territory, 1896, triggered an Alaskan gold rush.
- Alaska became a territory, 1912, and a state, 1959.
- A huge oil find at Prudhoe Bay, 1968, led to the construction of the Trans-Alaska Pipeline, 1974–77.
- The *Exxon Valdez* supertanker ran aground, 1989, and spilled about 11 million gallons of crude oil; the cleanup cost over $2.2 billion.
- A federal proposal to drill for oil in the Arctic National Wildlife Refuge has passed the U.S. House 12 times since 1995, most recently in 2006, but failed in the Senate.

This early 20th-century family is of Aleut descent.

TOPOGRAPHY

- Pacific and Arctic mountain systems
- Central plateau
- Arctic slope

Highest elevation: Mt. McKinley, 20,320 ft

Lowest elevation: sea level

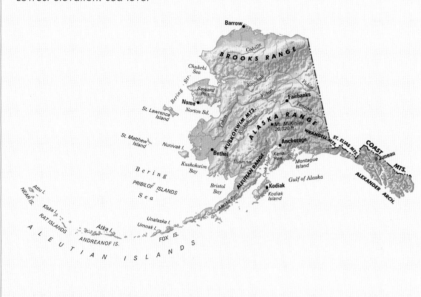

CAPITAL CITY: **JUNEAU**

Juneau ranks as Alaska's third largest city.

Glaciers preside near Homer, a small town on the Kenai peninsula, which began as a mining camp during the Gold Rush.

SPOTLIGHT CITY: **ANCHORAGE**

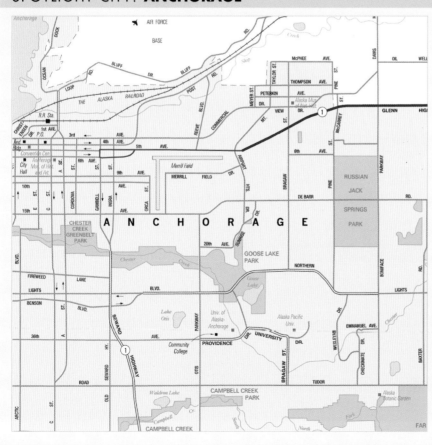

Overlooked by snowcapped mountains, Anchorage sits on Cook Inlet, which opens to the most northerly reaches of the Pacific Ocean. The city began as a hub for the construction of the Alaska Railroad, built between 1915 and 1923. Almost two-fifths of Alaskans live in Anchorage, and more than half, 339,000, live in the metro area. The discovery of oil in the north coast's Prudhoe Bay in 1968 brought about rapid growth to Anchorage, which receives 95 percent of the state's seaborne cargo.

Tourism and the military, in addition to oil, are important to the city's economy. North of Anchorage are Elmendorf Air Force Base and Fort Richardson.

Area: 1,697.2 sq mi

Population (2005): 275,043

Population density: 162 per sq mi

Per-capita income: $37,058

The summer solstice gives Anchorage nearly 20 hours of daylight.

Alaska

The highest mountain in North America, at 20,320 feet, Mount McKinley was named after U.S. president William McKinley in 1897. Most Alaskans still call the mountain Denali, meaning "the high one" in the Athabaskan dialect. Mount McKinley is a centerpiece of Denali National Park and Preserve.

Grizzlies (top), American bald eagles (center), and polar bears (above) all feed on pink salmon, which is native to northern Pacific and Arctic coastal waters. It is abundant in Alaska, spawning in streams between late June and mid-October.

ARIZONA

Ditat Deus (God enriches)

Settled: *1752*

Origin of name: *Spanish version of Pima Indian word for "little spring place," or Aztec arizuma, meaning "silver-bearing"*

Capital: *Phoenix*

Population (2005): *5,939,292 (ranked 18th in size)*

Population density: *52.3 per sq mi*

ECONOMY

Chief industries: *Manufacturing, construction, tourism, mining, agriculture*

Chief manufactured goods: *Electronics, printing and publishing, foods, metals, aircraft and missiles, apparel*

Chief crops: *Cotton, lettuce, cauliflower, broccoli, sorghum, barley, corn, wheat, citrus fruits*

Gross state product (2005): *$215.8 billion*

Employment (May 2006): *15.9% government; 19.2% trade/transportation/utilities; 7% manufacturing; 10.9% education/health; 15% professional/business services; 10.4% leisure/hospitality; 6.9% finance; 9.1% construction; 5.4% other services*

Per-capita income (2005): *$30,267*

STATE FLOWER	STATE BIRD

Saguaro cactus blossom	Cactus wren

THE GRAND CANYON STATE

Arizona is a "Four Corner" state, along with New Mexico, Colorado, and Utah, whose corners meet at the only place in the country where four states touch. The state is nicknamed for the vast canyon that is one of the seven natural wonders of the world. The Grand Canyon, in northwest Arizona, was formed by the action of the Colorado River, which flows westward. Arizona is arid, receiving the nation's highest percentage (86 percent) of sunshine. In the south, the Sonoran Desert, with its characteristic saguaro cactus, straddles the border with Mexico. Yet the landscape is not all desert. More than half of Arizona consists of mountains, plateaus, forests, and rivers. The climate varies with elevation. Manufacturing, tourism, farming, and mining are the chief industries.

A Brief History

- Paleoindians hunted large game in the area at least 12,000 years ago.
- Anasazi, Mogollon, and Hohokam civilizations lived there c. 300 BCE to 1300 CE; Navajo and Apache came c. 15th century.
- Marcos de Niza, a Franciscan, and Estevanico, a black former slave, explored, 1539; Spanish explorer Francisco Vázquez de Coronado visited, 1540.
- Eusebio Francisco Kino, a Jesuit missionary, taught Indians, 1692–1711, and left missions.
- Tubac, a Spanish fort, became the first European settlement, 1752.
- Spain ceded Arizona to Mexico, 1821; the United States took over, 1848, after the Mexican War. The area below the Gila River came from Mexico in the Gadsden Purchase, 1853.
- Arizona became a territory, 1863.
- Apache wars ended with Geronimo's surrender, 1886.
- Arizona became a state, 1912, and grew rapidly after 1960 with a fourfold rise in population over the next four decades.
- Barry Goldwater was a leading conservative voice in the U.S. Senate (1953–65, 1969–87).
- The border with Mexico is a major gateway for illegal immigration to the United States.

The San Xavier Mission, in Tucson, was founded in 1692.

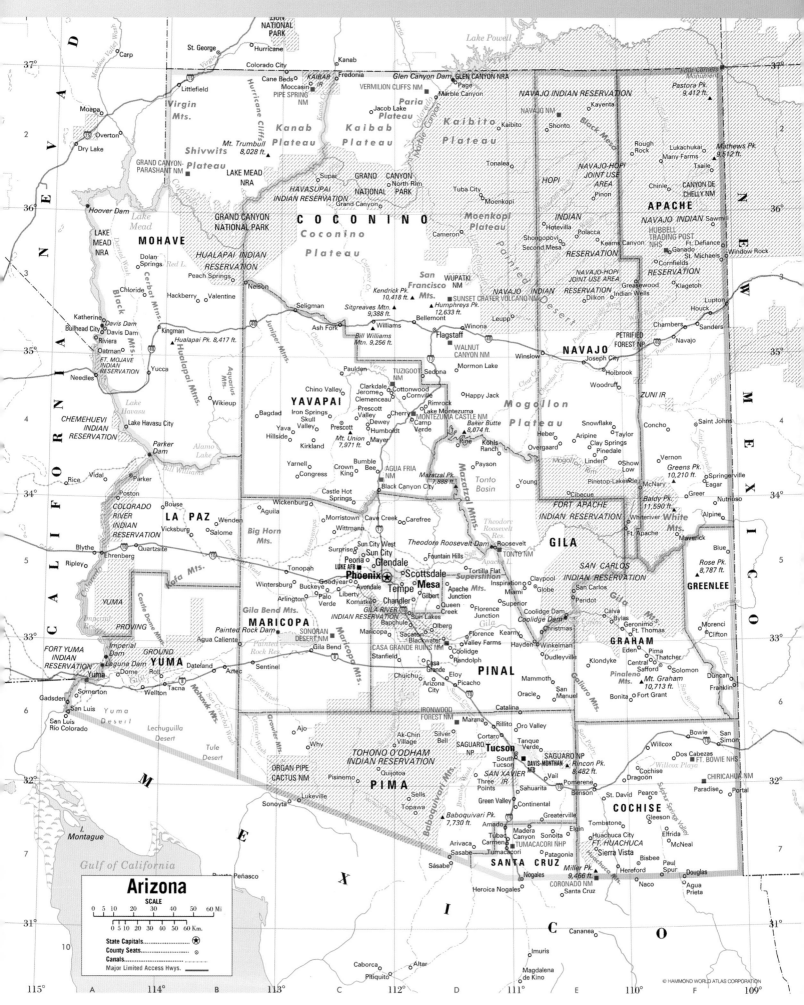

Arizona

SCALE

0 5 10   20   30   40   50   60 Mi

0 5 10 20 30 40 50 60 Km.

State Capitals...........................⊛
County Seats.............................◦
Canals....................................
Major Limited Access Hwys.

Arizona

FACTS & FIGURES

GEOGRAPHY

Total area: *113,998 sq mi (ranked 6th in size)*

Acres forested: *19.4 million*

CLIMATE

Clear and dry in the southern regions and northern plateau; high central areas have heavy winter snows

STATE TREE

Palo verde

AVERAGE TEMPERATURE

CITY	JUN	DEC
Flagstaff	60.1	30.2
Phoenix	88.6	54.3
Tucson	84.1	51.9
Winslow	72.1	34.1
Yuma	88.8	57.4

FAMOUS ARIZONANS

- Geronimo (1829–1909), Apache leader
- Zane Grey (1872–1939), novelist
- John McCain (b. 1936), U.S. senator
- William H. Pickering (1858–1938), astronomer
- Morris Udall (1922–1998), member of U.S. House of Representatives

Geronimo

ATTRACTIONS

Canyon de Chelly, *Chinle*

The Grand Canyon

The Painted Desert

Petrified Forest National Park

Meteor Crater, *near Winslow*

Navajo National Monument, *Navajo Nation*

Sedona

Arizona-Sonora Desert Museum; Saguaro National Park; San Xavier Mission, *Tucson*

TOPOGRAPHY

- Colorado plateau, containing the Grand Canyon, in the north
- Mexican Highlands running northwest to southeast
- Sonoran Desert in the southwest

Highest elevation: Humphreys Peak, 12,633 ft

Lowest elevation: Colorado River, 70 ft

Horseshoe Bend, near Page, Arizona, is a meander, formed by erosion, in the course of the Colorado River.

CAPITAL CITY: **PHOENIX**

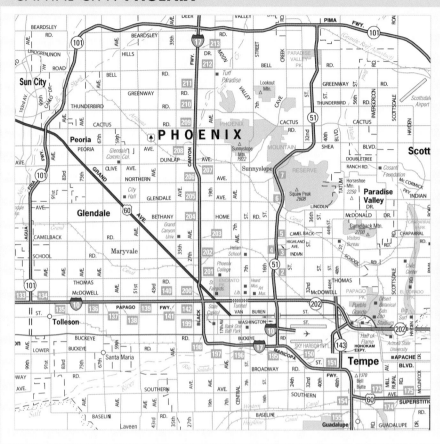

Arizona's largest city, Phoenix stands in the Salt River Valley, known as the "Valley of the Sun," and has the highest average summer temperature of any major city in the country. The temperature reaches 100° F at least 89 days of the year. The economy and population have grown rapidly since the late 20th century, making Phoenix the fifth largest city in the United States. The metro area is more than 4 million, 13th in the nation. Tourism is a key industry, with golf courses a main attraction.

Area: 474.9 sq mi

Population (2005): 1,461,575

Population density: 3,078 per sq mi

Per-capita income: $31,133

On average, Phoenix receives less than 8 inches of rain a year.

SPOTLIGHT CITY: **TUCSON**

At 2,389 feet above sea level, Arizona's second largest city is surrounded by mountain ranges. Landscapes include deserts, dry riverbeds, and pine-covered mountain peaks.

The city began as an 18th-century Spanish fort on the Santa Cruz River, which then flowed year-round but now is dry. With a growing metro population, Tucson depends on a 300-mile canal to carry much of its water. Conservation and water recycling are essential to its future sustainability.

Area: 194.7 sq mi

Population (2005): 515,526

Population density: 2,648 per sq mi

Per-capita income: $27,244

Saguaro cacti can grow to be 50 feet high.

Arizona

Antelope Canyon, in the Navajo Nation, is a slot canyon, a narrow canyon carved from sandstone by flash floods and wind.

Watson Lake, near Prescott, is surrounded by the Granite Dells, a region of unusual granite outcroppings.

The Colorado River runs 500 miles from the north to the south of the state.

The sedimentary rock making up the Grand Canyon is evident from the striations of the formations.

ARKANSAS

Regnat Populus (The people rule)

Settled: *1685*

Origin of name: *Algonquian name for the Quapaw Indians, meaning "south wind"*

Capital: *Little Rock*

Population (2005): *2,779,154 (ranked 32nd in size)*

Population density: *53.4 per sq mi*

ECONOMY

Chief industries: *Manufacturing, agriculture, tourism, forestry*

Chief manufactured goods: *Food products, chemicals, lumber, paper, plastics, electric motors, furniture, auto components, airplane parts, apparel, machinery, steel*

Chief crops: *Rice, soybeans, cotton, tomatoes, grapes, apples, commercial vegetables, peaches, wheat*

Chief ports: *Little Rock, Pine Bluff, Osceola, Helena, Fort Smith, Van Buren, Camden, Dardanelle, North Little Rock, West Memphis, Crossett, McGehee, Morrilton*

Gross state product (2005): *$86.8 billion*

Employment (May 2006): *17.6% government; 20.7% trade/transportation/utilities; 16.5% manufacturing; 12.5% education/health; 9.4% professional/business services; 8.2% leisure/hospitality; 4.4% finance; 4.7% construction; 5.2% other services*

STATE FLOWER

Apple blossom

STATE BIRD

Mockingbird

THE RAZORBACK STATE

Arkansas is the only place in North America where diamonds have been found, and so has been called the "Diamond State." It is also known as the "Hot Springs State," for the famous therapeutic springs that flow from Hot Springs Mountain in the western Ouachita Mountain Range. It is nicknamed the "Razorback State" after the state's feral pigs, known as razorbacks—the mascot of the University of Arkansas' teams. Northwest Arkansas is a plateau formed by the Ozark Mountains. In eastern Arkansas a plain rises westward from the Mississippi River, which forms the state's eastern border. Agriculture, automobile parts manufacturing, and tourism are major industries.

A Brief History

- Quapaw, Caddo, Osage, Cherokee, and Choctaw peoples lived in the area at the time of European contact.
- The first European explorers were Hernando de Soto, 1541; Jacques Marquette and Louis Jolliet, 1673; and René Robert Cavelier, Sieur de La Salle, 1682.
- French fur trader Henri de Tonty founded the first settlement, 1686, at Arkansas Post.
- The area was acquired as part of the Louisiana Purchase, 1803.
- Arkansas was made a territory, 1819, and entered the Union as a slave state, 1836.
- Arkansas seceded in 1861, after the Civil War began, and was readmitted, 1868.
- President Eisenhower sent federal troops, 1957, to keep Governor Orval Faubus from blocking racial integration in Little Rock.
- Wal-Mart, now the world's leading retailer, opened its first store at Rogers, 1962.
- Elected five times as governor, Bill Clinton later served two terms in the White House (1993–2001); his presidential library opened, 2004, in Little Rock.

Hot Springs National Park has been nicknamed "the American spa."

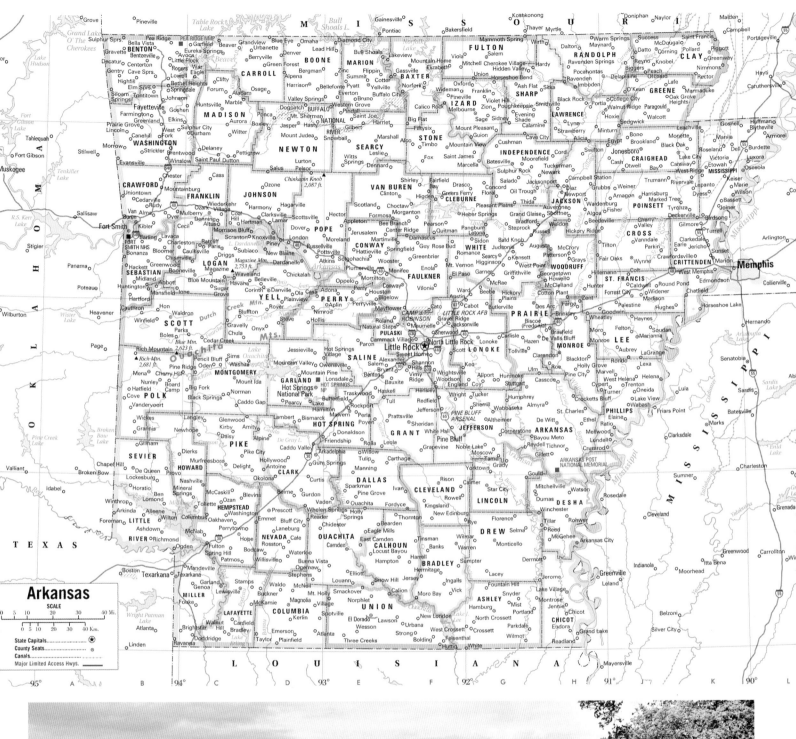

Arkansas

SCALE

0 5 10 20 30 40 Mi.

0 5 10 20 30 40 Km.

State Capitals..............★
County Seats..............◉
Canals..............
Major Limited Access Hwys.

Most of Arkansas's crops are grown in the southeastern part of the state, in the lowlands region known as the Delta and the Grand Prairie.

Arkansas

TOPOGRAPHY

- Eastern delta and prairie
- Southern lowland forests
- Northwestern highlands, which include the Ozark Plateau

Highest elevation:
Magazine Mountain, 2,753 ft

Lowest elevation:
Ouachita River, 55 ft

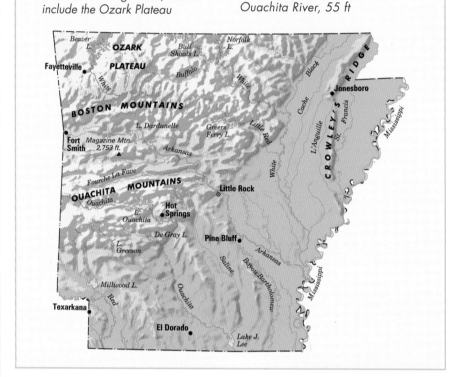

Lake Ouachita, in the Ouachita National Forest in western Arkansas, is the state's largest lake.

The Buffalo River was the first river in the country to be designated a national park, in 1972.

The Civilian Conservation Corps built this dam of native stone in the 1930s, forming 8-acre Lake Devil in the heart of northwest Arkansas' Devil's Den State Park in the Ozarks.

CAPITAL CITY: **LITTLE ROCK**

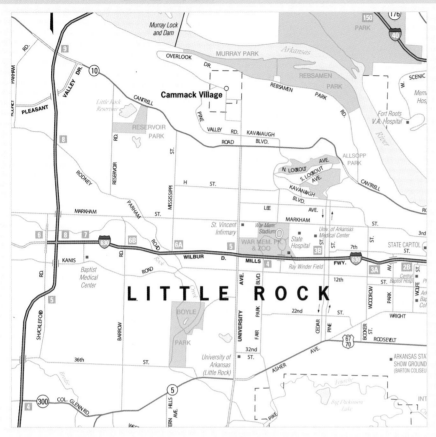

The "little rock" after which Arkansas' capital and most populous city was named was a natural stone formation—once an important landmark for travelers. At this point on the Arkansas River, which runs through the city of Little Rock, was a ford that marked the transition from the eastern plains to the foothills of the Ouachita Mountains.

Little Rock's six-county metro area has 652,000 residents and is near the state's geographic center.

The birthplace of World War II general Douglas MacArthur, Little Rock has the MacArthur Museum of military history. Another attraction is the presidential library of former Arkansas governor and 42nd president, Bill Clinton.

Area: 116.2 sq mi

Population (2005): 184,564

Population density: 1,575.9 per sq mi

Per-capita income: $23,209

Little Rock sits at the center of the Sun Belt.

Over millennia, the flowing waters of the Buffalo National River have carved a hole into this cavern to create the Glory Hole.

CALIFORNIA

CALIFORNIA REPUBLIC

Eureka (I have found it)

Settled: *1769*

Origin of name: *Bestowed by the Spanish conquistadors (possibly by Cortez), it was the name of an imaginary island, regarded as an earthly paradise, in a Spanish literary romance by Montalvo written in 1510.*

Capital: *Sacramento*

Population (2005): *36,132,147 (ranked 1st in size)*

Population density: *231.7 per sq mi*

ECONOMY

Chief industries: *Agriculture, tourism, apparel, electronics, telecommunications, entertainment*

Chief manufactured goods: *Electronic and electrical equipment, computers, industrial machinery, transportation equipment and instruments, food*

Chief crops: *Milk and cream, grapes, cotton, flowers, oranges, rice, nursery products, hay, tomatoes, lettuce, strawberries, almonds, asparagus*

Commercial fishing (2004): *$139 million*

Chief ports: *Long Beach, Los Angeles, San Diego, Oakland, San Francisco, Sacramento, Stockton*

Gross state product (2005): *$1.6 trillion*

Employment (May 2006): *16.5% government; 18.7% trade/transportation/utilities; 10% manufacturing; 10.8% education/health; 14.6% professional/ business services; 10.1% leisure/hospitality; 6.3% finance; 6.1% construction; 4.6% other services*

Per-capita income (2005): *$37,076*

STATE FLOWER	STATE BIRD

California poppy	California valley quail

THE GOLDEN STATE

The nickname for the nation's most populous state likely comes from the 1849 Gold Rush that made California world-famous. The Pacific coastline features wide beaches in the south and rugged cliffs where the coastal mountain ranges approach the water. The arid inland central valley has been irrigated to become one of the world's most productive agricultural regions. California's largest industry is agriculture. In the Sierra Nevadas, 14,494-foot Mount Whitney is the highest point in the lower 48 states, while North America's lowest point, 282 feet below sea level, is found in Death Valley. The climate is sunny year-round in the south and cooler and damper in the north. California's economy, led by Hollywood in entertainment and Silicon Valley in high-tech, dwarfs those of many countries.

A Brief History

- Early inhabitants included more than 100 different Native American tribes with multiple dialects.
- The first European explorers were Juan Rodríguez Cabrillo, 1542, and Francis Drake, 1579.
- The first settlement was the Spanish Alta California Mission at San Diego, 1769, first in a string founded by Franciscan Father Junipero Serra.
- California became a province of independent Mexico, 1821.
- U.S. traders and settlers arrived in the 19th century and staged the Bear Flag revolt, 1846, in protest against Mexican rule; later that year U.S. forces occupied California.
- At the end of the Mexican War, Mexico ceded the territory to the United States, 1848; that same year gold was discovered, and the famed Gold Rush began.
- California became a state, 1850.
- An economic downturn in the 1870s spurred riots against Chinese immigrants, who had come as laborers in the boom years.
- An earthquake and related fires devastated San Francisco, 1906.
- During World War II, Japanese Americans, many of them U.S. citizens, were held in detention camps, 1942–45.
- Ronald Reagan, a former movie actor, became state governor (1967–75) and U.S. president (1981–89).
- A budget crisis, 2003, resulted in the recall of Governor Gray Davis and the election of Arnold Schwarzenegger.

This drawing, c. 1854, by George Henry Burgess shows Butte City, California, an established mining community of about 40 buildings, near where Burgess camped while prospecting for gold with his brother.

California

FACTS & FIGURES

GEOGRAPHY

Total area: 163,696 sq mi (ranked 3rd in size)

Acres forested: 40.2 million

CLIMATE

Moderate temperatures and rainfall along the coast; extremes in the interior

STATE TREE

Coast redwood

AVERAGE TEMPERATURE

CITY	JUN	DEC
Los Angeles	70.5	58.5
Sacramento	71.5	45.8
San Diego	67.4	57.6
San Francisco	60.5	52.7
Santa Barbara	64.2	53.2

FAMOUS CALIFORNIANS

- Julia Child (1912–2004), chef
- Jack London (1876–1916), writer
- George Lucas (b. 1944), director
- Marilyn Monroe (1926–62), actress
- John Muir (1838–1914), preservationist
- Richard M. Nixon (1913–94), 37th U.S. president
- George S. Patton Jr. (1885–1945), World War II general
- Gregory Peck (1916–2003), actor
- Ronald Reagan (1911–2004), 40th U.S. president

George Lucas

ATTRACTIONS

Disneyland, *Anaheim*

J. Paul Getty Museum, *Los Angeles*

San Diego Zoo

Yosemite Valley

Lassen and Sequoia–Kings Canyon national parks

Lake Tahoe

Mojave and Colorado deserts

Napa Valley

Monterey Peninsula

Inyo National Forest, with a stand of bristlecone pines estimated to be 4,700 years old

TOPOGRAPHY

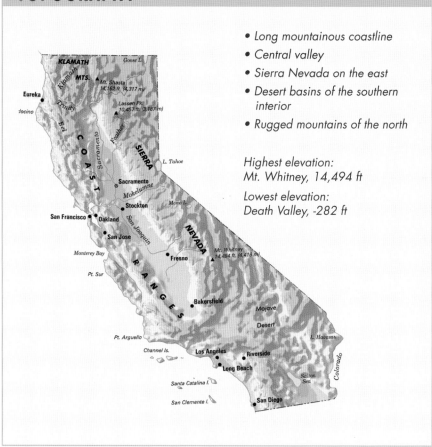

- Long mountainous coastline
- Central valley
- Sierra Nevada on the east
- Desert basins of the southern interior
- Rugged mountains of the north

Highest elevation:
Mt. Whitney, 14,494 ft

Lowest elevation:
Death Valley, -282 ft

CAPITAL CITY: **SACRAMENTO**

Sacramento was founded near where the American and Sacramento rivers converge.

SPOTLIGHT CITY: **SAN DIEGO**

California's second largest and southernmost city, San Diego is on the coast just north of Mexico. It is known for its beautiful surfing beaches. San Diego is home port to the world's largest naval fleet and has the world's greatest concentration of naval facilities. It is also home to the Coast Guard and Marines, a military presence that has brought major defense contractors to the city. Recently, San Diego has also become known as a leading center for biotechnology research.

Area: 324.3 sq mi

Population (2005): 1,255,540

Population density: 3,872 per sq mi

Per-capita income: $37,965

San Diego ranks as the second-largest city in the state.

The San Diego Zoo is known for its habitat exhibits and its efforts to breed endangered species.

An orca performs at SeaWorld, San Diego's marine mammal park.

California

The nation's second most densely populated city, San Francisco is famous for the cable cars that climb its steep hills and for the Golden Gate Bridge. One of the longest suspension bridges in the world, it spans the "Golden Gate," where the Pacific Ocean meets San Francisco Bay.

Sited on the tip of a peninsula, San Francisco has water on three sides, which often brings on a chilly fog. The city contains seven islands, the most famous being Alcatraz, formerly a notorious prison. Fisherman's Wharf and Chinatown are favorite tourist attractions.

In 1906, San Francisco was struck by a devastating earthquake and fire. The city was soon rebuilt, restoring the elegant Victorian structures that now stand alongside diverse modern architecture, giving San Francisco its distinctive, eclectic appearance.

Area: 46.7 sq mi

Population (2005): 739,426

Population density: 15,834 per sq mi

Per-capita income: $49,276

San Francisco's classic Victorian houses are known as painted ladies.

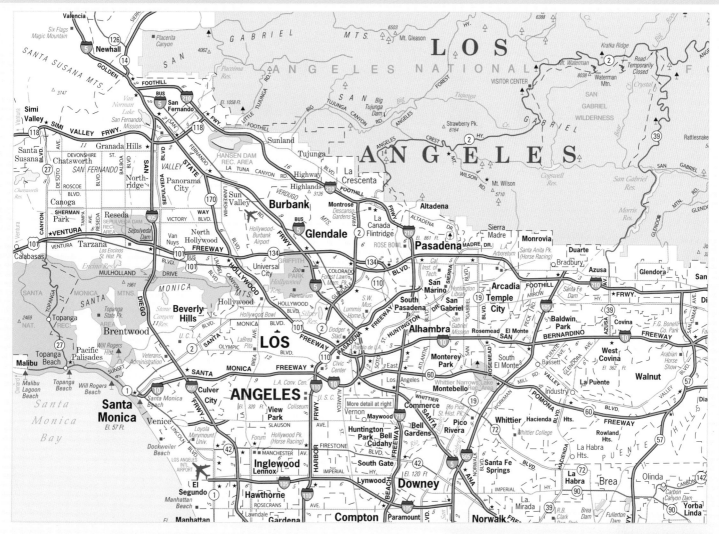

Los Angeles is the heart of the popular-entertainment industry, dominating in television, film, and music recording. The city is second only to New York in population; the five counties of Greater Los Angeles, however, have almost 18 million people, which is comparable to New York's metro area. Los Angeles is also the largest manufacturing center in the United States and is a leader in science and technology. The city is also a center for international trade, with the joint ports of Los Angeles and Long Beach among the busiest and most important in the world.

Los Angeles's original Spanish name, given to the city when it was founded in 1781, means, "Village of Our Lady, the Queen of the Angels of Porciuncula."

Area: 469.1 sq mi

Population (2005): 3,844,829

Population density: 8,196 per sq mi

Per-capita income: $35,188

The residential population of downtown L.A., the city's central business district, jumped by 20 percent between 2005 and 2007.

Hermosa Beach is the official birthplace of California surfing.

The original sign, erected in 1923, read: HOLLYWOODLAND.

California

Yosemite National Park, the nation's third oldest, was established in 1890. It is noted for its dramatic cliffs and waterfalls.

Monterey Bay supports one of the world's most diverse marine ecosystems, including huge forests of kelp. Marine mammals such as sea otters, harbor seals, and bottlenose dolphins live in the bay, and humpback and gray whales visit during migrations.

The ancient giant sequoias in Sequoia National Park are some of the tallest and longest-lived trees in the world.

COLORADO

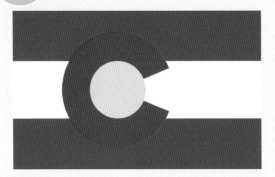

Nil Sine Numine (Nothing without Providence)

Settled: *1858*

Origin of name: *From Spanish for "red," a description first given to the Colorado River*

Capital: *Denver*

Population (2005): *4,665,177 (ranked 22nd in size)*

Population density: *45 per sq mi*

ECONOMY

Chief industries: *Manufacturing, construction, government, tourism, agriculture, aerospace, electronics equipment*

Chief manufactured goods: *Computer equipment and instruments, foods, machinery, aerospace products*

Chief crops: *Corn, wheat, hay, sugar beets, barley, potatoes, apples, peaches, pears, dry edible beans, sorghum, onions, oats, sunflowers, vegetables*

Gross state product (2005): *$216.1 billion*

Employment (May 2006): *16.6% government; 18.4% trade/transportation/utilities; 6.6% manufacturing; 10.1% education/health; 14.5% professional/business services; 11.2% leisure/hospitality; 7.1% finance; 7.4% construction; 7.3% other services*

Per-capita income (2005): *$37,946*

STATE FLOWER

Rocky Mountain columbine

STATE BIRD

Lark bunting

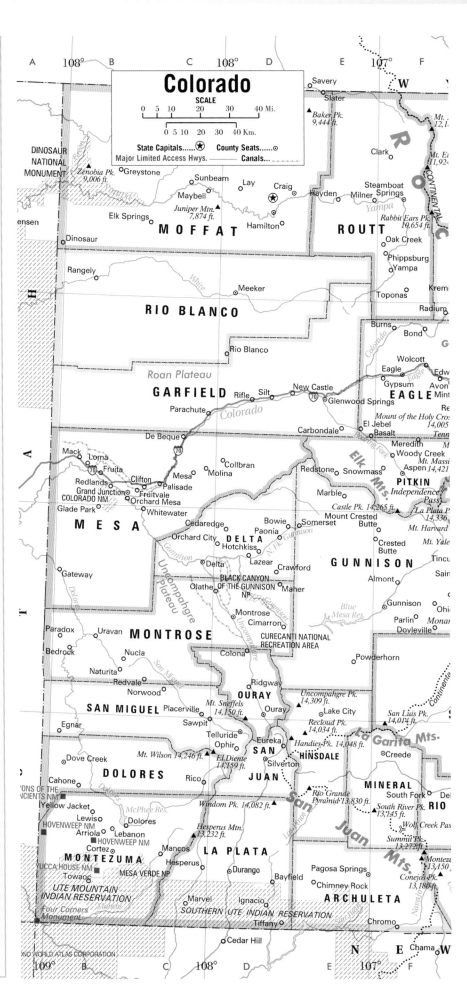

Colorado

AVERAGE TEMPERATURE		
CITY	JUN	DEC
Alamosa	59.4	17.1
Colorado Springs	64.4	29
Denver	67.6	30.3
Grand Junction	71.1	28.2
Pueblo	69.8	30.3

FAMOUS COLORADANS

Molly Brown

- Molly Brown (1867–1932), *Titanic* survivor
- M. Scott Carpenter (b. 1925), astronaut
- Jack Dempsey (1895–1983), boxer
- Mamie Eisenhower (1896–1979), First Lady
- Chief Ourey (1833–80), Native American leader
- Byron R. White (1917–2002), U.S. Supreme Court justice

ATTRACTIONS

Rocky Mountain and Black Canyon of the Gunnison national parks

Aspen ski resort

Garden of the Gods, *Colorado Springs*

Great Sand Dunes, Dinosaur, and Colorado national monuments

Pike's Peak and Mt. Evans highways

Mesa Verde National Park (ancient Anasazi cliff dwellings)

Grand Mesa National Forest

Mining towns of *Central City, Silverton,* and *Cripple Creek*

THE CENTENNIAL STATE

Colorado is known as the "Centennial State," since it became a state in 1876, the hundredth anniversary of the American Declaration of Independence. Colorado is divided, north to south, by the Colorado Rockies, which contain the highest city in the nation: Leadville, at 10,200 feet. With more than 50 peaks higher than 14,000 feet, the Rockies make up the highest portion of the lengthy North American Cordillera, the broad band of mountain ranges that runs from Alaska to Mexico. East of the mountains are the Great Plains, and west is the Colorado Plateau. The climate is dry and sunny, with Denver, on the east side of the mountains, receiving just 16 inches of rain a year. The chief 19th-century industries of mining and agriculture have been surpassed today by manufacturing. Tourism has also steadily grown, fueled by skiing and snowboarding.

A Brief History

- Paleoindians hunted big game in the area at least 11,000 years ago.
- Anasazi cliff dwellers flourished around Mesa Verde until c. 1300 CE; other Native Americans were the Ute, Pueblo, Cheyenne, and Arapaho.
- The region was claimed by Spain but passed to France, 1800.
- Eastern Colorado was acquired in the Louisiana Purchase, 1803.
- Lieutenant Zebulon M. Pike explored the area, 1806, sighting the peak that bears his name.
- After the Mexican War, 1846–48, U.S. immigrants settled in the east, former Mexicans in the south.
- Gold was discovered in 1858, causing a population boom.
- Colorado Territory was created by Congress, 1861.
- Conflict between newcomers and displaced Native Americans led to the Sand Creek Massacre, 1864, in which U.S. soldiers and settlers killed some 150 Cheyenne and Arapaho.
- Most Native Americans were later removed to Oklahoma Territory.
- The 1870s brought statehood, 1876, and rich silver finds that turned Leadville into a boomtown.
- Federal military and civilian employment in Colorado surged in the 1940s and 1950s; more recently, the economy has been fueled by tourism and high-tech industries.

Prospectors hoping to strike it rich headed for Pike's Peak during the Gold Rush.

TOPOGRAPHY

- Eastern dry high plains
- Hilly to mountainous central plateau
- Western Rocky Mountains of high ranges, with broad valleys and deep, narrow canyons

Highest elevation:
Mt. Elbert, 14,433 ft

Lowest elevation:
Arkansas River, 3,350 ft

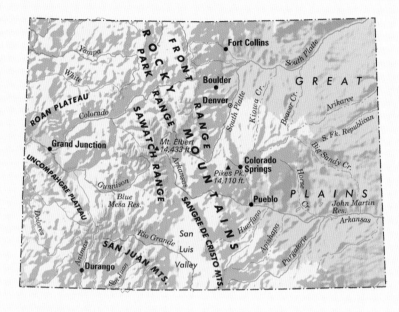

Hermosa Cliffs is north of Durango; hermosa is Spanish for "beautiful."

With more than 4,000 archeological sites, Mesa Verde has preserved the cliff dwellings of the Pueblo who lived there from 600 to 1300 CE.

CAPITAL CITY: **DENVER**

Colorado's capital and largest city, Denver sits on the western edge of the Great Plains, just east of the foothills of the Rocky Mountains. Called "the Mile-High City," Denver is more than 5,200 feet above sea level. The city is the financial, industrial, and cultural center of the Rocky Mountain region.

Established as a mining camp during the 1858 Gold Rush, its growth was spurred by the gold and silver boom.

Denver became the state capital in 1876, when Colorado joined the Union. Mining is still important to the local economy, as are oil and telecommunications. Denver's metro area has 2.92 million people, two-thirds of the state's population.

Area: 153.4 sq mi

Population (2005): 557,917

Population density: 3,637 per sq mi

Per-capita income: $40,939

Denver's location and mile-high elevation make a "one-bounce" satellite uplink possible to six continents in the same day.

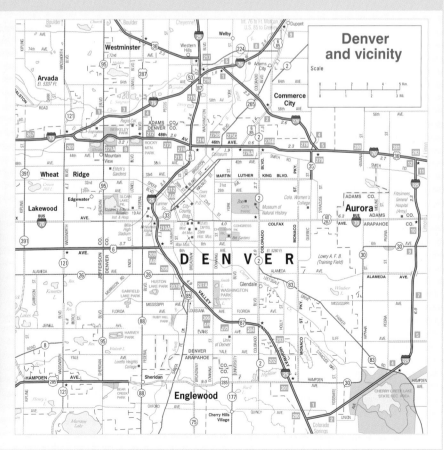

Colorado

Among the mountain peaks of Uncompahgre National Park lie abandoned ghost towns and mines, remnants of the mid-19th-century Gold Rush.

Mountain goats, introduced to Colorado in 1948, now thrive there.

Once a destination for gold and silver prospectors, Georgetown now draws hikers and mountain bikers.

Part of both the White River and Gunnison national forests, the Maroon Bells–Snowmass Wilderness is known for its beautiful mountain passes and alpine valleys and lakes.

CONNECTICUT

Qui Transtulit Sustinet (He who transplanted still sustains)

Settled: *1639*

Origin of name: *From Mohegan and other Algonquian words meaning "long river place"*

Capital: *Hartford*

Population (2005): *3,510,297 (ranked 29th in size)*

Population density: *724.5 per sq mi*

ECONOMY

Chief industries: *Manufacturing, retail trade, government, services, finances, insurance, real estate*

Chief manufactured goods: *Aircraft engines and parts, submarines, helicopters, machinery and computer equipment, electronics and electrical equipment, medical instruments, pharmaceuticals*

Chief crops: *Nursery stock, Christmas trees, mushrooms, vegetables, sweet corn, tobacco, apples*

Commercial fishing (2004): *$35.8 million*

Chief ports: *New Haven, Bridgeport, New London*

Gross state product (2005): *$194.5 billion*

Employment (May 2006): *14.9% government; 18.5% trade/transportation/utilities; 11.5% manufacturing; 16.5% education/health; 12.1% professional/business services; 8% leisure/hospitality; 8.5% finance; 3.8% construction; 6% other services*

Per-capita income (2005): *$47,819*

STATE FLOWER	STATE BIRD

Mountain laurel	American robin

THE CONSTITUTION STATE

Connecticut is the richest state, ranked first in both per-capita income and median household income. Much of that wealth belongs to businesspeople who commute to New York City. Southern Connecticut is suburban, while the northwest and northeast are rural. The Connecticut River flows southward, opening into a broad floodplain near Hartford, which is at sea level. The climate is mild—warmer and more humid near the coast. Although just 48th in size (only Delaware and Rhode Island are smaller), Connecticut has more than 200 miles of coastline on the Long Island Sound, an arm of the Atlantic Ocean. Until the late 20th century, fishing and boatbuilding figured large in the economy. Today, manufacturing, finance, and tourism are the chief industries. Connecticut is known as the "Constitution State" because in 1638 the colonists adopted one of the world's first democratic constitutions. Its other nickname, "Nutmeg State," recalls itinerant Connecticut peddlers who sold nutmegs—sometimes wooden ones.

A Brief History

- Inhabitants of the area at the time of European contact were Algonquian peoples, including the Mohegan and Pequot.
- Dutch explorer Adriaen Block was the first European visitor, 1614.
- By 1634, settlers from Plymouth Bay had started colonies along the Connecticut River; in 1637 they defeated the Pequots.
- The Colony of Connecticut was chartered by England, 1662, adding New Haven, 1665.
- A Patriot stronghold in the American Revolution, the state actively supported the antislavery movement and the Union cause in the Civil War.
- The state economy prospered in the 20th century from insurance- and defense-related industries.
- *Nautilus,* the first nuclear-powered submarine, was launched at Groton, in Connecticut's Thames River, 1954.

This portrait of Cinqué, or Cinquez, the leader of the Amistad rebellion, was done as he awaited trail in New Haven. Thanks to John Quincy Adams's eloquent defense, the kidnapped Africans were acquitted and returned to Africa.

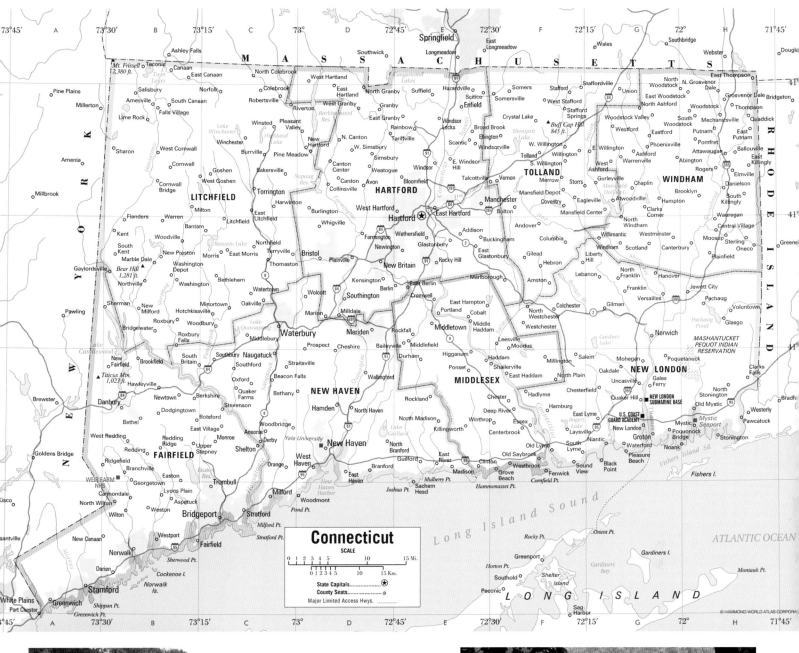

Connecticut

SCALE

0 1 2 3 4 5   10   15 Mi.

0 1 2 3 4 5   10   15 Km.

State Capitals..................... ★
County Seats..................... ⊚
Major Limited Access Hwys. _____

The Mohegan tribe once called the upper Thames River and its tributaries home.

Yantic Falls, known as Indian Leap, powered a gristmill in the 1600s.

Connecticut

FACTS & FIGURES

GEOGRAPHY

Total area: 5,543 sq mi (ranked 48th)

Acres forested: 1.9 million

CLIMATE

Moderate; winters average slightly below freezing; warm, humid summers

STATE TREE

White oak

AVERAGE TEMPERATURE

CITY	JUN	DEC
Bridgeport	68	35.1
Hartford	68.5	30.8

FAMOUS "NUTMEGGERS"

- Ethan Allen (1738–89), Revolutionary War hero
- Samuel Colt (1814–62), inventor
- Nathan Hale (1755–76), Revolutionary War hero
- J. Pierpont Morgan (1837–1913), financier
- Wallace Stevens (1879–1955), poet
- P.T. Barnum (1810–91), circus founder

Mark Twain

- Mark Twain (1835–1910), writer
- Noah Webster (1758–1843), lexicographer
- Eli Whitney

ATTRACTIONS

Mark Twain House, *Hartford*

Yale University Art Gallery; Peabody Museum, *New Haven*

Mystic Seaport, Mystic Marine Life Aquarium, *Mystic*

P. T. Barnum Museum, *Bridgeport*

Gillette Castle, *East Haddam*

USS *Nautilus* Memorial (1st nuclear-powered submarine), *Groton*

Mashantucket Pequot Museum & Research Center, *Ledyard*

The Maritime Museum, *Norwalk*

TOPOGRAPHY

- Western upland, the Berkshires, in the northwest, highest elevations
- Narrow central lowland north-south; hilly eastern upland drained by rivers

Highest elevation: Mt. Frisell, 2,380 ft

Lowest elevation: Long Island Sound, sea level

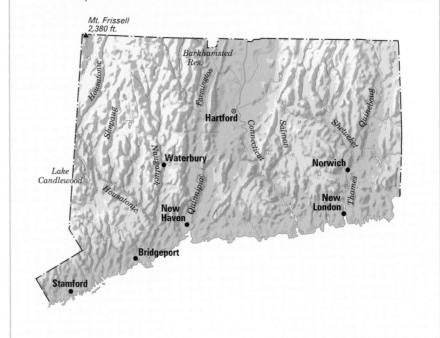

Founded in 1929, Mystic Seaport is the country's leading maritime museum.

Though the Thimble Islands number in the hundreds, all but the southernmost Outer Island are privately owned.

Using local fieldstone, a crew of 20 men worked for five years to build Gillette Castle in East Haddam.

CAPITAL CITY: **HARTFORD**

Connecticut's capital was a Dutch trading post in the early 17th century until English colonists arrived in 1635, outnumbered the Dutch, and took possession of it.

During the American Revolution and the nation's early years, Hartford often was a convention site for meetings of the elected leaders of the New England states. In the 19th century, the city became one of the East Coast's major manufacturing centers as well as a cultural and intellectual focal point. It was a center of abolitionist activity. In the 1870s and 1880s, Mark Twain wrote both *Huckleberry Finn* and *Tom Sawyer* while living in Hartford. The Twain home is a significant historic site, as is the Wadsworth Atheneum, the nation's oldest art museum.

By the 20th century, Hartford was known as the "insurance capital of the world" because so many insurance companies had headquarters there.

Area: 18 sq mi

Population (2005): 124,397

Population density: 7,189.8 per sq mi

Per-capita income: $13,428

Founded by Reverend Thomas Hooker in 1636, close to an earlier Dutch fort, Hartford was originally called House of Hope.

SPOTLIGHT CITY: **NEW HAVEN**

New Haven was founded in 1638 by Puritans from the Massachusetts Bay Colony seeking more religious freedom. They named their settlement in the hope that it would be a place of security for them.

New Haven is one of the oldest examples of town planning. The original grid design established the "Nine Squares," a block pattern that still shapes the center of downtown. The "Ninth Square" area has undergone revitalization, with new and renovated residences and upscale restaurants and nightclubs. New Haven is noted for its architecture and well-preserved historic districts. The 16-acre New Haven Green is a downtown historic landmark harking back to colonial times. Also downtown is Yale University, the city's largest employer.

Area: 20.3 sq mi

Population (2005): 124,791

Population density: 6,601.9 per sq mi

Per-capita income: $16,393

Yale was named for Welsh merchant Elihu Yale, who donated 417 books and a portrait of King George I in addition to money.

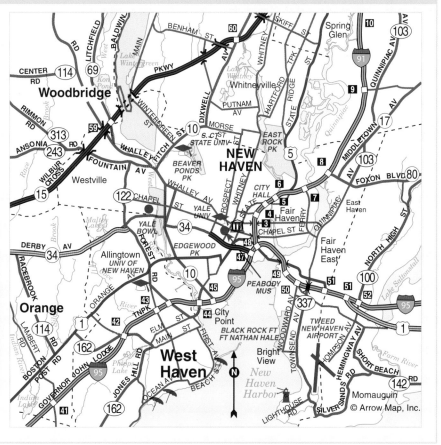

© Arrow Map, Inc.

DELAWARE

FACTS & FIGURES

DECEMBER 7, 1787

Liberty and independence

Settled: *1627*

Origin of name: *Named for Lord De La Warr, early governor of Virginia: first applied to Delaware River, then to native inhabitants (Lenni Lenape), and then to the state*

Capital: *Dover*

Population (2005): *843,524 (ranked 45th in size)*

Population density: *431.8 per sq mi*

ECONOMY

Chief industries: *Chemicals, agriculture, finance, poultry, shellfish, tourism, auto assembly, food processing, transportation equipment*

Chief manufactured goods: *Nylon, apparel, luggage, foods, autos, processed meats and vegetables, railroad and aircraft equipment*

Chief crops: *Soybeans, potatoes, corn, mushrooms, lima beans, green peas, barley, cucumbers, wheat, corn, grain sorghum, greenhouse and nursery*

Commercial fishing (2004): *$5.4 million*

Chief port: *Wilmington*

Gross state product (2005): *$54.4 billion*

Employment (May 2006): *14% government; 18.9% trade/transportation/utilities; 7.3% manufacturing; 12.7% education/health; 14.6% professional/business services; 9.6% leisure/hospitality; 10.2% finance; 6.6% construction; 6.3% other services*

Per-capita income (2005): *$37,065*

STATE FLOWER	STATE BIRD

Peach blossom	Blue hen chicken

THE FIRST STATE

One of the original 13 colonies, Delaware was named for the bay and river, which were named after the Virginia colonist and governor Lord De La Warr. As its nickname suggests, Delaware was the first state to ratify the United States Constitution, in 1787. With fine bays, beaches, and harbors, Delaware is part of the Atlantic Coastal Plain; its highest elevation is just 450 feet. The ocean moderates the climate, which is humid subtropical in the south. The second-smallest state (after Rhode Island), Delaware shares the 180-mile-long Delmarva Peninsula with parts of Virginia and Maryland. Delaware ranks 46th in population but is the 9th most densely populated state, with more than 430 people per square mile. The state is prosperous, ranking 9th in per-capita income. Delaware's major employers are chemical and pharmaceutical companies and financial institutions. Dover Air Force Base, one of the nation's largest, is also a leading employer.

A Brief History

- The Lenni Lenape (Delaware) people lived in the region at the time of European contact.
- Henry Hudson located the Delaware River, 1609, and in 1610, English explorer Samuel Argall entered Delaware Bay, naming the area after Virginia's governor, Lord De La Warr.
- Dutch, Swedish, and Finnish settlers were followed by the British, who took control in 1664.
- After 1682, Delaware became part of Pennsylvania, and in 1704 it was granted its own assembly.
- It adopted a constitution as the state of Delaware, 1776, and was first to ratify the federal Constitution, 1787.
- Although it remained in the Union during the Civil War, Delaware allowed slavery until the 13th Amendment abolished it in 1865.
- The DuPont Company, founded as a gunpowder mill in 1802, became an industrial giant in the 20th century, making nylon, Teflon, and other synthetics.
- The enactment of pro-business finance laws encouraged many out-of-state firms to incorporate in Delaware.

John Rubens Smith's 1830 painting "Mill on the Brandywine" depicts a paper mill, one of the many types of mills powered by the river during the American Industrial Revolution.

Delaware

FACTS & FIGURES

GEOGRAPHY

Total area: *2,489 sq mi
(ranked 49th in size)*

Acres forested: *0.4 million*

CLIMATE

*Moderate; transitional zone
between northern part of state
and humid, subtropical climate
in south; relatively hot and
humid summers*

STATE TREE

American holly

AVERAGE TEMPERATURE

CITY	JUN	DEC
Wilmington	71.5	36.4

FAMOUS DELAWAREANS

E. I. du Pont

- Thomas F. Bayard
  (1828–98),
  Grover Cleveland's
  secretary of state
- Joseph Biden (b. 1942),
  U.S. senator
- Henry Heimlich
  (b. 1920), physician
- E. I. du Pont
  (1771–1834), chemist
- John P. Marquand
  (1893–1960),
  novelist
- Caesar Rodney
  (1728–84), signer
  of the Declaration of
  Independence

ATTRACTIONS

Fort Christina Monument, site of founding of New
Sweden, and Holy Trinity (Old Swedes) Church,
erected in 1698, the oldest Protestant church in
the United States still in use, *Wilmington*

Hagley Museum; Winterthur Museum and
Gardens, *near Wilmington*

Historic district, *New Castle*

John Dickinson "Penman of the Revolution" home,
Dover

Rehoboth Beach

A view of Old New Castle Courthouse in 1936.

TOPOGRAPHY

- Piedmont plateau to the north,
  sloping to a near sea-level plain

Highest elevation: 448 ft
Lowest elevation: sea level

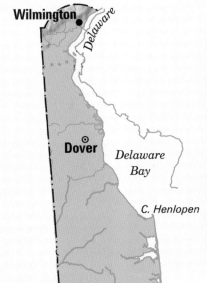

Delaware Bay

CAPITAL CITY: **DOVER**

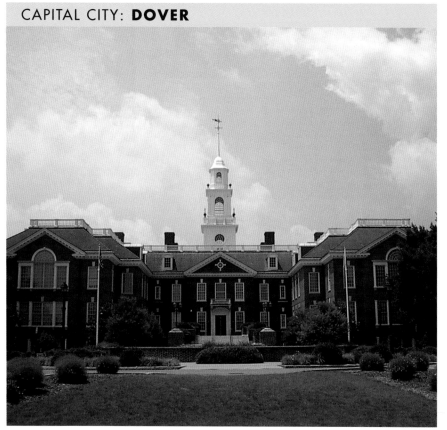

The town of Dover was founded in 1683 by William Penn. It became the capital in 1777 because its inland
location was considered safe from British raiders on the Delaware River. Dover's Legislative Hall, with its
Georgian Revival architecture, emulating colonial style, was built in 1931.

SPOTLIGHT CITY: **WILMINGTON**

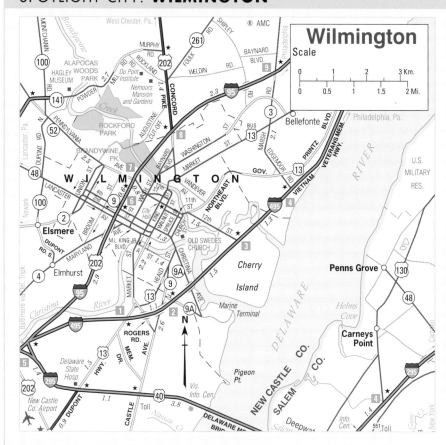

Wilmington

Scale

| 0 | 1 | 2 | 3 Km. |
| 0 | 0.5 | 1 | 1.5 | 2 Mi. |

Wilmington was settled in 1638 by Swedish colonists who built a trading post on the Christina River, which flows into the Delaware. That first colony was taken over by the Dutch in 1655 and by the English 9 years later. Delaware's largest city, Wilmington grew rapidly during the Civil War, when her workshops turned out ships, railroad cars, tents, uniforms, and gunpowder for the Union.

Heavy manufacturing and chemicals remained key to the city's prosperity, but financial institutions began to flourish in the late 20th century. This growth was stimulated by legislation liberalizing banking and incorporation laws. Wilmington has become a national center for the credit card industry. As part of the accompanying new construction and development, former shipyards have been renovated into the Wilmington Riverfront, with cultural venues, luxury residences, and shops.

Area: 10.9 sq mi

Population (2005): 72,644

Population density: 6,698.1 per sq mi

Per-capita income: $20,236

In the 17th century, Wilmington was under Swedish and Dutch rule before it was claimed by the British.

The largest freshwater pond in the state, Lums Pond was created to supply water to the locks of the Chesapeake and Delaware Canal when it was built in the early 19th century.

Scientists at the University of Delaware have been working to improve grazing land for horses, which have been a familiar sight in Delaware since Europeans first settled there in the early 17th century. Agricultural pursuits remain critical to Delaware's economy.

The Delaware estuary consists of salt marshes, tidal rivers, and woodlands.

FLORIDA

FACTS & FIGURES

In God we trust

Settled: *1565*

Origin of name: *Named Pascua Florida, or "Flowery Easter," by Spanish explorer Ponce de León on Easter Sunday in 1513*

Capital: *Tallahassee*

Population (2005): *17,789,864 (ranked 4th in size)*

Population density: *329.9 per sq mi*

ECONOMY

Chief industries: *Tourism, agriculture, manufacturing, construction, services, international trade*

Chief manufactured goods: *Electric and electronic equipment, transportation equipment, food, printing and publishing, chemicals, instruments, industrial machinery*

Chief crops: *Citrus fruits, vegetables, melons, greenhouse and nursery products, potatoes, sugarcane, strawberries*

Chief ports: *Pensacola, Tampa, Manatee, Miami, Port Everglades, Jacksonville, St. Petersburg, Canaveral*

Commercial fishing (2004): *$190.6 million*

Gross state product (2005): *$674 billion*

Employment (2006): *13.7% government; 19.9% trade/transportation/utilities; 5% manufacturing; 12% education/health; 17.1% professional/business services; 11.5% leisure; 6.7% finance; 7.7% construction; 6.3% other services*

Per-capita income (2005): *$33,219*

STATE FLOWER

Orange blossom

STATE BIRD

Mockingbird

THE SUNSHINE STATE

With the Gulf of Mexico on its west and the Atlantic Ocean on its east, Florida's famous peninsula forms one of the largest states east of the Mississippi. Today, it is the fourth most populous state in the country, with an economy that relies heavily on tourism. Warm weather and hundreds of miles of beaches, as well as Disney World and SeaWorld, attract about 60 million visitors to the state every year. Agriculture is a major industry. Florida produces roughly two-thirds of the citrus fruit grown in the United States and 95 percent of the orange juice. Florida is also where many Major League Baseball teams—known as the "Grapefruit League"—warm up for the season during spring training.

A Brief History

- Florida has been inhabited for at least 12,000 years. Timucua, Apalachee, and Calusa peoples were living in the region when the Europeans first came.
- Later the Seminole migrated from Georgia to Florida, becoming dominant there in the early 18th century.
- The first European to see Florida was Ponce de León, 1513.
- France established a colony, Fort Caroline, on the St. Johns River, 1564.
- Spain settled St. Augustine, 1565, and Spanish troops massacred most of the French.
- Britain's Sir Francis Drake burned St. Augustine, 1586.
- In 1763, Spain ceded Florida to Great Britain, which held the area for 20 years before returning it to Spain.
- After Andrew Jackson led a U.S. invasion, 1818, Spain ceded Florida to the United States, 1819.
- One of the Seminole Wars, 1835–42, resulted in the removal of most Native Americans to Oklahoma Territory.
- Florida joined the Union in 1845, seceded in 1861, and was readmitted in 1868.
- In the late 19th century, hotel and rail-road builder Henry M. Flagler laid the foundations of the tourism industry.
- The state experienced phenomenal population growth in the 20th century, especially after 1950.
- The first U.S. astronaut was launched into space from Cape Canaveral, 1961.
- Walt Disney World opened near Orlando, 1971.

St. Augustine is the oldest permanent European settlement in the United States.

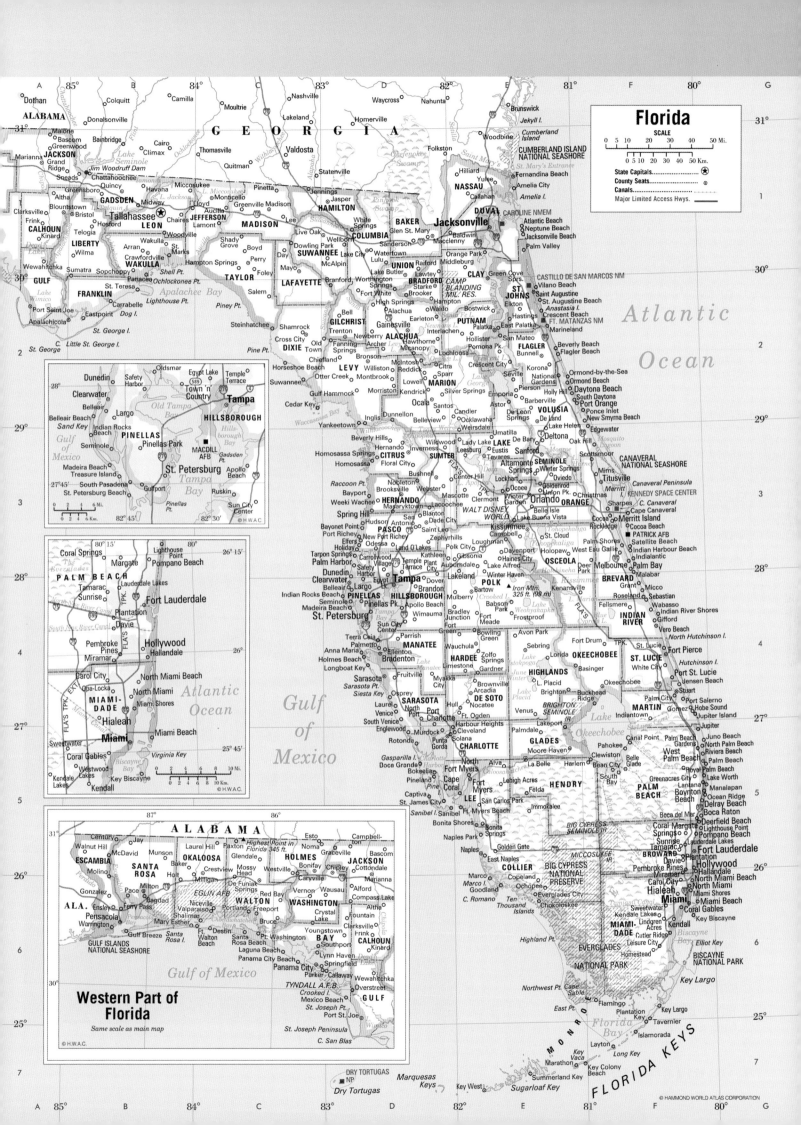

Florida

FACTS & FIGURES

GEOGRAPHY

Total area: *65,755 sq mi (ranked 22nd in size)*

Acres forested: *16.3 million*

CLIMATE

Subtropical north of Bradenton–Lake Okeechobee–Vero Beach line; tropical south of line

STATE TREE

Sabal palmetto palm

AVERAGE TEMPERATURE		
CITY	JUN	DEC
Jacksonville	79.1	55.0
Miami	82.4	69.9
Orlando	81.2	63.0
Tallahassee	80.4	53.7
Tampa	81.5	63.3

FAMOUS FLORIDIANS

- Zora Neale Hurston (1891–1960), writer
- James Weldon Johnson (1871–1938), poet
- Osceola (1804–38), Seminole leader
- Marjorie Kinnan Rawlings (1896–1953), writer
- Janet Reno (b. 1938), 1st female U.S. attorney general

Chief Osceola

- Joseph W. Stilwell (1883–1946), U.S. Army general

ATTRACTIONS

John F. Kennedy Space Center; NASA-Kennedy Space Center's Spaceport USA, *Cape Canaveral*

Everglades National Park

Miami Beach

Walt Disney World's Magic Kingdom; EPCOT Center; Disney-MGM Studios; Animal Kingdom; SeaWorld; Universal Studios, *near Orlando*

Ringling Museum of Art and Ringling Museum of the Circus, *Sarasota*

Castillo de San Marcos, *St. Augustine*

Busch Gardens, *Tampa*

TOPOGRAPHY

- Land is flat or rolling
- Highest point is in the northwest

Highest elevation: 345 ft
Lowest elevation: sea level

Key West, Florida

CAPITAL CITY: **TALLAHASSEE**

State capital since 1824, Tallahassee was the only capital east of the Mississippi to avoid capture in the Civil War. The new statehouse, built in 1977, faces the old capitol building, now a museum.

Everglades National Park is the largest subtropical wilderness in the United States.

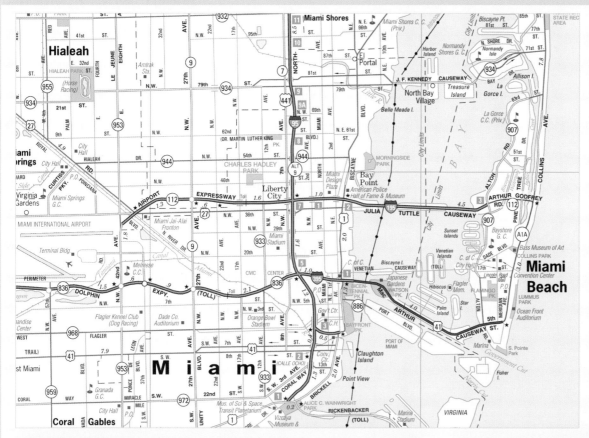

Known as the "Gateway to the Americas," Miami is a major financial and cultural center with strong ties to Latin America. The city is also called the "Cruise Capital of the World" because of its many luxury ships.

Founded as a fort in 1836, Miami is in southeastern Florida between the Everglades and the Atlantic. Almost 66 percent of the city's population is of Latino descent, more than half of which is Cuban. The metro population is 5.4 million, seventh in the nation.

In the 21st century, a new-construction boom in high-rises made Miami's skyline the third highest, after New York's and Chicago's.

Area: 35.7 sq mi

Population (2005): 386,417

Population density:
10,824 per sq mi

Per-capita income: $34,278

A winter destination for over a century, Miami Beach is famous for its nightclubs and expensive beachfront hotels, which draw millions of tourists every year.

South Beach, one of the richest sections of Miami, is known for its characteristic Art Deco architecture.

One of the country's most important financial centers, Miami has an extremely high concentration of multinational corporations and international banks.

Florida

SPOTLIGHT CITY: **ORLANDO**

With its famous tourist attractions, theme parks, and resorts, Orlando is one of the most popular vacation destinations in the world. Walt Disney World, SeaWorld, and Universal Orlando Resort (the former Universal Studios) attract more than 52 million visitors annually. Orlando, with its booming hotel industry, is one of the busiest cities in the country with conferences and conventions.

In 1838, during a war with the Seminole Indians, Fort Gatlin was built just south of present-day Orlando. The city was incorporated in 1875. Today, the Orlando–Kissimmee metro area is the third largest in Florida, with 1.97 million people.

Area: 93.5 sq mi

Population (2005): 213,223

Population density: 2,280 per sq mi

Per-capita income: $29,576

To accommodate the millions of tourists who come each year from all over the world, the city of Orlando has the second largest number of hotel rooms in the country.

One of SeaWorld's main attractions, Dolphin Cove is a 700,000-gallon lagoon that several Atlantic bottlenose dolphins call home.

Flamingos use their curved bills to filter mud and silt from the shrimp and other small crustaceans that they eat.

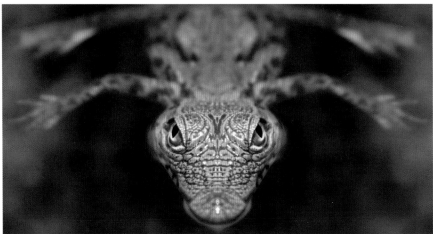

Florida is the only state in the United States where American crocodiles are found. They live in sheltered bays, coastal mangrove swamps, and inland freshwater swamps.

SPOTLIGHT CITY: **TAMPA**

Tampa, on the west coast of Florida, was founded in 1823 as a military post in Seminole territory. The fort was surrounded by swamps and often-hostile Seminoles, who opposed military intrusion into their lands.

Late in the 19th century Tampa was famous as a major producer of cigars. Today tourism is the leading industry. The city grew rapidly after 1950. The Tampa Bay area includes the cities of St. Petersburg and Clearwater, with a combined population of 2.7 million.

Tampa has the distinction of being the "Lightning Capital of the United States" because of its severe thunderstorms during the hot, wet summers.

Area: 112.1 sq mi

Population (2005): 333,040

Population density:
2,707 per sq mi

Per-capita income: $29,379

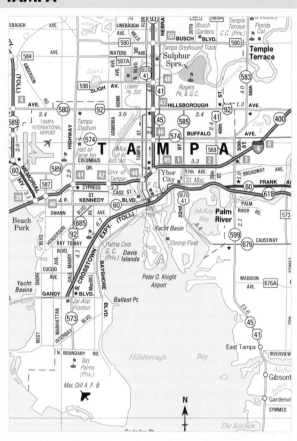

Tampa is bordered by bays that flow into the Gulf of Mexico.

Tampa's growth was spurred by the arrival of the railroad in the late 19th century and a surge of immigration.

SPOTLIGHT CITY: **JACKSONVILLE**

Jacksonville, in northeast Florida, is the state's largest city. The greater metro area has 1.3 million people.

The first settlement, founded on the St. Johns River in 1791, was named Cowford because it was a cattle-fording place. In 1822 it was renamed for Andrew Jackson, Florida Territory's military governor.

During the Civil War, Jacksonville's busy port was blockaded by the Union. Today this port, with three naval bases, is the second largest on the East Coast.

Jacksonville is the largest city in land area in the lower 48 states. Its urban park system, which includes Atlantic Coast beaches, is also the largest in the country.

Area: 757.7 sq mi

Population (2005): 782,623

Population density:
1,033 per sq mi

Per-capita income: $32,283

The St. Johns River, stretching 310 miles through eastern Florida, runs north through the city of Jacksonville to the Atlantic Ocean.

GEORGIA

Wisdom, justice and moderation

Settled: *1733*

Origin of name: *Named for King George II of England, by General James Oglethorpe, colonial administrator, in 1732*

Capital: *Atlanta*

Population (2005): *9,072,576 (ranked 9th in size)*

Population density: *156.7 per sq mi*

ECONOMY

Chief industries: *Services, manufacturing, retail trade*

Chief manufactured goods: *Textiles, apparel, food, and kindred products, pulp and paper products*

Chief crops: *Peanuts, cotton, corn, tobacco, hay, soybeans*

Commercial fishing (2004): *$11.3 million*

Chief ports: *Savannah, Brunswick*

Gross state product (2005): *$364.3 billion*

Employment (May 2006): *16.2% government; 21.2% trade/transportation/utilities; 11% manufacturing; 10.6% education/health; 13.4% professional/business services; 9.5% leisure/hospitals; 5.6% finance; 5.3% construction; 6.1% other services*

Per-capita income (2005): *$31,121*

STATE FLOWER	STATE BIRD

Cherokee rose	Brown thrasher

THE PEACH STATE

While half of all the peanuts grown in the United States are grown in Georgia, the state is nicknamed for its famous peaches. Agriculture and tourism are leading industries. Georgia's manufacturing output is diverse, from paper products to textiles and chemicals. A dozen major military installations also bolster the economy of one of the fastest growing states in the country. Northern Georgia is in the Blue Ridge Mountains, while the state's central region lies in the foothills. The southeast half of the state is coastal plain reaching to the Atlantic Ocean. In Georgia's southeast corner is the largest swamp in North America, the Great Okefenokee Swamp, comprising 700 square miles. An immense, peat-filled bog, it was named "quivering earth" by the native Choctaw because of the trembling of the deep watery beds of peat.

A Brief History

- Creek and Cherokee peoples were living in the region when Spaniards founded Santa Catalina mission, 1566, on Saint Catherines Island.
- General James Oglethorpe established a colony at Savannah, 1733, for the poor and religiously persecuted.
- Oglethorpe defeated a Spanish army from Florida at Bloody Marsh, 1742.
- Georgia was a battleground in the American Revolution, with the British finally evacuating Savannah in 1782.
- When Georgia entered the Union, 1788, its plantation economy relied on slaves to grow rice and cotton.
- The Cherokee were removed to Oklahoma Territory, 1832–38; thousands died on the long march, known as the Trail of Tears.
- By 1860 the number of slaves exceeded 462,000 (44 percent of the population).
- Georgia seceded from the Union, 1861, and was invaded by Union forces, 1864, under General William T. Sherman, who took Atlanta, September 2, and proceeded on his famous "march to the sea," ending in December, in Savannah.
- Georgia was readmitted, 1870.
- Born in Atlanta, 1929, Martin Luther King Jr. made the city his home base during the 1960s and the struggles of the Civil Rights Movement.
- Atlanta became the leading city of the "New South," world headquarters of Coca-Cola and CNN, and host of the 1996 Summer Olympic Games.

General Oglethorpe defeated Spanish troops invading Georgia from Florida in 1742.

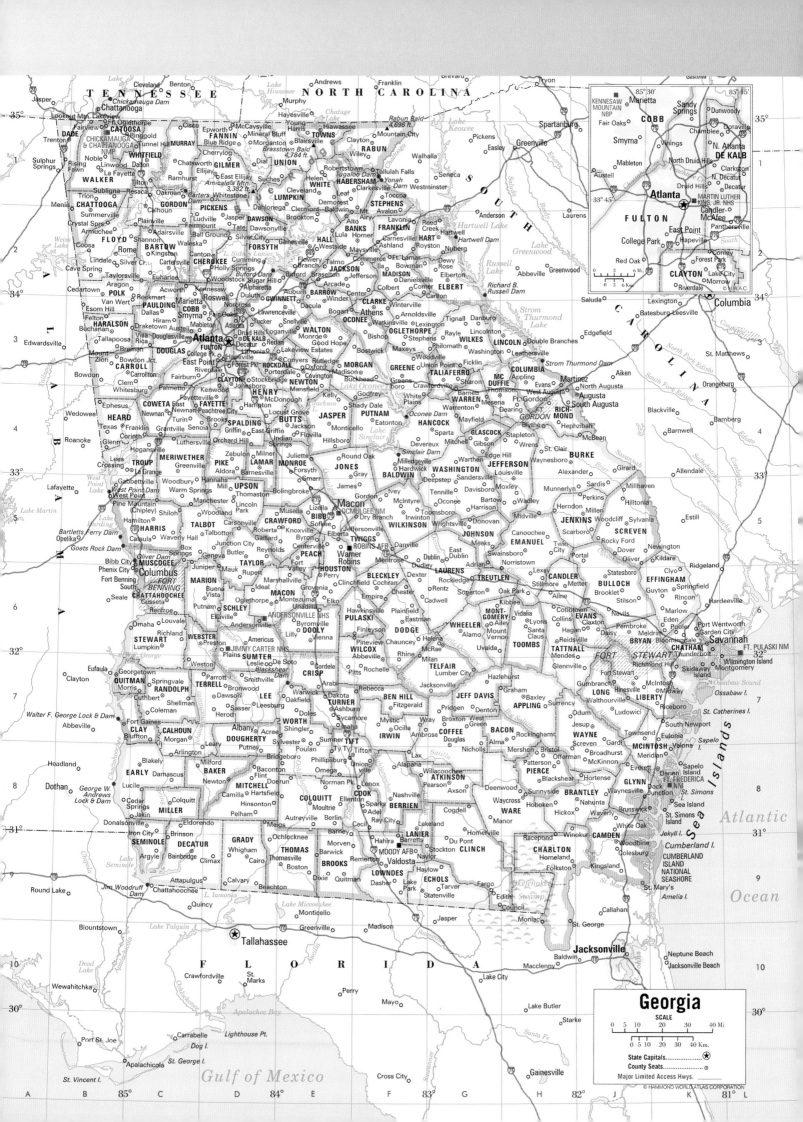

Georgia

FACTS & FIGURES

GEOGRAPHY
Total area: *59,425 sq mi* (ranked 24th in size)

Acres forested: *24.4 million*

CLIMATE
Maritime tropical air masses dominate in summer; polar air masses in winter; east central area drier

STATE TREE

Live oak

AVERAGE TEMPERATURE

CITY	JUN	DEC
Atlanta	76.8	45.4
Augusta	77.5	46.9
Savannah	78.8	51.4

FAMOUS GEORGIANS

- James Brown (1993–2006), singer
- Jimmy Carter (b. 1924), 39th U.S. president
- Ray Charles (1930–2004), singer
- Jasper Johns (b. 1930), painter
- Martin Luther King Jr. (1929–68), leader of Civil Rights Movement
- Gladys Knight (b. 1944), singer
- Otis Redding (1941–67), singer
- Jackie Robinson (1919–72), baseball player
- Clarence Thomas (b. 1948), U.S. Supreme Court justice

Ray Charles

ATTRACTIONS

State Capitol; Stone Mountain Park; Kennesaw Mountain National Battlefield Park; Martin Luther King Jr. National Historic Site; Jimmy Carter Library and Museum, *Atlanta*

Chickamauga and Chattanooga National Military Park, *near Dalton*

Chattahoochee National Forest

Brasstown Bald Mountain

Lake Lanier

Historic riverfront district, *Savannah*

Okefenokee Swamp, *near Waycross*

Jekyll Island; St. Simons Island; *Cumberland Island National Seashore*

TOPOGRAPHY

- Blue Ridge Mts. cover the northeast and north central part of the state
- Central Piedmont extends to the fall line of rivers
- Coastal plain levels to the coast flatlands

  Highest elevation: Brasstown Bald Mt., 4,784 ft

  Lowest elevation: sea level

One of the oldest rivers in the United States, the Chattahoochee runs along the Brevard Fault Zone, which extends from Alabama to Virginia. The river flows easily through the zone's sheared and fractured rock.

The southern terminus of the 2,160-mile Appalachian Trail is at Georgia's Springer Mountain.

CAPITAL CITY: **ATLANTA**

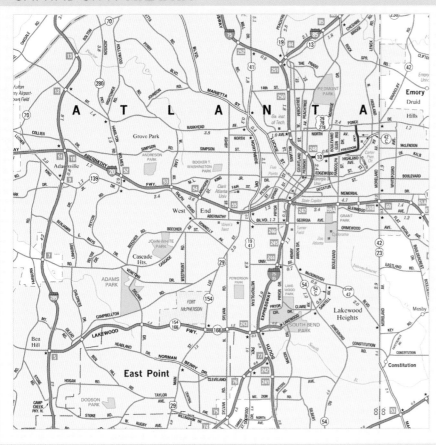

Founded in 1846 as a railroad station linking the South to the Midwest, Atlanta was originally named "Terminus."

The city became a boom town and soon developed into a focal point for commerce and railroads.

Atlanta's importance cost her dearly during the Civil War, when she was captured and burned by Union forces.

Georgia's capital (since 1877) and largest city, Atlanta, with a metro population of 5.13 million, keeps growing rapidly. As the South's leading city for business, and a major airline hub, Atlanta has become internationally influential. New York and Houston are the only cities with more Fortune 500 company headquarters than Atlanta. One of the companies the city is home to is Coca-Cola, which began there with the invention of the drink in 1884.

Area: 131.7 sq mi

Population (2005): 470,688

Population density: 3,574 per sq mi

Per-capita income: $33,838

As the third American city to host the Summer Olympics, in 1996, Atlanta undertook major improvements of the city's parks.

SPOTLIGHT CITY: **SAVANNAH**

Georgia's fourth-largest city, Savannah was the first capital of both the colony and the state. Named for the Savannah River, the city has a marshy, flat topography requiring canals and pumps to prevent flooding.

Savannah became an industrial center late in the 19th century, but it had already amassed great wealth as a port city. By 1820, annual exports of agricultural products from the plantations were valued at more than $18 million.

Since colonial times Savannah has had a cosmopolitan mix of people and cultures. Jews from Spain and Portugal arrived soon after the settlement's founding in 1733, and many non-British immigrants followed: Huguenots, Irish Catholics, and Greek Orthodox.

In the 19th century the city emulated Paris in its decorative use of parks and fountains. Savannah's spirit of historic preservation has saved magnificent homes and sites ranging from cotton warehouses to a colonial graveyard.

Area: 78.1 sq mi

Population (2005): 128,500

Population density: 1,759.5 per sq mi

Per-capita income: $16,921

Known for its architectural beauty, Savannah, one of the first planned cities, was founded the same year as the state, in 1733.

HAWAII

The life of the land is perpetuated in righteousness

Settled: *Polynesians from islands 2,000 miles to the south settled Hawaii between 300 and 600 CE*

Origin of name: *Possibly derived from native word for homeland, Hawaiki or Owhyhee*

Capital: *Honolulu*

Population (2005): *1,275,194 (ranked 42nd in size)*

Population density: *198.5 per sq mi*

ECONOMY

Chief industries: *Tourism, defense, sugar, pineapples*

Chief manufactured goods: *Processed sugar, canned pineapple, clothing, foods, printing and publishing*

Chief crops: *Sugarcane, pineapples, macadamia nuts, coffee, vegetables, floriculture*

Commercial fishing (2004): *$57.2 million*

Chief ports: *Honolulu, Hilo, Kailua*

Gross state product (2005): *$53.7 billion*

Employment (May 2006): *20% government; 19.6% trade/transportation/utilities; 2.5% manufacturing; 11.5% education/health; 12.4% professional/business services; 17.4% leisure/hospitals; 4.8% finance; 5.8% construction; 6% other services*

Per-capita income (2005): *$34,539*

STATE FLOWER

Yellow hibiscus

STATE BIRD

Hawaiian goose

THE ALOHA STATE

Before the eight main islands of the Hawaiian archipelago became a United States territory in 1898, Hawaii had been a kingdom of Polynesian people. *Aloha* is one of several Hawaiian words (along with *ukulele, luau,* and *lei*) adopted into the American vernacular. *Aloha* has a number of meanings, including "hello," "good-bye," "love," and "peace." Not only is Hawaii the newest state in the Union (admitted in 1959), but its islands are among the youngest on the globe. The many active volcanoes, whose eruptions created Hawaii, attest to this newness. Famed for natural beauty and a tropical climate, Hawaii has a thriving tourism industry, although government is the main employer. Hawaii is the southernmost state, the islands and atolls stretching for 1,500 miles across the Pacific region known as Oceania.

A Brief History

- Polynesians from islands 2,000 miles to the south settled the Hawaiian Islands, probably 300–600 CE.
- The first European visitor was British captain James Cook, 1778.
- King Kamehameha I united the islands by 1810.
- Christian missionaries arrived, 1819, bringing Western culture.
- Under the reign of King Kamehameha III, 1825–54, a constitution, legislature, and public school system were instituted.
- Sugar production began, 1835, and soon became the dominant industry.
- Queen Liliuokalani was deposed, 1893, and a republic established, 1894.
- The islands were annexed by the United States in 1898.
- The Japanese attack on Pearl Harbor, December 7, 1941, brought the United States into World War II.
- Hawaii attained statehood, 1959.
- Hurricane Iniki pounded Kauai, 1992, causing about $1 billion in damage.
- In 2006, President George W. Bush designated the Northwestern Hawaiian Islands National Monument, a marine area of 140,000 square miles.

The 1941 battleground of Pearl Harbor is a war memorial today.

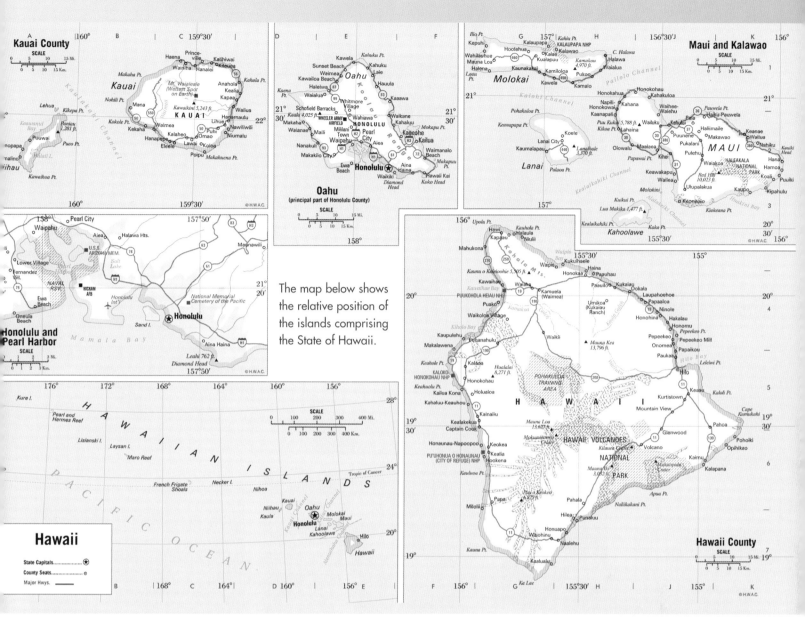

Kauai County

SCALE

Kauai

Mt. Waialeale
(Wettest Spot
on Earth!)

Kawaikini 5,243 ft.

KAUAI

Niihau

Lehua

Honolulu and Pearl Harbor

SCALE

Honolulu

The map below shows the relative position of the islands comprising the State of Hawaii.

Oahu
(principal part of Honolulu County)

SCALE

Honolulu

Diamond Head

Koko Head

Maui and Kalawao

SCALE

Molokai

Lanai

Lanai City

Kahoolawe

MAUI

HALEAKALA NATIONAL PARK

Red Hill 10,023 ft.

HAWAIIAN ISLANDS

PACIFIC OCEAN

Tropic of Cancer

Kure I.
Pearl and Hermes Reef
Lisianski I.
Laysan I.
Maro Reef
French Frigate Shoals
Necker I.
Nihoa

Kauai
Niihau
Kaula
Oahu
Honolulu
Molokai
Lanai
Maui
Kahoolawe
Hilo
Hawaii

Hawaii

State Capitals.................. ✪
County Seats.................. ◉
Major Hwys. ——

HAWAII

Mauna Kea 13,796 ft.

Mauna Loa 13,677 ft.

Hualalai 8,271 ft.

HAWAII VOLCANOES NATIONAL PARK

Kilauea Crater

Hilo

Hawaii County

SCALE

© H.W.A.C.

Kawili Beach, in Halawa Beach Park, offers calm waters in summer and good surfing in winter.

Hawaii

FACTS & FIGURES

GEOGRAPHY

Total area: 10,931 sq mi
(ranked 43rd in size)

Acres forested: 1.7 million

CLIMATE

Subtropical, with wide
variations in rainfall;
Waialeale, on Kauai,
is the wettest spot in the
United States.

STATE TREE

Kukui (candlenut)

AVERAGE TEMPERATURE

CITY	JUN	DEC
Hilo	75.1	72.2
Honolulu	79.5	74.8
Kahului	77.6	73.4
Lihue	77.7	73.3

FAMOUS ISLANDERS

- Duke Kahanamoku
  (1890–1968),
  Olympic swimmer
- King Kamehameha I
  (1758–1819),
  1st ruler of united
  Kingdom of Hawaii
- Don Ho (1930–2007),
  musician
- Daniel K. Inouye
  (b. 1924), senator
- Queen Liliuokalani
  (1838–1917),
  last monarch of
  Kingdom of Hawaii

Queen Liliuokalani

- Ellison Onizuka
  (1946–86),
  astronaut on the
  Challenger shuttle

ATTRACTIONS

Hawaii Volcanoes National Park

Haleakala National Park

National Memorial Cemetery of the Pacific,
Waikiki Beach

Diamond Head, *Honolulu*

USS *Arizona* Memorial, *Pearl Harbor*

Hanauma Bay

Polynesian Cultural Center, *Laie*

Nu'uanu Pali

Waimea Canyon

Wailoa and Wailuku River state parks

TOPOGRAPHY

- Islands are tops of a chain of
  submerged volcanic mountains
- Active volcanoes are Mauna Loa
  and Kilauea

Highest elevation:
Puu Wekiu, 13,796 ft

Lowest elevation:
Pacific Ocean, sea level

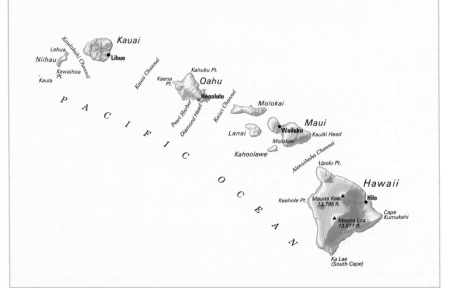

The force of the Akaka Falls plummeting 442 feet
has created a gorge in the rock below it.

Volcanic activity and erosion by wind, rain, and ocean
have shaped Hawaii's topography.

CAPITAL CITY: **HONOLULU**

In the 19th century, when Honolulu was capital of the Kingdom of Hawaii, its port was an essential stopover for any ships sailing between North America and Asia. The meaning of Honolulu is "sheltered bay."

As a state capital in modern times, Honolulu receives most visitors by airline, including millions of tourists annually. Visitors are attracted to the Waikiki district, with its world-famous beach, just a short hike to the volcanic cone, Diamond Head, an icon of Hawaii.

Honolulu was the scene of disaster in December 1941, when a surprise Japanese air assault on Pearl Harbor's naval base crippled the U.S. fleet and brought America into World War II. Memorials to those lost on that day are among the main tourist attractions.

Honolulu stands on Oahu, the third largest Hawaiian island (almost 600 sq mi). The island has 900,000 people, 75 percent of the state's population.

Area: 85.7 sq mi

Population (2005): 377,379

Population density: 4,403 per sq mi

Per-capita income (2004): $34,911

Named the capital of the Hawaiian kingdom in 1850, Honolulu now serves as the capital of the 50th state.

Geographically the oldest of Hawaii's islands, Kauai is the only island not to have been conquered by King Kamehameha I.

Hawaii

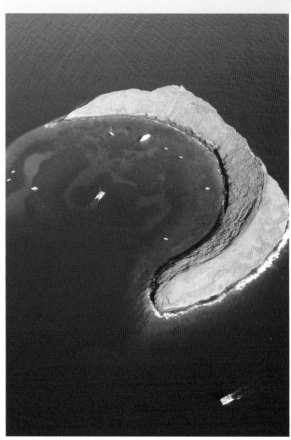

Located just off the coast of Maui, the crescent-shaped Molokini Crater has some of the best snorkeling and diving around. Because the island is now a wildlife preserve, people are no longer allowed on the island.

The island of Kauai is known for its lush tropical foliage and its wildlife preserves for endangered species of birds. Many native forest and song birds are only found above 3,000 feet.

The Koko Crater, on the island of Oahu, has the highest tuff ring in Hawaii. Tuff rings are created by volcanic material cooling in water.

The Haleakala Crater (meaning "House of the Sun") boasts the largest dormant volcano in the world.

The Na Pali Coast is a rugged series of narrow valleys, carved by the island's streams and waterfalls, and pali, or cliffs, only accessible to hikers.

IDAHO

FACTS & FIGURES

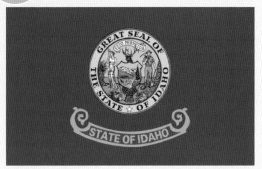

Esto Perpetua (It is perpetual)

Settled: *1842*

Origin of name: *Said to have been coined for the new mining territory of the Pacific Northwest to mean "gem of the mountains." An alternative theory is that Idaho was a Kiowa Apache term for the Comanche.*

Capital: *Boise*

Population (2005): *1,429,096 (ranked 39th in size)*

Population density: *17.3 per sq mi*

ECONOMY

Chief industries: *Manufacturing, agriculture, tourism, lumber, mining, electronics*

Chief manufactured goods: *Electronic components, computer equipment, processed foods, lumber and wood products, chemical products, primary metals, fabricated metal products, machinery*

Chief crops: *Potatoes, peas, dry beans, sugar beets, alfalfa seed, lentils, wheat, hops, barley, plums and prunes, mint, onions, cherries, apples, hay*

Chief port: *Lewiston*

Gross state product (2005): *$47.2 billion*

Employment (May 2006): *18.7% government; 19.7% trade/transportation/utilities; 9.9% manufacturing; 10.9% education/health; 12.8% professional/business services; 9.5% leisure/hospitals; 5% finance; 8.2% construction; 4.8% other services*

Per-capita income (2005): *$28,158*

STATE FLOWER	STATE BIRD

Syringa	Mountain bluebird

THE GEM STATE

The Rocky Mountains occupy most of Idaho; the Snake River Plateau cuts through the state's southern regions. Fertile farmland and open grazing land border the Snake River, which flows westward over the plains, then turns northward to become part of Idaho's western border. Hydroelectric plants on the Snake and its tributaries generate most of the state's electricity. As with other western states, Idaho's economy depends on agriculture, lumber, tourism, and mining. Idaho produces one third of the nation's silver. Called the "Gem State," Idaho has deposits of 72 types of precious and semiprecious stones, more than anywhere in the world but Africa. Famous for its potatoes, Idaho grows one-fourth of the nation's crop. The state also leads the country in commercially raised trout. Idaho's northern mountains protect it from cold Arctic air, and westerly winds from the Pacific moderate temperatures. Idaho has an annual average rainfall of only 12 inches.

A Brief History

- At the time of European exploration, inhabitants included Shoshone, Northern Paiute, Bannock, and Nez Perce peoples.
- Lewis and Clark explored the region, 1805–06, followed by American and European fur traders, 1809–34, and missionaries, 1830s to 1850s.
- Mormons made their first permanent settlement at Franklin, 1860.
- Idaho's gold rush began in 1860 and brought thousands of settlers. A series of Indian wars followed, including a campaign by Chief Joseph and the Nez Perce that ended with his surrender in Montana, 1877.
- Idaho became a territory, 1863, and a state, 1890.
- In the 20th century, Idaho began to lead in potato, lumber, and silver output.
- The opening of the Sun Valley ski resort, 1936, boosted tourism; the startup of Lewiston's river port, 1975, opened Idaho to oceangoing trade.
- Driven by growth in high-tech industry, the population jumped 10.4 percent from 2000 to 2005.

Edward S. Curtis photographed this Nez Perce tribesman on horseback about the year 1910.

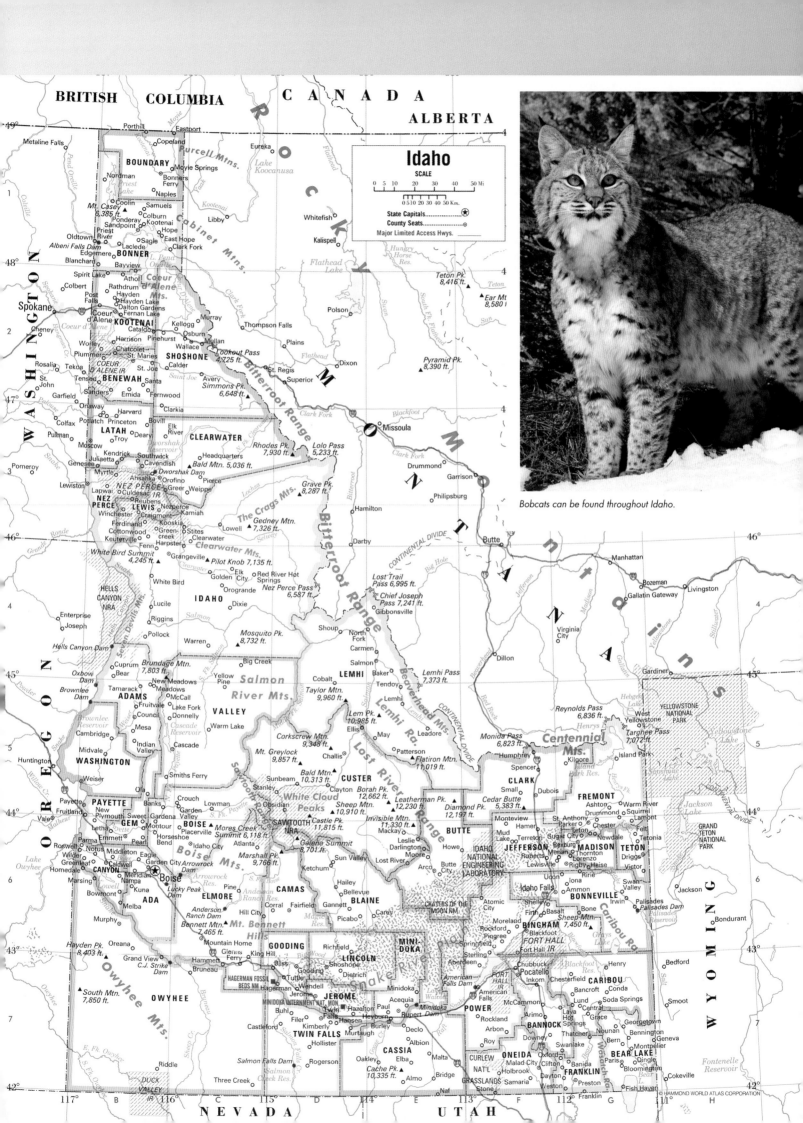

Bobcats can be found throughout Idaho.

Idaho

FACTS & FIGURES

GEOGRAPHY

Total area: 83,570 sq mi (ranked 14th in size)

Acres forested: 21.6 million

CLIMATE

Mountain state tempered by Pacific westerly winds; drier, colder, continental climate in southeast; altitude an important factor

STATE TREE

White pine

AVERAGE TEMPERATURE

CITY	JUN	DEC
Boise	67.2	30.6
Lewiston	65.8	33.9
Pocatello	62	25.3

FAMOUS IDAHOANS

- Frank Church (1924–84), senator
- Chief Joseph (1840–1904), Nez Perce chief
- Harmon Killebrew (b. 1936), baseball Hall-of-Famer
- Ezra Pound (1885–1972), poet
- Sacagawea (1787–1812), Shoshone guide
- Picabo Street (b. 1971), skier

Ezra Pound

ATTRACTIONS

Crystal Falls Cave, *American Falls*

River of No Return Wilderness Area

World Center for Birds of Prey, *Boise*

Hells Canyon, deepest gorge in North America

Lava Hot Springs

Craters of the Moon, *near Pocatello*

Sun Valley; Redfish Lake, *in Sawtooth Mountains*

Shoshone Falls, *east of Twin Falls*

Lake Pend Oreille, *Sandpoint*

Lake Coeur d'Alene

Sawtooth National Recreation Area, *Ketchum*

TOPOGRAPHY

- Snake River Plain in the south
- Central region of mountains, canyons, and gorges
- Subalpine northern region

Highest elevation: Borah Peak, 12,662 ft

Lowest elevation: Snake River, 710 ft

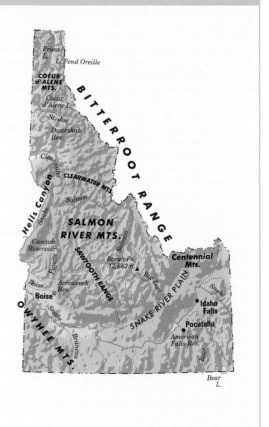

Wheat field, eastern Idaho

Idaho's City of Rocks features granite spires more than 60 stories in height, some more than 2 million years old.

The Snake River's Shoshone Falls are 212 feet high, 36 feet higher than Niagara Falls.

The Snake River's name is attributed to Shoshone tribesmen who made snakelike movements with their hands to signify swimming salmon. After crossing southern Idaho, the river enters Hells Canyon.

CAPITAL CITY: **BOISE**

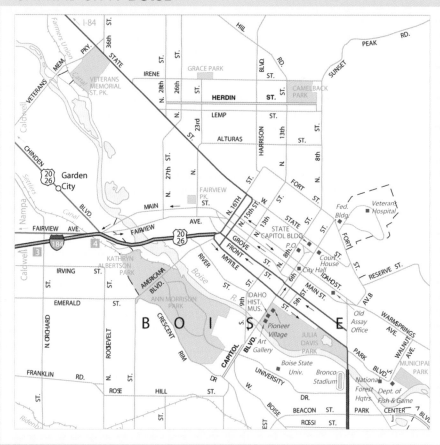

Idaho's capital, Boise, is the state's only city with a population greater than 100,000. Set along the Boise River in the southwest, Boise stands near the foot of the mountains to the north. The region's shady, tree-lined riverbanks were a welcome respite to travelers crossing the arid Snake River Plateau. Fort Boise was established by the federal government in 1863 to protect the community and to serve the gold miners as well as the wagon trains journeying to Oregon and California.

The nearby Boise National Forest has many abandoned mines and ghost towns. The construction of railroads and reservoirs in the 20th century promoted Boise's development as a commercial center for wholesale trade and trucking.

Area: 64 sq mi

Population (2005): 216,248

Population density: 3,379 per sq mi

Per-capita income: $31,249

The city of Boise was named by French-Canadian trappers, who made reference to its plentiful trees (boisé is French for "wooded").

Central Idaho's Sawtooth Mountains have been called the American Alps. The Sawtooth National Forest's 2.1 million acres contain more than 3,000 miles of rivers and streams.

ILLINOIS

FACTS & FIGURES

ILLINOIS

State sovereignty—national union

Settled: *1720*

Origin of Name: *French for Illini, or "land of Illini," Algonquian word meaning "men" or "warriors"*

Capital: *Springfield*

Population (2005): *12,763,371 (ranked 5th in size)*

Population density: *229.6 per sq mi*

ECONOMY

Chief industries: *Services, manufacturing, travel, wholesale and retail trade, finance, insurance, real estate, construction, health care, agriculture*

Chief manufactured goods: *Machinery, electric and electronic equipment, metals, chemical products, printing and publishing, food*

Chief crops: *Corn, soybeans, wheat, sorghum, hay*

Chief ports: *Chicago*

Gross state product (2005): *$560.2 billion*

Employment (May 2006): *14.4% government; 20% trade/transportation/utilities; 11.4% manufacturing; 12.7% education/health; 14.3% professional/business services; 9.1% leisure/hospitals; 6.9% finance; 4.7% construction; 6.4% other services*

Per-capita income (2005): *$36,120*

STATE FLOWER	STATE BIRD

Native violet	Cardinal

THE PRAIRIE STATE

Known as the "Prairie State" for the vast grasslands that cover almost 90 percent of the land, Illinois is also called the "Land of Lincoln," honoring Abraham Lincoln's residence there before he became president in 1861. One of the Great Lakes States, Illinois is at the southwest end of Lake Michigan, with less than 75 miles of lakefront. Along that lakeshore sprawls the Chicago metropolitan area, the third largest in the United States. Illinois is the sixth most populous state, with more than 12.7 million residents. Northern Illinois is a leading manufacturing region—notably of farm and earth-moving equipment—while the southern part of the state is a major producer of agricultural products, second only to Iowa in corn production.

A Brief History

- Seminomadic Algonquian peoples (the Peoria, Illinois, Kaskaskia, and Tamaroa) lived there at the time of European contact.
- European fur traders were followed by French explorers Jolliet and Marquette, 1673, and La Salle, 1680, who built a fort near present-day Peoria.
- French priests established the first permanent settlements, at Cahokia, 1699, and Kaskaskia, 1703.

Jesuit missionary Jacques Marquette was one of the first Europeans to travel to Illinois.

- France ceded the area to Britain, 1763; in 1778, American General George Rogers Clark took Kaskaskia from the British without firing a shot.
- Illinois became a separate territory, 1809, and a state, 1818.
- The defeat of Native American tribes in the Black Hawk War, 1832, and canal, rail, and road construction brought rapid change.
- The Great Chicago Fire, 1871, destroyed the city's downtown.
- Illinois became a center for the labor movement, leading to bitter conflicts such as the Haymarket riot, 1886, and Pullman strike, 1894.
- Social reformer Jane Addams founded Hull House, 1889, to aid the poor.
- From 1900 through the 1960s, as manufacturing expanded, many African-Americans arrived from the South.
- Senator Barack Obama (D–IL), elected in 2004, is the first male African-American Democrat to serve in the U.S. Senate.

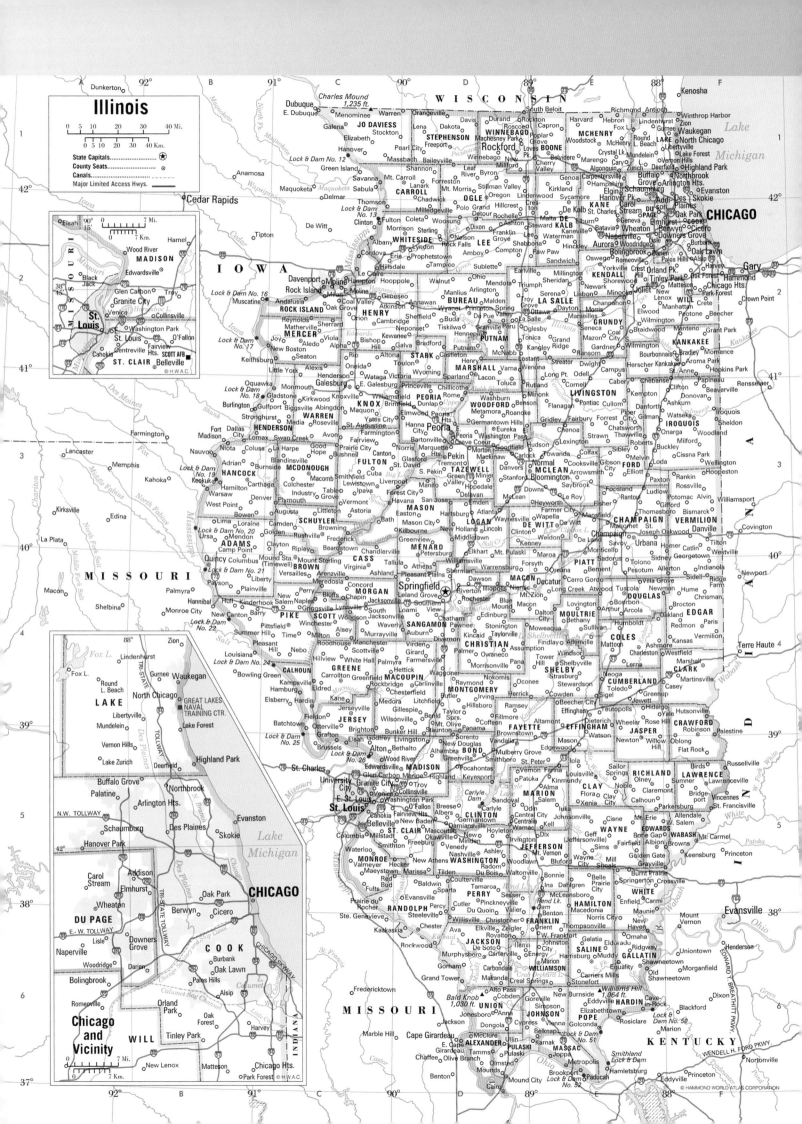

Illinois

FACTS & FIGURES

GEOGRAPHY

Total area: 57,914 sq mi (ranked 25th in size)

Acres forested: 4.3 million

CLIMATE

Temperate; typically cold, snowy winters, hot summers

STATE TREE

White oak

AVERAGE TEMPERATURE

CITY	JUN	DEC
Chicago	68.2	27.4
Moline	71.2	26.4
Peoria	71.1	27.8
Rockford	68.8	24.4
Springfield	72.6	30.3

FAMOUS ILLINOISANS

- Saul Bellow (1915–2005), author
- Ray Bradbury (b. 1920), author
- Hillary Rodham Clinton (b. 1947), U.S. senator
- Clarence Darrow (1857–1938), lawyer
- Betty Friedan (1921–2006), feminist and author
- James Watson (b. 1928), molecular biologist
- Frank Lloyd Wright (1865–1959), architect

Frank Lloyd Wright

ATTRACTIONS

Field Museum of Natural History; Art Institute; Pritzker Pavilion, Millenium Park, *Chicago*

Cahokia Mounds, *Collinsville*

Dickson Mounds Museum, *between Havana and Lewistown*

Crab Orchard Wildlife Refuge, *Marion*

Mormon settlement, *Nauvoo*

Lincoln shrines, *New Salem, Sangamon County, Springfield*

Shawnee National Forest

Illinois State Museum, *Springfield*

TOPOGRAPHY

- Prairie and fertile plains throughout
- Open hills in the southern region

Highest elevation: Charles Mound, 1,235 ft

Lowest elevation: Mississippi River, 279 ft

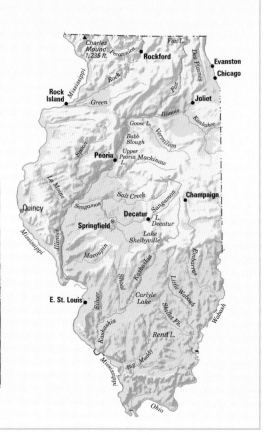

Cornfields have replaced open prairie land in much of Illinois.

Home to over 500 species of wildlife, the Shawnee National Forest is an ecological success story, the result of a remarkable, human-driven transformation of exhausted farmland into 270 thousand acres of forest.

The rock formations of Southern Illinois' Garden of the Gods, in the Shawnee National Forest, occur in an area in which the sedimentary rock is over 4 miles deep.

Cahokia, near Collinsville, Illinois, is the site of the largest Pre-Columbian earthwork in North America. The terraced mound is over 100 feet high. It supported a complex of buildings and is thought to have been the ceremonial center of the major city of Mississippian culture.

Illinois

CAPITAL CITY: **SPRINGFIELD**

Abraham Lincoln led a group of state legislators who in 1837 successfully lobbied for Springfield to become the capital of Illinois. Lincoln moved that year to Springfield and lived there until he was elected president in 1860. Today, Lincoln's legacy is key to the city's character and heritage.

The Civil War brought Springfield an economic boom, as new businesses and industries developed, followed by railroad lines and coal mining.

Springfield is in one of the nation's richest farming regions, serving as a commercial hub for wholesale trade and shipping. The Illinois State Fair held here annually is one of the largest in the country. Insurance companies, health care, the service industry, and education are leading businesses.

Area: 60 sq mi

Population (2000): 189,000

Population density: 2,064 per sq mi

Per-capita income: $29,664

Springfield's most famous citizen, Abraham Lincoln, lived there from 1837 to 1860. The 16th president's tomb and home are popular local historic sites.

Museum Campus, a 57-acre lakefront park, is home to three nationally recognized museums: the Adler Planetarium, which was the first significant planetarium built in the Western Hemisphere; the Shedd Aquarium, the world's largest indoor aquarium; and the Field Museum of Natural History.

Built in 2004, the revolutionary sound system of Frank Gehry's Pritzker Pavilion is designed to carry sound equally over 4,000 seats and the lawn beyond, which can hold 7,000 people.

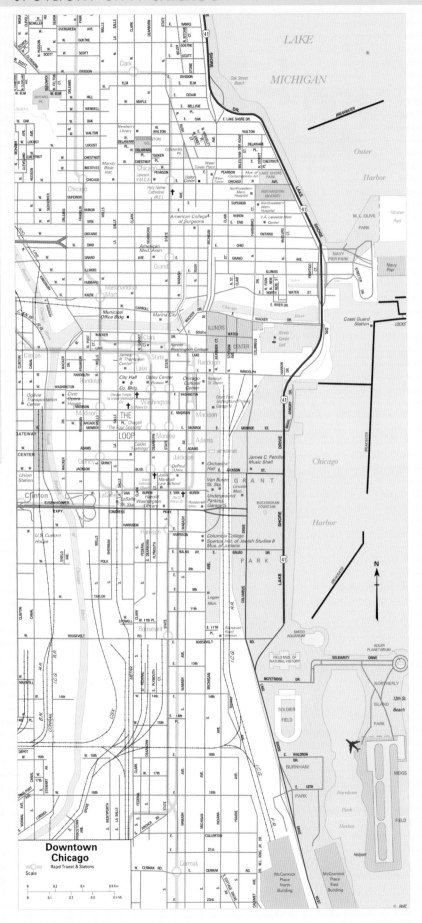

Downtown Chicago

Rapid Transit & Stations

Scale

0   0.2   0.4   0.6 Km.

0   0.2   0.4   0.4 Mi.

Fur trappers and traders of the colonial period knew Chicago by its original native name, "Es-chica-gou," meaning "the place of onions," for the wild onions that grew there. After the opening of the Erie Canal in 1825, the frontier settlement of Chicago grew swiftly as a center for trade and commerce.

After rising from the ashes of a great fire in 1871, the city became one of the world's leading industrial and commercial centers by the first years of the 20th century.

Famous for meat-packing, Chicago was called the "hog butcher to the world." The city enjoyed sustained prosperity, raising the world's first skyscraper (1885) and creating an imposing skyline along the lake. In the 1920s and 1930s, Chicago earned notoriety for underworld criminal organizations and gangster violence.

As the city thrived, its suburbs spread into the prairie lands, while the lakeside downtown became the heart of a dynamic metropolitan area that reaches eastward to Gary, Indiana, and encompasses more than 8 million people.

Area: 227.1 sq mi

Population (2005): 2,842,518

Population density: 12,517 per sq mi

Per-capita income: $37,169

Widely recognized as one of the great American cities, Chicago has been a center of culture, science, and politics for well over a century.

INDIANA

Crossroads of America

Settled: *1730*

Origin of name: *Means "land of the Indians"*

Capital: *Indianapolis*

Population (2005): *6,271,973* *(ranked 15th in size)*

Population density: *174.9 per sq mi*

ECONOMY

Chief industries: *Manufacturing, services, agriculture, government, wholesale and retail trade, transportation and public utilities*

Chief manufactured goods: *Primary metals, transportation equipment, motor vehicles and equipment, industrial machinery and equipment, electronic and electric equipment*

Chief crops: *Corn, soybeans, wheat, nursery and greenhouse products, vegetables, popcorn, fruit, hay, tobacco, mint*

Chief ports: *Burns Harbor, Portage; Mt. Vernon; Jeffersonville*

Gross state product (2005): *$238.6 billion*

Employment (May 2006): *14.6% government; 19.5% trade/transportation/utilities; 19.1% manufacturing; 12.8% education/health; 9.2% professional/business services; 9.6% leisure/hospitals; 4.7% finance; 5.1% construction; 5.1% other services*

Per-capita income (2005): *$31,276*

STATE FLOWER	STATE BIRD

Peony	Cardinal

THE HOOSIER STATE

Since pioneer days, Indiana and its capital, Indianapolis, have been busy with travelers—journeying at first by wagon and flatboat, and today by automobile and truck on the interstate highways. The state has three topographical regions: a narrow strip of low-lying country along Lake Michigan in the north; a plain of rich soil and low hills in the center of the state; and limestone hills in the south. The Ohio River, flowing southwest, defines Indiana's southern boundary. The Wabash River, which forms part of the western border, flows southward and meets the Ohio at Indiana's southwestern tip. Indiana's principal businesses are manufacturing and agriculture, while its quarries produce more building limestone than any other state. Most industry is in the north, where finished products—including cars and trucks and transportation equipment—can be carried over the Great Lakes. Corn and soybeans are the chief crops. Though the origin of the name "Hoosier" is unclear, Indianans have taken to it proudly.

A Brief History

- When the Europeans arrived, Miami, Potawatomi, Kickapoo, Piankashaw, Wea, and Shawnee peoples inhabited the region.
- French explorer La Salle visited the present South Bend area, 1679.
- The first French fort was built near present-day Lafayette, 1717; a French trading post was established, 1731–32, at Vincennes.
- France ceded the area to Britain, 1763.
- During the Revolution, American General George Rogers Clark defeated British forces, 1779.
- Indiana became a territory, 1800, and a state, 1816.
- The Miami were beaten, 1794, at Fallen Timbers, and General William H. Harrison defeated Tecumseh's Indian confederation, 1811, at Tippecanoe.
- Manufacturing grew after the Civil War.
- U.S. Steel founded Gary, 1906.
- An automotive test track was the site of the first Indianapolis 500 race, 1911.
- The auto industry remains key to the economy; in 2006, Honda announced plans for a $550 million plant near Greensburg.

René Robert Cavelier, Sieur de La Salle (1643–87) explored the Mississippi Valley for France.

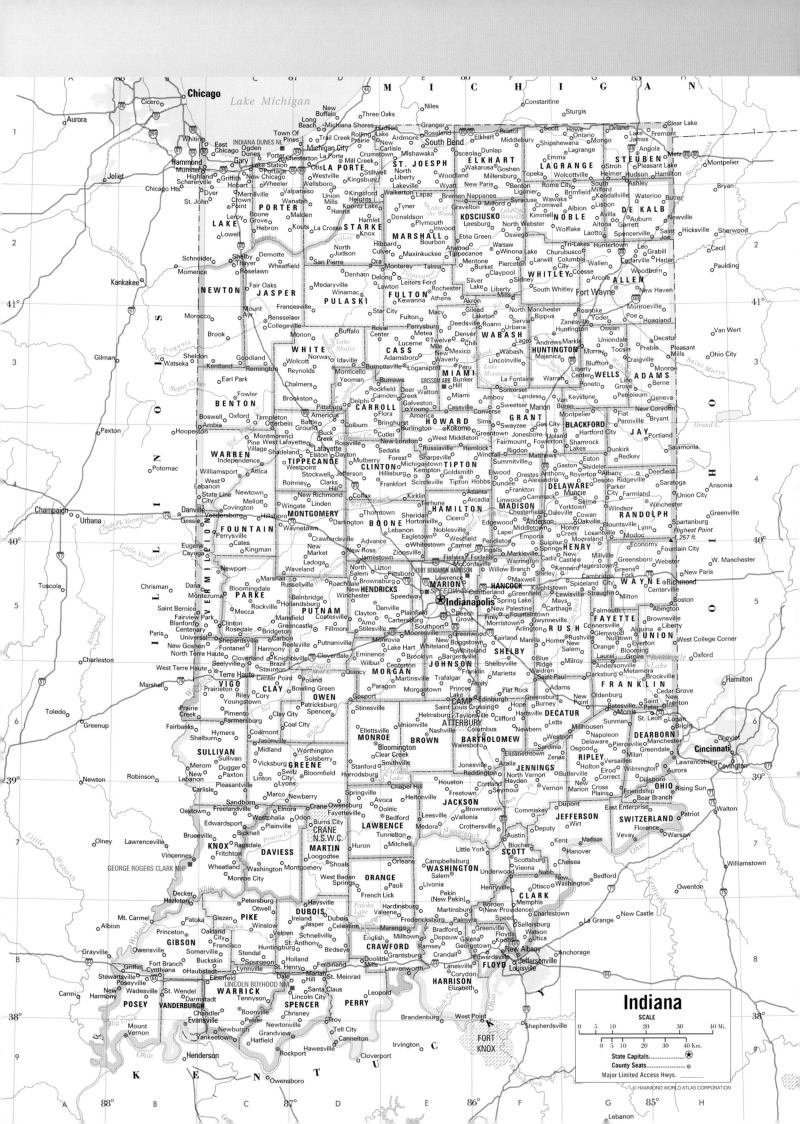

Indiana
SCALE

State Capitals .... ★
County Seats .... ○
Major Limited Access Hwys. _____

© HAMMOND WORLD ATLAS CORPORATION

Indiana

FACTS & FIGURES

GEOGRAPHY

Total area: *36,418 sq mi (ranked 38th in size)*

Acres forested: *4.5 million*

CLIMATE

Four distinct seasons with a temperate climate

STATE TREE

Tulip poplar

AVERAGE TEMPERATURE

CITY	JUN	DEC
Evansville	74.8	35.6
Fort Wayne	69.7	29
Indianapolis	71.7	31.6
South Bend	69	28.7

FAMOUS "HOOSIERS"

Cole Porter

- Larry Bird (b. 1956), basketball player
- James Dean (1931–55), actor
- Theodore Dreiser (1871–1945), author
- Jeff Gordon (b. 1971), race car driver
- Benjamin Harrison (1833–1901), 23rd U.S. president
- Gil Hodges (1924–72), baseball player
- Cole Porter (1891–1964), composer
- Kurt Vonnegut (1922–2007), novelist

ATTRACTIONS

Lincoln Log Cabin Historic Site, *near Charleston*

Indiana Dunes, *near Chesterton*

Hoosier National Forest

Wyandotte Cave; Tippecanoe Battlefield Memorial Park; Benjamin Harrison home; Indianapolis 500 raceway and museum, *Indianapolis*

National College Football Hall of Fame, *South Bend*

George Rogers Clark Park, *Vincennes*

TOPOGRAPHY

- Hilly southern region
- Fertile rolling plains of central region
- Flat, heavily glaciated north
- Dunes along shore of Lake Michigan

Highest elevation: Hoosier Hill, 1,257 ft

Lowest elevation: Ohio River, 320 ft

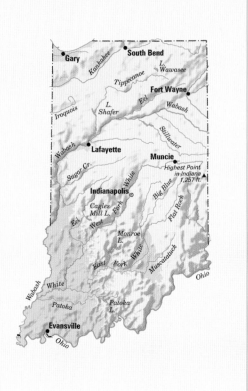

The flat lands of eastern Indiana.

Sand in the Indiana dunes "sings" when walked on, a characteristic shared with only a few beaches in the world.

The Nextel Cup Series, held in Indianapolis, is the highest level of competition sanctioned by the National Association for Stock Car Auto Racing (NASCAR).

CAPITAL CITY: **INDIANAPOLIS**

Indiana, known as the "Crossroads of America," has always been a busy avenue for commerce. Located at the center of the state and its web of highways is Indianapolis. It was chosen to be the capital in 1825, 9 years after Indiana achieved statehood.

From the start, travelers were key to the city's prosperity, as the opening of the National Road in 1827 sent hundreds of thousands of westward-bound emigrants passing through. Railroads followed, and with the discovery of natural gas late in the century, industry benefited from the availability of cheap fuel and good transportation. By the 20th century, the manufacture of automobiles became an economic cornerstone. The state and city's passion for the automobile is attested to each Memorial Day by the famous Indy 500 race held at the Indianapolis Motor Speedway.

Area: 361.5 sq mi

Population (2005): 784,118

Population density: 2,169 per sq mi

Per-capita income: $35,266

Constructed in 1985, the Indianapolis Canal Walk was rebuilt from the southern part of the older Central Canal, first conceived in 1836.

SPOTLIGHT CITY: **FORT WAYNE**

Indiana's second largest city lies in the heart of the state's industrial district, near Lake Michigan. Fort Wayne is divided into three parts by rivers that are spanned by more than 20 bridges.

The city was established as a French trading post in the late 1680s near a major town of the Miami Indians, important partners in the fur trade. For much of the next century, frontier warfare raged between French and British colonials, with native fighters taking sides as allies. In the mid-1790s, American soldiers occupied the fort and named it after their general. The construction of canals and railroads in the mid-1800s brought industrial growth and economic prosperity.

The legendary missionary Johnny Appleseed (John Chapman), who died in 1845, is buried in Fort Wayne.

Area: 79 sq mi

Population (2005): 223,341

Population density: 2,827 per sq mi

Per-capita income: $30,214

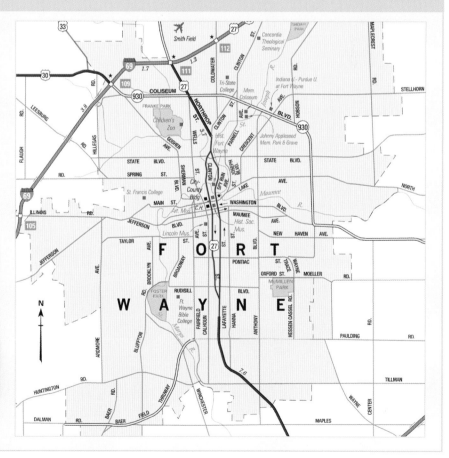

Named for one of the Revolution's most colorful generals, "Mad" Anthony Wayne, Fort Wayne has changed hands several times since the initial 17th-century Miami Indian settlement.

IOWA

IOWA

Our liberties we prize, and our rights we will maintain

Settled: *1788*

Origin of name: *Indian word variously translated as "here I rest" or "beautiful land." Named for the Iowa River, which was named for the Iowa peoples.*

Capital: *Des Moines*

Population (2005): *2,966,334 (ranked 30th in size)*

Population density: *53.1 per sq mi*

ECONOMY

Chief industries: *Agriculture, communications, construction, finance, insurance, trade, services, manufacturing*

Chief manufactured goods: *Processed food products, tires, farm machinery, electronic products, appliances, household furniture, chemicals, fertilizers, auto accessories*

Chief crops: *Silage and grain corn, soybeans, oats, hay*

Gross state product (2005): *$114.3 billion*

Employment (May 2006): *16.8% government; 20.4% trade/transportation/utilities; 15.4% manufacturing; 13.2% education/health; 7.6% professional/business services; 8.9% leisure/hospitality; 6.6% finance; 5.1% construction; 5.8% other services*

Per-capita personal income (2005): *$32,315*

STATE FLOWER

Wild rose

STATE BIRD

Eastern goldfinch

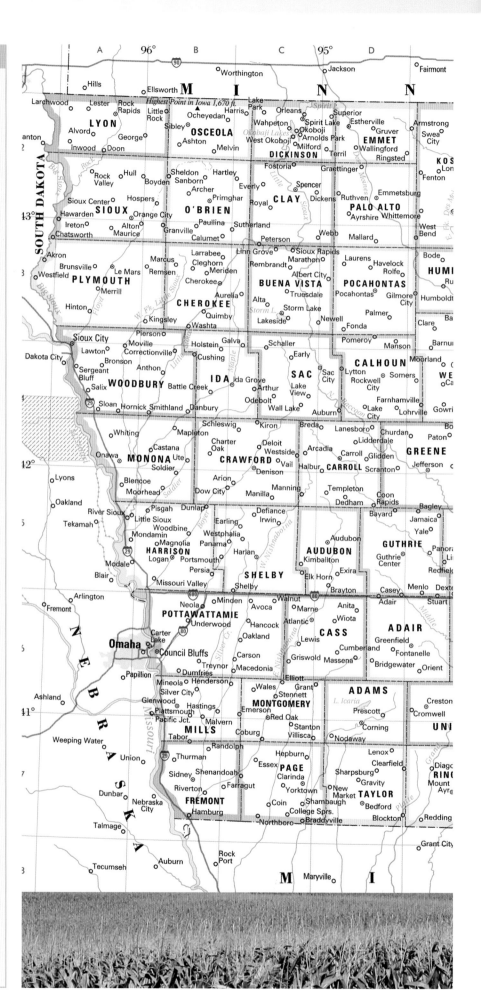

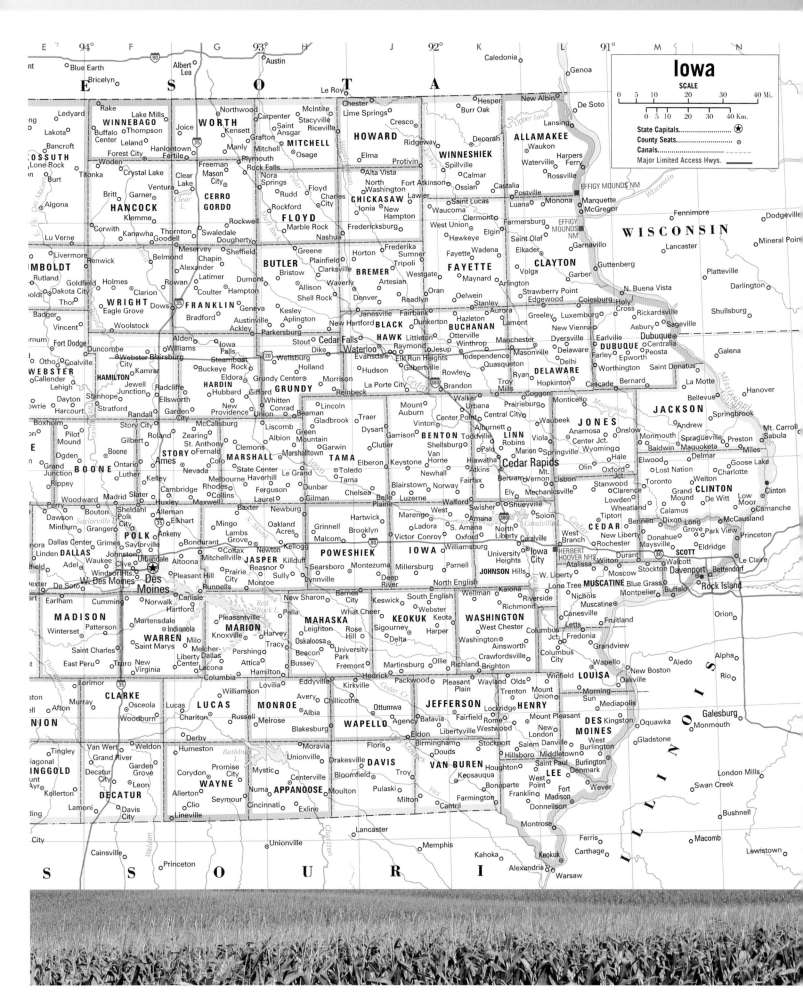

Iowa

FACTS & FIGURES

GEOGRAPHY

Total area:
56,272 sq mi
(ranked 26th in size)

Acres forested:
2.1 million

CLIMATE

Humid, continental

STATE TREE

Oak

AVERAGE TEMPERATURE

CITY	JUN	DEC
Des Moines	71.4	24.9
Dubuque	68.3	22.5
Sioux City	70.5	22.3
Waterloo	69.9	21.6

FAMOUS IOWANS

- Buffalo Bill Cody (1846–1917), soldier and bison hunter
- Herbert Hoover (1874–1964), 31st U.S. president
- Carl Van Vechten (1880–1964), writer
- Henry Wallace (1888–1965), 33rd U.S. vice president
- John Wayne (1907–79), actor
- Meredith Willson (1902–84), composer and playwright
- Grant Wood (1891–1942), painter

Buffalo Bill Cody

ATTRACTIONS

Adventureland, *Altoona*

Boone & Scenic Valley Railroad, *Boone*

Amana Colonies; Grant Wood's paintings and memorabilia, Davenport Municipal Art Gallery; Living History Farms, *Des Moines*

Effigy Mounds National Monument, prehistoric Indian burial site, *Marquette*

Iowa Great Lakes, *Okoboji*

Herbert Hoover birthplace and library, *West Branch*

THE HAWKEYE STATE

Iowa is named for its native people, but the origin of the nickname "Hawkeye State" is unclear. There is, however, an obvious reason for Iowa's other nickname, "Corn State": Iowa produces more corn than any other state in the country. With its rich, nearly level land, Iowa is ideal for growing the crop. Also the nation's leader in soybean and hog production, Iowa is one of the country's leading food exporters and is a center for research into plant hybrids and fertilizers. Unlike its land, Iowa's climate varies in extremes, with the temperature sometimes changing by 50° F in a day. Farming has been Iowa's leading industry for many decades, but mechanization and farm-consolidation have reduced the agricultural opportunities for young people, many of whom move out of the state. Iowa is bordered by the Missouri River to the west and the Mississippi to the east.

A Brief History

- Early inhabitants were Mound Builders who dwelt on Iowa's fertile plains. Later, Iowa and Yankton Sioux lived in the area.
- French explorers Louis Jolliet and Jacques Marquette gave France its claim to the area, 1673.
- The region was included in the Louisiana Purchase, 1803, and became part of the United States at that time.
- Native American Sauk and Fox tribes moved into the area but relinquished their land in defeat after the 1832 uprising led by the Sauk chieftain Black Hawk.
- Iowa became a territory, 1838, and entered as a free state, 1846, strongly supporting the Union.
- Fertile land lured farmers from eastern states, 1850–1900, and the population rose rapidly.
- Growth slowed in the 20th century, as farming became mechanized.
- Surging demand for ethanol fuel from corn contributed more than $2.6 billion to the state economy in 2005.

Sauk chieftain Black Hawk led an unsuccessful uprising against the United States in 1832.

TOPOGRAPHY

- Watershed from northwest to southeast
- Soil especially rich and land level in the north central counties

Highest elevation: Hawkeye Point, 1,670 ft

Lowest elevation: Mississippi River, 480 ft

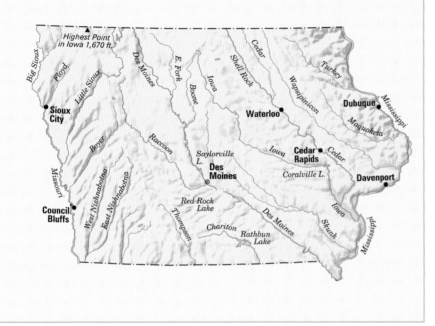

Iowa is one of eight states with a border determined by the course of the Mississippi River.

Rock Creek Lake, in central Iowa's Rock Creek State Park, is known for its fishing and boating. The 602-acre lake has 15 miles of shoreline.

CAPITAL CITY: **DES MOINES**

Founded on the Des Moines River in the south-central part of the state, Des Moines developed along with the steady increase in river traffic in the mid-19th century. The river was Iowa's main commercial artery until the arrival of railroads after the Civil War.

First established as Fort Des Moines in 1843, the post soon opened settlement to white civilians, and a town grew up. Des Moines became the state capital in 1857, and the business of government helped develop manufacturing, retailing, wholesaling, and publishing enterprises. Early in the 20th century

the discovery of coalfields brought on further expansion, and the city became a communications center and the headquarters for major insurance companies.

The origin of the name is uncertain. It possibly derived from the French pronunciation of the native name for the river, *Moingona*.

Area: 76 sq mi

Population (2005): 194,163

Population density: 2,621 per sq mi

Per-capita income: $32,745

Des Moines, a major insurance and financial center, was ranked by Forbes magazine as the "4th Best Place for Business" in 2007.

KANSAS

FACTS & FIGURES

Ad Astra per Aspera (To the stars through difficulties)

Settled: 1831

Origin of name: *Sioux for "south wind people"*

Capital: *Topeka*

Population (2005): *2,744,687 (ranked 33rd in size)*

Population density: *33.5 per sq mi*

ECONOMY

Chief industries: *Manufacturing, finance, insurance, real estate, services*

Chief manufactured goods: *Transportation equipment, machinery and computer equipment, food and kindred products, printing and publishing*

Chief crops: *Wheat, sorghum, corn, hay, soybeans, sunflowers*

Chief ports: *Kansas City*

Gross state product (2005): *$105.4 billion*

Employment (May 2006): *19.4% government; 19.2% trade/transportation/utilities; 13.3% manufacturing; 12.3% education/health; 9.8% professional/business services; 8.4% leisure/hospitality; 5.2% finance; 5% construction; 6.8% other*

Per-capita personal income (2005): *$32,836*

STATE FLOWER

Native sunflower

STATE BIRD

Western meadowlark

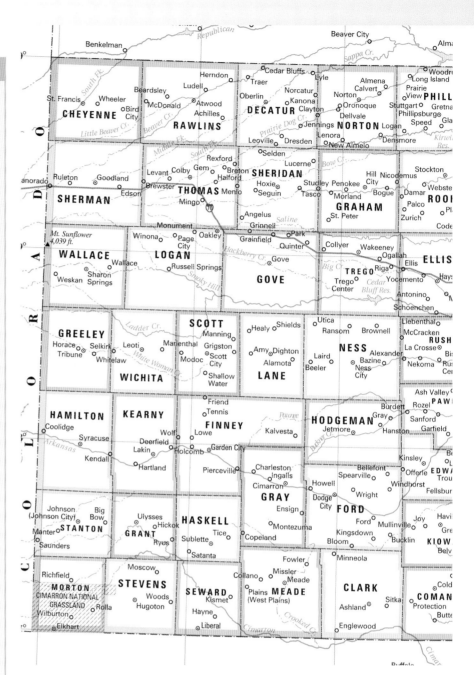

THE SUNFLOWER STATE

Kansas is known as the Sunflower State because of the quarter million acres of wild sunflowers that bloom during the hot, dry summers in this Great Plains State. Kansas has the country's largest stretch of tallgrass prairie, a 5-million acre region named Flint Hills. As the slogan "Midway U.S.A." suggests, Kansas is located at the geographical center of the 48 contiguous states. The exact point is marked with a limestone shaft near the state's northern border with Nebraska. Covered by a sea in prehistoric times, Kansas is rich with fossils. The state's reputation as a leading wheat and livestock producer was surpassed in the 1950s by its growth in industrial production. Kansas is still in the agricultural heartland, while its industries are led by manufacturing—transportation, machinery, and computer components—as well as finance, insurance, and real estate.

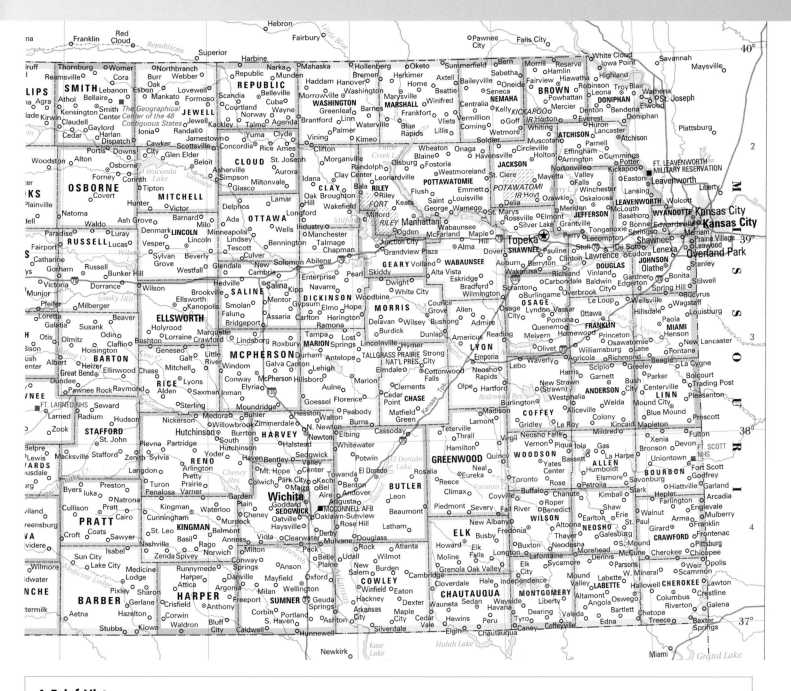

A Brief History

- Wichita, Pawnee, Kansa, and Osage peoples were living in the area when Francisco Vázquez de Coronado, the Spanish explorer and conquistador, explored it, 1541.
- These Native Americans—hunters who also farmed—were joined on the Plains by the nomadic Cheyenne, Arapaho, Comanche, and Kiowa tribes, about 1800.
- The United States bought the region in the Louisiana Purchase, 1803.
- After 1830, thousands of Native Americans were removed from more eastern states to Kansas.
- Organized as a territory, 1854, it came to be known as "Bleeding Kansas" as a result of violent clashes between pro- and antislavery settlers.
- In 1861, Kansas entered the Union as a free state.
- After the Civil War, rail construction and huge cattle drives from Texas turned Abilene and Dodge City into cowboy capitals.
- Carry Nation launched her antisaloon crusade in the 1890s.
- Part of the "Dust Bowl," the state experienced terrible drought and economic depression in the 1930s.
- Topeka was the focus of the famous *Brown v. Board of Education* decision, 1954, that led to desegregation of public schools in the United States.

Russian Mennonite immigrants brought a new strain of winter wheat with them in 1874, transforming Kansas agriculture.

Kansas

FACTS & FIGURES

GEOGRAPHY

Total area: 82,277 sq mi (ranked 15th in size)

Acres forested: 1.5 million

STATE TREE

Cottonwood

CLIMATE

Temperate but continental, with great extremes between summer and winter

AVERAGE TEMPERATURE

CITY	JUN	DEC
Concordia	73.4	30.2
Dodge City	74.3	33.1
Goodland	69.6	29.6
Topeka	73.9	31.4
Wichita	75.5	33.6

FAMOUS KANSANS

- Gwendolyn Brooks (1917–2000), poet
- George Washington Carver (1864–1943), educator
- Robert Dole (b. 1923), U.S. senator
- Amelia Earhart (1897–1939), aviator
- Wyatt Earp (1848–1929), lawman
- Dwight D. Eisenhower (1890–1969), 34th U.S. president
- Wild Bill Hickok (1837–76), army scout and lawman

Robert Dole

ATTRACTIONS

Eisenhower Center, Abilene

Agricultural Hall of Fame and National Center, Bonner Springs

Dodge City-Boot Hill and Frontier Town

Fort Scott and Fort Larned, restored 1800s cavalry forts

Kansas Cosmosphere and Space Center, Hutchinson

U.S. Cavalry Museum, Fort Riley

Old Cowtown Museum, Wichita

TOPOGRAPHY

- Hilly Osage plains in the east
- Central region of level prairie and hills
- High plains in the west

Highest elevation: Mt. Sunflower, 4,039 ft

Lowest elevation: Verdigris River, 679 ft

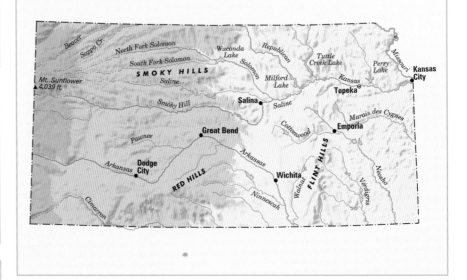

CAPITAL CITY: TOPEKA

The name Topeka came from a Native American word meaning "a good place to grow potatoes." Little more than a river-crossing in the 1840s, the town quickly developed into a transportation hub by the 1860s.

SPOTLIGHT CITY: **WICHITA**

The largest city in Kansas, Wichita was established as a trading post in 1864 on the Arkansas River site of a village of Wichita Native Americans. The cattle trade and railroads drove early development, followed by the growth of services to agricultural communities that rose up along the railroad lines.

Oil refining and aircraft manufacture boomed in the 20th century. Since the 1950s Wichita has been closely identified with nearby McConnell Air Force Base, named after three local brothers, all World War II pilots. McConnell is a key base for midair refueling and airlift operations. Home to several major aircraft manufacturing companies, Wichita calls itself the Air Capital of the World. The city is also rich in culture, with notable music festivals and museums.

Area: 135.8 sq mi

Population (2005): 354,865

Population density: 2,613 per sq mi

Per-capita income: $31,781

Wichita is ranked as one of the top 10 U.S. cities in which to live.

Most of Kansas is still farmland. It is one of the nation's most productive agricultural states.

Monument Rocks, or Chalk Pyramids, in western Kansas, rise out of what was once an inland sea. They were created 80 million years ago and are rich in fossils.

KENTUCKY

United we stand, divided we fall

Settled: *1774*

Origin of name: *Indian word, variously translated as "dark and bloody ground," "meadowland," and "land of tomorrow"*

Capital: *Frankfort*

Population (2005): *4,173,405 (ranked 26th in size)*

Population density: *105.0 per sq mi*

ECONOMY

Chief industries: *Manufacturing, services, finance, insurance and real estate, retail trade, public utilities*

Chief manufactured goods: *Transportation and industrial machinery, apparel, printing and publishing, food products, electric and electronic equipment*

Chief crops: *Tobacco, corn, soybeans*

Chief ports: *Paducah, Louisville, Covington, Owensboro, Ashland, Henderson County, Lyon County, Hickman-Fulton County*

Gross state product (2005): *$140.4 billion*

Employment (May 2006): *17.3% government; 20.7% trade/transportation/utilities; 14% manufacturing; 12.9% education/health; 9.3% professional/business services; 9.4% leisure/hospitality; 4.8% finance; 4.7% construction; 5.7% other services*

Per-capita income (2005): *$28,513*

STATE FLOWER	STATE BIRD

Goldenrod	Cardinal

THE BLUEGRASS STATE

The northernmost of the South Central States, Kentucky extends from the Appalachian Mountains in the east to the Mississippi River plains in the west. The state has a moderate climate, with prevailing winds from the south. Plentiful rainfall and good soil make for diverse vegetation—notably the bluegrass that earned Kentucky its nickname. Rivers border the state on the east and north, with the Ohio to the north and the Big Sandy River to the east. The eastern mountains have long been a leading coal-mining district, with tobacco and cotton produced in the central and southwest regions. Manufacturing is led by transportation and industrial machinery, with apparel, printing and publishing, and food products as other major enterprises. Livestock breeding is an important business, as Kentucky leads the nation in the breeding of thoroughbred saddle horses and racehorses.

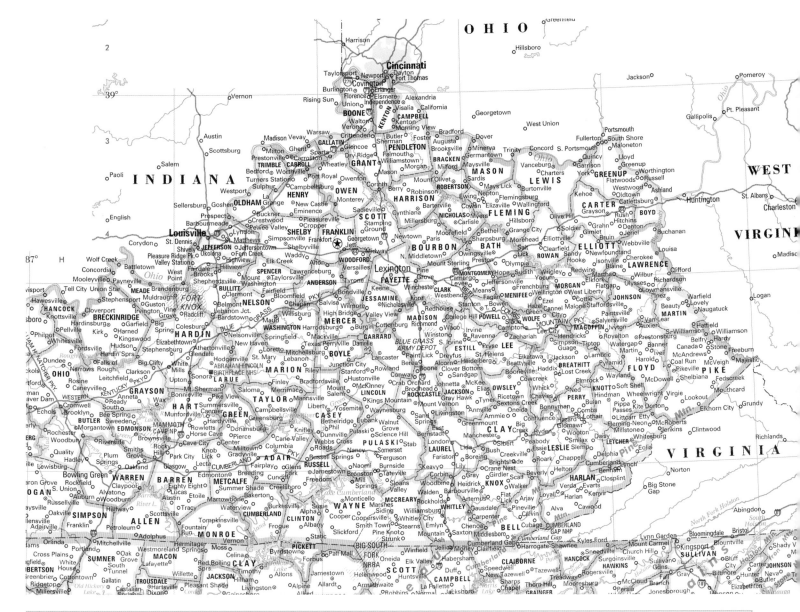

A Brief History

- Paleoindians first arrived about 14,000 years ago. At the time of European exploration, Shawnee, Wyandot, Delaware, and Cherokee peoples inhabited the area.
- Explored by Dr. Thomas Walker of Virginia and Christopher Gist of Maryland, 1750–51, Kentucky was the first area west of the Alleghenies to be settled by American pioneers.
- The first permanent settlement was Harrodsburg, 1774.
- Daniel Boone blazed the Wilderness Trail through the Cumberland Gap and founded Fort Boonesborough, 1775.
- Clashes with Native Americans were frequent, 1774–94.
- Virginia dropped its claims to the region, and Kentucky became a state, 1792.

- A slave state, Kentucky tried to stay neutral in the Civil War but then opted for the Union; many Kentuckians sided with the Confederacy.
- The U.S. gold depository at Fort Knox opened, 1937.
- Led by Toyota, Ford, and GM, auto manufacturing has grown in recent decades; about 10 percent of U.S. cars and trucks each year are made in Kentucky.

Tobacco growing, horse breeding, coal mining, and bourbon whiskey making were major industries in the 19th century.

Daniel Boone founded one of the first settlements west of the Appalachian Mountains.

Kentucky

FACTS & FIGURES

GEOGRAPHY

Total area: *40,409 sq mi* (ranked 37th in size)

Acres forested: *12.7 million*

CLIMATE

Moderate, with plentiful rainfall

STATE TREE

Tulip poplar

AVERAGE TEMPERATURE

CITY	JUN	DEC
Greater Cincinnati	72.0	34.6
Jackson	71.4	38.3
Lexington	72.2	36.3
Louisville	74.2	37.6
Paducah	74.5	36.9

FAMOUS KENTUCKIANS

- Muhammad Ali (b. 1942), boxer
- John J. Audubon (1785–1851), ornithologist and painter
- Daniel Boone (1734–1820), pioneer
- Louis D. Brandeis (1856–1941), Supreme Court justice
- Abraham Lincoln (1809–65), 16th U.S. president
- Zachary Taylor (1784–1850), 12th U.S. president
- Robert Penn Warren (1905–89), author

John James Audubon

ATTRACTIONS

Kentucky Derby, *Louisville*

Land Between the Lakes National Recreation Area, *Golden Pond*

Mammoth Cave National Park and Echo River, *Cave City*

Lincoln's birthplace, *Hodgenville*

My Old Kentucky Home State Park, *Bardstown*

Cumberland Gap National Historical Park, *Middlesboro*

Shaker Village, *Pleasant Hill*

TOPOGRAPHY

- Mountainous in the east
- Rounded hills of the Knobs in the north
- Bluegrass, heart of state
- Wooded rocky hillsides of the Pennyroyal
- Western coalfield
- The fertile Purchase in the southwest

Highest elevation: Black Mountain, 4,145 ft

Lowest elevation: Mississippi River, 257 ft

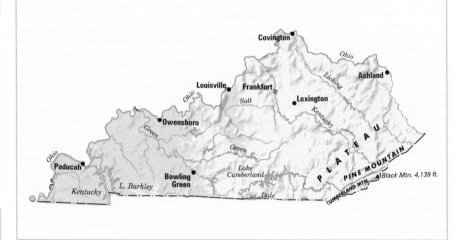

CAPITAL CITY: **FRANKFORT**

With a population of only 28,000, Frankfort is a small but picturesque city, rich in history, architecture (much of which dates to the late 19th century), and natural beauty.

SPOTLIGHT CITY: **LEXINGTON**

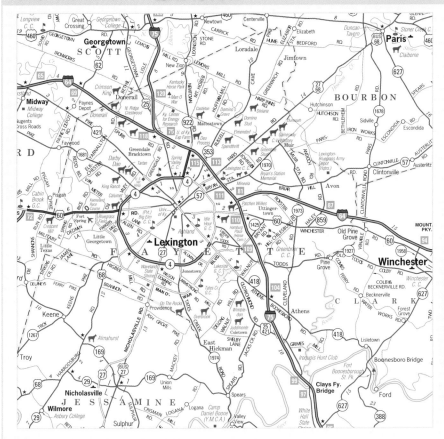

After Louisville, Kentucky's largest urban center is Lexington. Settled in 1775 and incorporated in 1832, Lexington is consistently rated among the top 10 cities nationwide for business and quality of life. The city has ranked high for relocation of business head-quarters and for small-business growth.

Lexington is also near the top for health care and for its "kid-friendliness," which is defined by education, health conditions, safety, libraries, parks, and environmental cleanliness. The city is in the heart of the lovely Bluegrass region, with its horse farms, stone fences, and grazing thoroughbreds.

In contrast to its bucolic surroundings, Lexington is a bustling manufacturing hub as well as a focal point for thousands of students at the region's colleges and the University of Kentucky. Almost 36 percent of Fayette County residents have bachelor's degrees, placing the city 8th among the country's 75 largest cities.

Area: 284.5 sq mi

Population (2005): 268,080

Population density: 942 per sq mi

Per-capita income: $32,722

Nowhere in America is horse racing as popular as in Kentucky, which hosts the world-famous Kentucky Derby every year.

Though tobacco is a longtime staple of Kentucky's economy, farmers have encountered growing pressure as a result of the significant health threats posed by use of cigarettes and other tobacco products.

The expression "sold down the river" refers to Kentucky slaves being sold and transported via the Ohio River to the deeper South.

LOUISIANA

FACTS & FIGURES

Union, justice, and confidence

Settled: *1699*

Origin of name: *Named after King Louis XIV of France by French explorer La Salle*

Capital: *Baton Rouge*

Population (2005): *4,523,628 (ranked 24th in size)*

Population density: *103.8 per sq mi*

ECONOMY

Chief industries: *Wholesale and retail trade, tourism, manufacturing, construction, transportation, communication, public utilities, finance, insurance, real estate, mining*

Chief manufactured goods: *Chemical products, foods, transportation equipment, electronic equipment, petroleum products, lumber, wood, and paper*

Chief crops: *Soybeans, sugarcane, rice, corn, cotton, sweet potatoes, pecans, sorghum, aquaculture*

Commercial fishing (2004): *$274.4 million*

Chief ports: *New Orleans, Baton Rouge, Lake Charles, Port of S. Louisiana (La Place), Shreveport, Plaquemine, St. Bernard, Alexandria*

Gross state product (2005): *$166.3 billion*

Employment (May 2006): *21% government; 20.5% trade/transportation/utilities; 8.1% manufacturing; 12% education/health; 9.6% professional/business services; 9.9% leisure/hospitality; 5.3% finance; 6.1% construction; 4.9% other services*

Per-capita income (2005): *$24,820*

STATE FLOWER

Magnolia

STATE BIRD

Eastern brown pelican

THE PELICAN STATE

Long-beaked pelicans were numerous in the bayous and swamps of Louisiana when French explorers arrived in the 1600s. Pelicans suffered greatly from chemical pollution and pesticides in the late 20th century, but lately their populations have begun to recover. Louisiana is marshy, and its largest city, New Orleans, is below sea level, protected by levees from the Mississippi River, which empties into the Gulf of Mexico. Much of the shoreline is sandy delta, deposited by Mississippi waters flowing from the heart of the country. Although vulnerable to destructive hurricanes, Louisiana also benefits from a warm, humid climate, ideal for growing sugarcane, cotton, and rice. Mild winters promote tourism as a leading industry, with hundreds of thousands of visitors coming to New Orleans each year. The state's economy is also driven by mining, fishing, lumber, oil, and natural gas.

A Brief History

- Caddo, Tunica, Choctaw, Chitimacha, and Chawash peoples lived in the region at the time of European contact.
- In the early 16th century, Spanish explorers reached the mouth of the Mississippi.
- French explorer René Robert Cavelier, Sieur de La Salle, claimed the region for France, 1682.
- The United States bought the region from France, 1803, in the Louisiana Purchase.
- Admitted as a state in 1812, Louisiana witnessed the Battle of New Orleans, 1815, in which American troops soundly defeated the British.
- Cotton and sugar plantations relied on black slaves, who made up 47 percent of the population in 1860, on the eve of the Civil War.
- Louisiana seceded, 1861, and was readmitted, 1868.

- Jazz was born in New Orleans in the early 20th century.
- As governor (1928–32), Huey Long pushed populist programs.
- The offshore oil and gas industry developed after World War II.
- Many tropical storms and floods have battered Louisiana, including Hurricane Katrina, 2005, which devastated New Orleans.

The most famous of New Orleans's neighborhoods, the French Quarter dates to 1718.

Hurricanes may provide ecological benefits, but they are a dreaded price to pay for citizens who live in their path.

Louisiana

SCALE

| 5 | 10 | 20 | 30 | 40 Mi. |

| 0 | 5 | 10 | 20 | 30 | 40 Km. |

State Capitals.........................★
Parish Seats.........................◎
Canals.............................
Major Limited Access Hwys. ──

The swamps and bayous (slow-moving waterways) of Louisiana draw thousands of tourists every year.

Louisiana

FACTS & FIGURES

GEOGRAPHY

Total area: 51,840 sq mi (ranked 31st in size)

Acres forested: 13.8 million

CLIMATE

Subtropical, affected by continental weather patterns

STATE TREE

Cypress

AVERAGE TEMPERATURE

CITY	JUN	DEC
Baton Rouge	79.7	52.4
Lake Charles	80.5	53.3
New Orleans	80.7	55.1
Shreveport	79.9	48.4

FAMOUS LOUISIANANS

- Louis Armstrong (1901–71), jazz musician
- Pierre Beauregard (1818–93), Confederate army general
- Kate Chopin (1850–1904), author
- Fats Domino (b. 1928), musician and songwriter
- Lillian Hellman (1905–84), playwright
- Huey Long (1893–1935), governor of Louisiana and U.S. senator
- Eli and Peyton Manning (b. 1981, b. 1976), football players
- Edward D. White Jr. (1845–1921), U.S. Supreme Court chief justice

Louis Armstrong

ATTRACTIONS

Kent House Museum, *Alexandria*

USS *Kidd* Memorial, *Baton Rouge*

Battle of New Orleans site, *Chalmette*

Hodges Gardens, *Natchitoches*

French Quarter, *New Orleans*

Longfellow-Evangeline Memorial Park, *St. Martinville*

TOPOGRAPHY

- Lowlands of marshes and Mississippi River floodplain
- Red River Valley lowlands; upland hills in the Florida parishes

Highest elevation: Driskill Mt., 535 ft

Lowest elevation: New Orleans, –8 ft

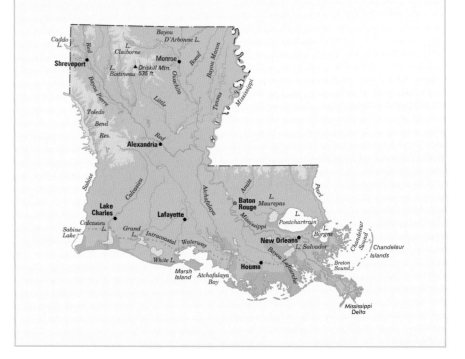

Common to the swamps, bayous, and other wetlands of Louisiana, the American alligator makes swimming a risky proposition. The larger of two existing alligator species, American "gators" are typically 13–18 feet.

CAPITAL CITY: **BATON ROUGE**

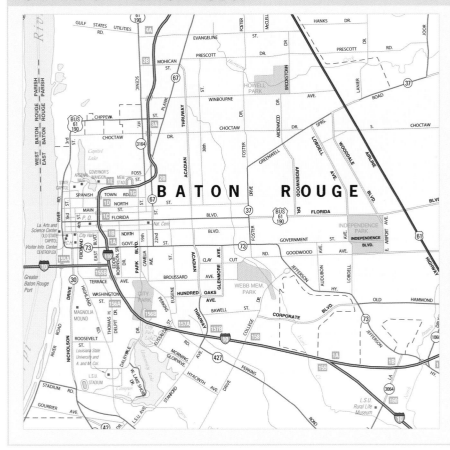

The state capital stands on the east side of the Mississippi River, on the first bluff upriver from the Mississippi delta. The original settlement was claimed by Spain at the time of the Louisiana Purchase in 1803, which acquired from France much of the Mississippi River and its tributaries.

Residents rebelled in 1810 and won their independence. In 1849 Baton Rouge—meaning "red stick"—became the capital of Louisiana. The city has two universities: Louisiana State University and Southern University.

In 2005, when major hurricanes struck, the city suffered a population loss of 2.5 percent. Since then, rapid job growth has pushed the city up more than 200 places, to 59th, on a national survey of the best places to do business. Baton Rouge is undergoing a renewed development effort, spurred by federal "Gulf Opportunity Zone" financial aid and tax-exemption programs to encourage the rebuilding of businesses and local economies after the storms.

Area: 79 sq mi

Population (2004): 224,097

Population density: 2,965 per sq mi

Per-capita income: $29,351

The Old Louisiana State Capitol building, now a National Historic Landmark, was in use from its construction in 1850 until 1932, surviving Union occupation during the Civil War.

SPOTLIGHT CITY: **NEW ORLEANS**

This colorful city at the mouth of the Mississippi, founded by the French in 1718, was purchased by the United States in 1803. As the South's greatest city, New Orleans was captured and held by the Union throughout the Civil War.

Its seaport is among the world's largest, busy transporting agricultural products, raw materials, manufactured goods, petroleum, and natural gas. The city is internationally famous for its jazz music and its Mardi Gras celebration. After Hurricane Katrina devastated New Orleans in 2005, the population of 454,000 was cut in half as tens of thousands of homeless residents were forced to move. Many returned as the city struggled to recover. The Mardi Gras festival remains a symbol of the city's cultural heritage, largely defined by a rich combination of African-American, Cajun (descendants of colonial French settlers), and Native American cultures.

Area: 180.6 sq mi

Population (2006): Estimated at 210,000 in spring 2006. Since then many residents have returned, but no new formal surveys have been conducted.

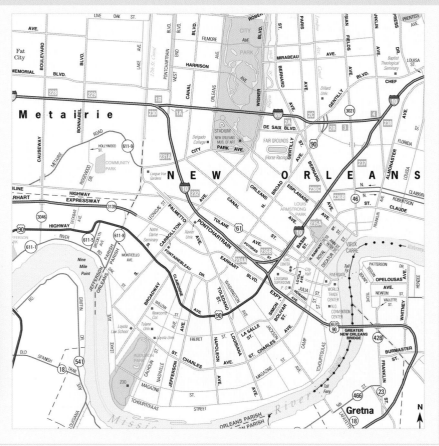

Mardi Gras (literally, "Fat Tuesday") is celebrated vibrantly and wildly in New Orleans, drawing thousands of visitors every year.

MAINE

THE PINE TREE STATE

In the northeastern tip of the United States, Maine is larger than all five other New England states combined. The climate of its hilly interior and mostly rocky shoreline is influenced by air masses from the south and west. Winters are snowy in the northerly regions, which receive more than 100 inches annually. The largest conifer in the Northeast, the eastern white pine, serves as Maine's state tree. Known as the "Pine Tree State," Maine is the most heavily forested state and is a leading producer of timber and lumber, mostly pine, spruce, and fir. Famous for its potatoes, the state also produces 99 percent of all wild blueberries in the country. Almost 90 percent of American lobster are trapped in Maine, but fishing was overtaken long ago as the state's largest industry by manufacturing and agriculture. Tourism is another significant source of employment and state income.

A Brief History

- Maine was inhabited by Algonquian peoples, including the Abenaki, Penobscot, and Passamaquoddy, at the time of European contact.
- Both the French settlement, 1604, at the St. Croix River, and the English, c. 1607, on the Kennebec, failed.
- A royal charter, 1691, made Maine part of Massachusetts.
- Maine broke off, 1819, and became a separate state, 1820.
- Drawing on vast forest resources, the pulp and paper industry developed after the Civil War.
- Bath Iron Works began building U.S. Navy vessels and other ships in the 1890s.
- Mail-order and retail giant L.L. Bean was founded, 1912.
- Margaret Chase Smith became the first woman to serve in both the House, 1940–49, and the Senate, 1949–73.

The first ships built by the Bath Iron Works, founded in 1884 by a Civil War veteran, were two iron gunboats for the U.S. Navy. The shipyard (shown here in 1940) recently built one of the most advanced warships in the world, an Arleigh Burke class destroyer, built entirely of steel.

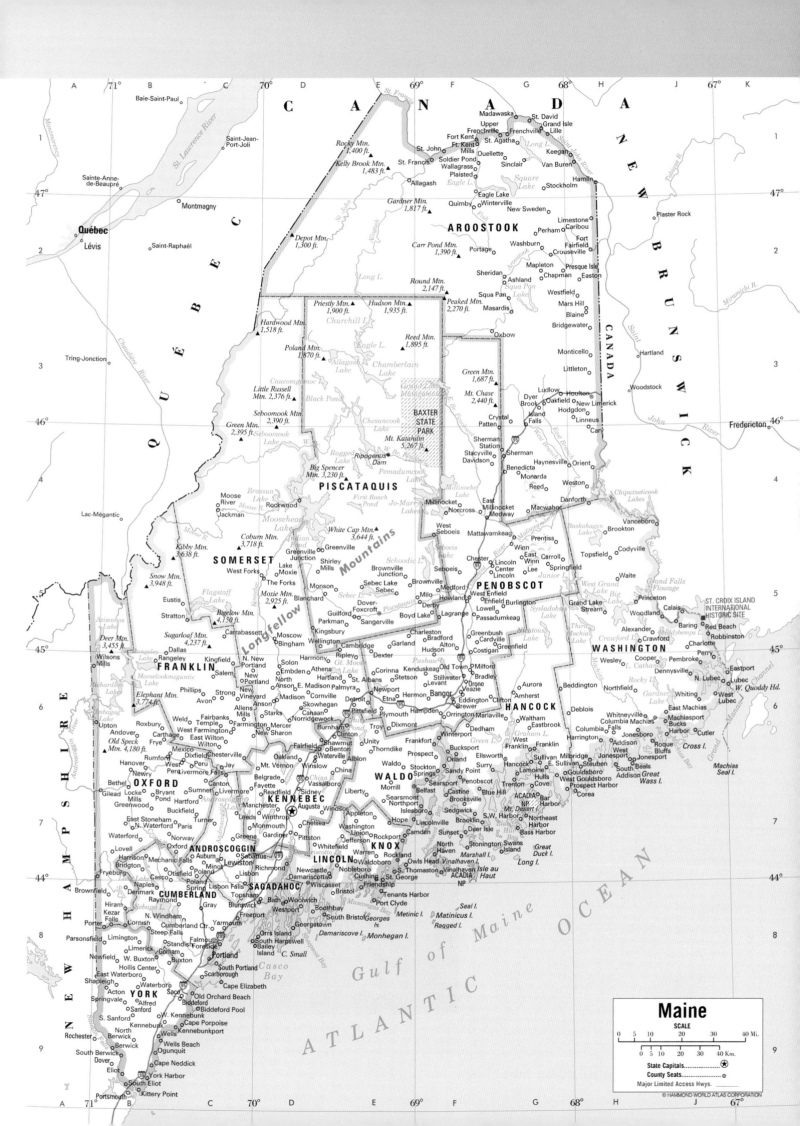

Maine

SCALE

State Capitals.............⊛
County Seats.............⊗
Major Limited Access Hwys.

© HAMMOND WORLD ATLAS CORPORATION

Maine

FACTS & FIGURES

GEOGRAPHY

Total area: 35,385 sq mi (ranked 39th in size)

Acres forested: 17.7 million

CLIMATE

Southern interior and coastal, influenced by air masses from the south and west; northern clime harsher, averaging over 100 inches of snow in winter

STATE TREE

Eastern white pine

AVERAGE TEMPERATURE		
CITY	JUN	DEC
Caribou	60.8	16.4
Portland	62.9	27.6

FAMOUS "DOWN EASTERS"

- Stephen King (b. 1947), novelist
- Henry Wadsworth Longfellow (1807–82), poet
- Edna St. Vincent Millay (1892–1950), poet and playwright
- George Mitchell (b. 1933), U.S. senator
- Edmund Muskie (1914–96), U.S. senator and secretary of state
- Edwin Arlington Robinson (1869–1935), poet
- Joan Benoit Samuelson (b. 1957), Olympic gold medalist

Henry Wadsworth Longfellow

ATTRACTIONS

Acadia National Park; Bar Harbor, on Mt. Desert Island

Mt. Katahdin, Baxter State Park

Kennebunkport

Old Orchard Beach

Portland's Old Port

Portland Head Light, Cape Elizabeth

Common Ground Country Fair, Unity

TOPOGRAPHY

- Appalachian Mts. extend through state
- Western borders have rugged terrain
- Long sand beaches on southern coast
- Northern coast mainly rocky promontories, peninsulas, fjords

Highest elevation: Mt. Katahdin, 5,267 ft

Lowest elevation: sea level

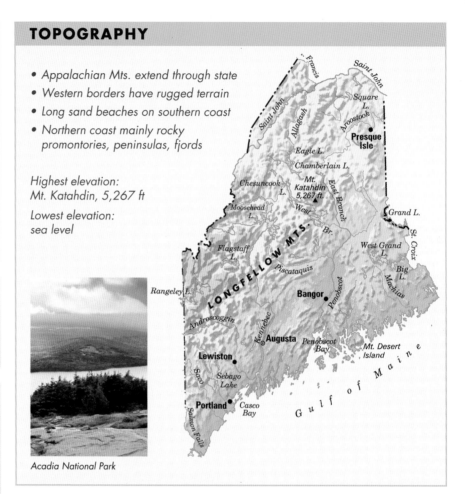

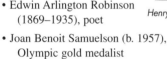

Acadia National Park

CAPITAL CITY: **AUGUSTA**

The Maine State House, designed by Charles Bulfinch, was built in 1829, two years after Augusta was designated the state capital. Sitting on the Kennebec River at the "head of the tide," the city is the easternmost state capital in the United States.

SPOTLIGHT CITY: **PORTLAND**

Portland, in the southwest region of Maine, is the largest city in the state, with a surrounding county population of 265,000, more than twice any other county in the state. The city is Maine's cultural and economic capital.

Standing on two hilly peninsulas overlooking scenic Casco Bay, Portland is a busy harbor town with seaborne commerce, mainly commercial fishing and the transshipping of oil piped from Canada. Industry includes paper products, manufacturing, and tourism, but the economy has steadily become service-based.

Settled by the English in 1632, the town suffered from attacks and destruction during colonial conflicts with the French and later, in the American Revolution, was burned by the British. Incorporated as a city in 1786, Portland again suffered a devastating fire in 1866. The city seal appropriately depicts a phoenix rising from the ashes.

Area: 53 sq mi

Population (2000): 64,249

Population density: 3,029 per sq mi

Per-capita income: $31,772

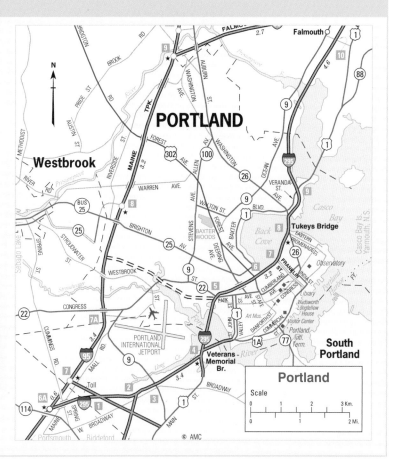

No longer dependent economically on the fishing industry, Portland still boasts an impressive array of fishing boats.

The Portland Head Light, one of four colonial lighthouses that are still standing, was begun in 1787, under George Washington's direction. Until 1855, when a Fresnel lens was installed, it was lit using whale oil lamps.

Maine

Acadia National Park, a wooded cluster of islands off the coast of Maine, is in a transition zone between eastern deciduous and northern coniferous forests. Surrounded by ocean, it has over 40 miles of rocky shoreline (right, top and bottom), with a 10–12 foot tidal range. Jordan Pond (above) was formed by glaciers.

MARYLAND

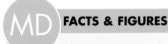

Fatti Maschii, Parole Femine (Manly deeds, womanly words)

Settled: *1634*

Origin of name: *From Queen Henrietta Maria, wife of King Charles I of England*

Capital: *Annapolis*

Population (2005): *5,600,388 (ranked 19th in size)*

Population density: *573.0 per sq mi*

ECONOMY

Chief industries: *Manufacturing, biotechnology and information technology, services, tourism*

Chief manufactured goods: *Electric and electronic equipment; food and kindred products, chemicals and allied products, printed materials*

Chief crops: *Greenhouse and nursery products, soybeans, corn*

Commercial fishing (2004): *$49.2 million*

Chief port: *Baltimore*

Gross state product (2005): *$244.9 billion*

Employment (May 2006): *18.3% government; 18.2% trade/transportation/utilities; 5.3% manufacturing; 14% education/health; 15.1% professional/business services; 9.2% leisure/hospitality; 6.2% finance; 7.2% construction; 6.5% other services*

Per-capita income (2004): *$41,760*

STATE FLOWER

Black-eyed Susan

STATE BIRD

Baltimore oriole

THE OLD LINE STATE

This northern Tidewater State (states surrounding the Chesapeake Bay) encompasses the Bay and the north shore of the Potomac River. In 1790, Washington, D.C.—a square 10 miles on each side—was carved out of Maryland, centrally locating the national capital on the Atlantic seaboard. Nicknamed the "Old Line State" in honor of its Revolutionary War heritage, Maryland also was the scene of some of the Civil War's bloodiest battles. Exploring that military legacy, preserved in battlefield parks, helps make tourism a major feature of Maryland's economy—as do its revitalized harbors and popular waterways. Fishing is both a tourist attraction and a major industry. Chesapeake Bay, the largest estuary in the United States, produces half the nation's prized blue crabs. It is also home to 29 species of waterfowl and is a major resting ground for migrating birds over the winter. The state's climate is warm and mild, moderated by the Atlantic and the Bay.

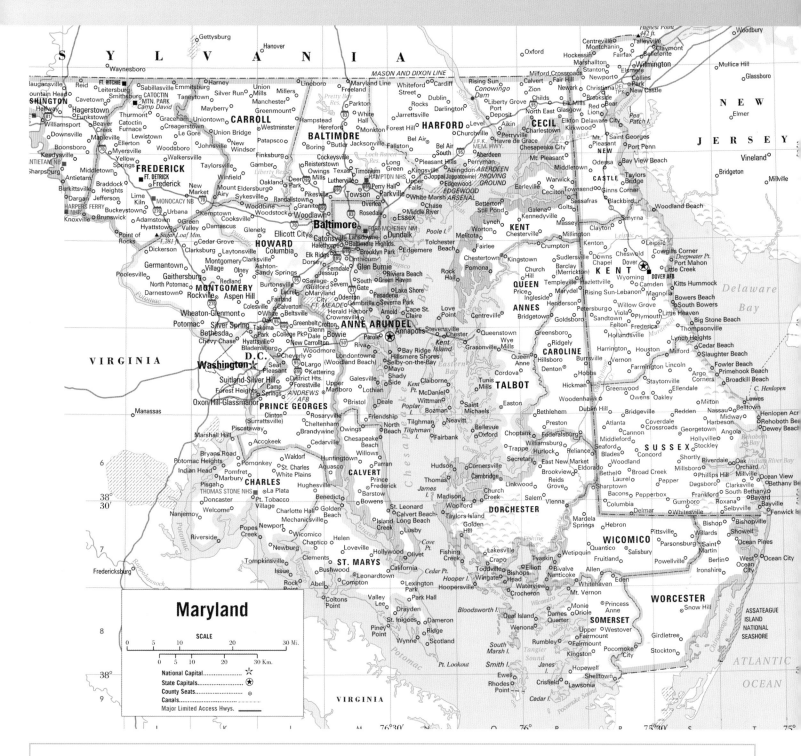

Maryland

SCALE

0	5	10	20	30 Mi.

0	5	10	20	30 Km.

National Capital.................☆
State Capitals.....................⊛
County Seats.....................◎
Canals...............................
Major Limited Access Hwys. ▬

A Brief History

- Algonquian-speaking Nanticoke and Piscataway and Iroquois-speaking Susquehannock lived in the area at the time of European contact.
- Italian explorer Giovanni da Verrazzano reached the Chesapeake region in the early 16th century.
- English Captain John Smith explored and mapped the area, 1608.
- William Claiborne of England set up a trading post in Chesapeake Bay, 1631.
- King Charles I granted land to Cecilius Calvert, Lord Baltimore, 1632; Calvert's brother Leonard, with about 200 settlers, founded St. Marys, 1634.
- Francis Scott Key wrote "The Star-Spangled Banner" after witnessing the British attack on Fort McHenry during the War of 1812.
- Frederick Douglass, born into slavery in 1818, became a leading abolitionist.
- Although a slave state, Maryland stayed in the Union during the Civil War; in the war's bloodiest day of battle, 23,000 soldiers were killed, wounded, or missing at Antietam, 1862.
- Israeli and Egyptian leaders reached a peace accord at Camp David, 1978.

Marylander Francis Scott Key peers at the American flag still flying over Fort McHenry.

Maryland

FACTS & FIGURES

GEOGRAPHY

Total area: 12,407 sq mi (ranked 42nd in size)

Acres forested: 2.6 million

CLIMATE

Continental in the west; humid subtropical in the east

STATE TREE

White oak

AVERAGE TEMPERATURE

CITY	JUN	DEC
Baltimore	71.8	36.7

FAMOUS MARYLANDERS

Upton Sinclair

- Benjamin Banneker (1731–1806), mathematician, clock-maker, astronomer, and publisher
- Francis Scott Key (1779–1843), author and songwriter
- H. L. Mencken (1880–1956), writer
- Kweisi Mfume (b. 1948), N.A.A.C.P. president and U.S. congressman
- Charles Willson Peale (1741–1827), painter
- William Pinkney (1764–1822), statesman, diplomat, and U.S. congressman
- Edgar Allan Poe (1809–49), writer
- Cal Ripken Jr. (b. 1960), Hall of Fame baseball player
- Babe Ruth (1895–1948), Hall of Fame baseball player
- Upton Sinclair (1878–1968), writer

ATTRACTIONS

South Mountain Battlefield, *near Frederick*

U.S. Naval Academy; Maryland State House (1772), the oldest still in legislative use in the United States, *Annapolis*

The Preakness at Pimlico track; restored Fort McHenry, near which Francis Scott Key wrote "The Star-Spangled Banner"; Edgar Allan Poe house; National Aquarium, Harborplace, *Baltimore*

Antietam Battlefield, *near Hagerstown*

TOPOGRAPHY

- Eastern Shore and Maryland Main regions are coastal plains
- Piedmont Plateau, and the Blue Ridge, separated by the Chesapeake Bay

Highest elevation: Backbone Mt., 3,360 ft

Lowest elevation: sea level

Great Falls National Park

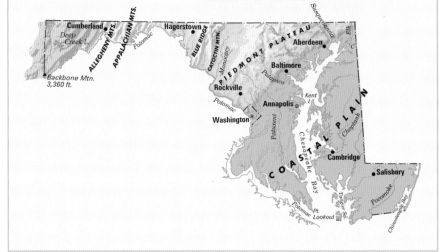

Harpers Ferry, on the banks of the Potomac and Shenandoah rivers, is the site where West Virginia, Virginia, and Maryland all meet.

The Chesapeake Bay Bridge is among the world's longest bridges, with a shore-to-shore span of 4.3 miles.

Ocean City is a resort town popular for its luxury hotels, amusement parks, and striking beaches.

CAPITAL CITY: **BALTIMORE**

Baltimore, Maryland's largest city, is the closest major Atlantic port to the Midwest. Established in 1729, the city became an industrial center, with one of the first railroads in the country, the Baltimore and Ohio, or B&O.

Baltimore's metropolitan area has 2.6 million people, about half the state's population. While the city's population has been declining, the growing suburbs have created the greater Baltimore-Washington metro area, with 8.1 million residents. Nearby is the U.S. Naval Academy at Annapolis, founded in 1845 to educate and train elite officers.

Baltimore attracts thousands of tourists to its Inner Harbor, National Aquarium, and restored Fort McHenry, the scene of Francis Scott Key's inspiration for "The Star-Spangled Banner" during the War of 1812. The city is home to more than 30 universities and colleges, which are among the region's largest individual employers.

Area: 80.8 sq mi

Population (2005): 635,815

Population density: 7,869 per sq mi

Per-capita income: $38,813

Baltimore lies at the head of the Patapsco River estuary, 15 miles above the Chesapeake Bay.

Located near Olney, west of Columbia, Triadelphia Reservoir covers 800 acres and can hold up to 6.4 billion gallons of water. It is a particularly popular destination for boaters.

Rock Point Beach, in the town Point of Rocks, looks out over the Potomac River, which eventually flows into the Chesapeake Bay.

MASSACHUSETTS

MA FACTS & FIGURES

Ense Petit Placidam Sub Libertate Quietem
(By the sword we seek peace, but peace only under liberty)

Settled: *1620*

Origin of name: *From the Indian tribe named after the "large hill place"*

Capital: *Boston*

Population (2005): *6,398,743
(ranked 13th in size)*

Population density: *816.2 per sq mi*

ECONOMY

Chief industries: *Services, trade, manufacturing*

Chief manufactured goods: *Electric and electronic equipment, instruments, industrial machinery and equipment, printing and publishing, fabricated metal products*

Chief crops: *Cranberries, greenhouse, nursery, vegetables*

Commercial fishing (2004): *$326.1 million*

Chief ports: *Boston, Fall River, New Bedford, Salem, Gloucester, Plymouth*

Gross state product (2005): *$328.5 billion*

Employment (May 2006): *13% government;
17.5% trade/transportation/utilities;
9.4% manufacturing; 18.4% education/health;
14.5% professional/business services;
9.2% leisure/hospitality; 6.9% finance;
4.5% construction; 6.4% other services*

Per-capita income (2005): *$44,289*

STATE FLOWER

Mayflower

STATE BIRD

Chickadee

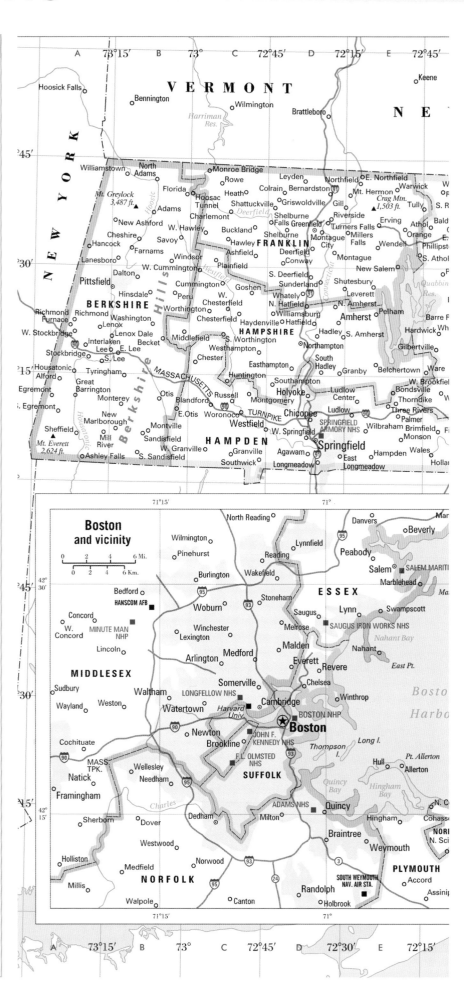

Massachusetts

SCALE

0 5 10 15 20 Mi.

0 5 10 15 20 Km.

State Capitals..........................★
County Seats..........................⊙
Canals..........................
Major Limited Access Hwys._____

Massachusetts

FACTS & FIGURES

GEOGRAPHY

Total area: *10,555 sq mi (ranked 44th in size)*

Acres forested: *3.1 million*

CLIMATE

Temperate, with colder and drier clime in western region

STATE TREE

American elm

AVERAGE TEMPERATURE		
CITY	JUN	DEC
Boston	68.0	34.8
Worcester	64.7	28.9

FAMOUS "BAY STATERS"

- John Adams (1735–1826), 2nd U.S. president
- John Quincy Adams (1767–1848), 6th U.S. president
- Samuel Adams (1722–1803), Revolutionary War hero
- Louisa May Alcott (1832–88), novelist
- Susan B. Anthony (1820–1906), suffragette activist
- Alexander Graham Bell (1847–1922), inventor
- Emily Dickinson (1830–86), poet
- Ralph Waldo Emerson (1803–82), essayist
- Nathaniel Hawthorne (1804–64), writer
- John F. Kennedy (1917–63), 35th U.S. president
- Paul Revere (1734–1818), Revolutionary War hero
- Henry David Thoreau (1817–62), essayist
- James McNeil Whistler (1834–1903), painter

Henry David Thoreau

ATTRACTIONS

Freedom Trail, Gardner Museum, Museum of Fine Arts, Children's Museum, Museum of Science, New England Aquarium, JFK Library, *Boston*

Tanglewood, Jacob's Pillow Dance Festival, Hancock Shaker Village, Berkshire Scenic Railway Museum, Norman Rockwell Museum, Edith Wharton and Herman Melville homes, *the Berkshires*

Cape Cod

Naismith Memorial Basketball Hall of Fame, *Springfield*

Plymouth Rock, Mayflower II, Plimouth Plantation, *Plymouth*

THE BAY STATE

Beginning with colonial times, Massachusetts has been a maritime leader, prospering from merchant shipping and fishing. Although shipping and commercial fishing have gone into decline, the state entered the 21st century with a robust manufacturing sector. Also important to the economy are biotechnology, information technology, electronic equipment, and computer-related businesses. Tourism is the second largest industry and benefits the entire state. Massachusetts offers a variety of scenery and settings, from Cape Cod beaches on the Atlantic to the western Berkshire Hills. The most popular tourist attraction is Boston, with its historic sites and sports and performing arts venues. Boston is New England's largest city, and considered the unofficial capital of the region. Massachusetts is not known for its agriculture, with one exception: cranberries. Early settlers were so successful growing cranberries in lowland bogs that Massachusetts now produces the largest crop of cranberries in the world.

A Brief History

- Early inhabitants were Algonquian peoples: Nauset, Wampanoag, Massachuset, Pennacook, and Nipmuc.
- Pilgrims settled in Plymouth, 1620; first precursor to Thanksgiving Day holiday celebrated, 1621.
- From 1630 to 1640 about 20,000 new settlers arrived.
- Colonist-Native American relations deteriorated and led to King Philip's War, 1675–76, won by the colonists.
- Witch trials at Salem, 1692, led to the execution of 19 people.
- Demonstrations against British restrictions set off the Boston Massacre, 1770, and the Boston Tea Party, 1773.
- Lexington saw the first bloodshed of the American Revolution, 1775.
- After statehood, Massachusetts prospered from shipbuilding, seafaring, and the making of textiles, shoes, and metal goods, while artists, writers, and social reformers flourished.
- After World War II, old industries declined, knowledge-intensive enterprises thrived; the Kennedys became a dominant political family.

The Boston Tea Party, the colonists' protest against Britain's excessive taxation, took place on December 16, 1773.

TOPOGRAPHY

- Jagged indented coast from Rhode Island around Cape Cod
- Flat land yields to stony upland pastures near central region and gentle hilly country in west
- Except in west, land is rocky, sandy, and not fertile

Highest elevation: Mt. Greylock, 3,487 ft

Lowest elevation: sea level

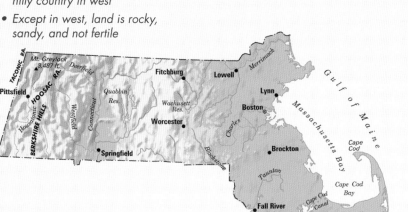

Provincetown, located at the extreme tip of Cape Cod, has the largest natural harbor on the East Coast.

The cliffs of Gloucester rise from the water, overlooking rocky shores. In 1713, the first schooner was built in Gloucester, still an important shipbuilding center.

CAPITAL CITY: **BOSTON**

Known as the "cradle of liberty" for its prominent role in the American Revolution, Boston is the capital of Massachusetts and its largest city, with a population of almost 560,000. The Greater Boston metro area has 4.4 million people.

Settled in 1630 by Puritans who established the Massachusetts Bay Colony in the 1620s, Boston became the capital and center of commerce. The Revolution's first important engagements took place in and around the city, an historical heritage that is at the heart of Boston's identity. Meticulously restored buildings and cobblestone back streets evoke colonial times, and the culture of old-fashioned New England "Yankee-ness" is perpetuated and cultivated—for both tourists and residents.

Boston is especially famed for its institutions of higher education, with 31 universities and colleges in the metro area. Its more than 374,000 students rank Boston first as a college destination.

Area: 48.4 sq mi

Population (2005): 559,034

Population density: 11,550 per sq mi

Per-capita income: $46,060

Founded on the Shawmut peninsula by Puritan colonists, Boston is surrounded by the waters of the Massachusetts Bay and Back Bay, an estuary of the Charles River.

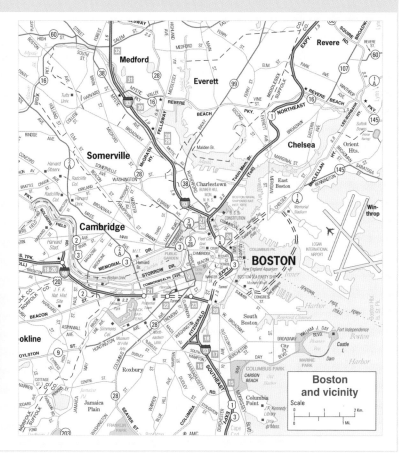

Boston and vicinity

MICHIGAN

FACTS & FIGURES

Si Quaeris Peninsulam Amoenam, Cirumspice
(If you seek a pleasant peninsula, look about you)

Settled: *1831*

Origin of name: *From Chippewa mici gama, meaning "great water"*

Capital: *Lansing*

Population (2005): *10,120,860 (ranked 8th in size)*

Population density: *178.2 per sq mi*

ECONOMY

Chief industries: *Manufacturing, services, tourism, agriculture, forestry/lumber*

Chief manufactured goods: *Automobiles, transportation equipment, machinery, fabricated metals, food products, plastics, office furniture*

Chief crops: *Corn, wheat, soybeans, dry beans, hay, potatoes, sweet corn, apples, cherries, sugar beets, blueberries, cucumbers, grapes*

Commercial fishing (2004): *$6.2 million*

Chief ports: *Detroit, Saginaw River, Escanaba, Muskegon, Sault Ste. Marie, Port Huron, Marine City*

Gross state product (2005): *$377.9 billion*

Employment (May 2006): *15.6% government; 18% trade/transportation/utilities; 15% manufacturing; 13.1% education/health; 13.6% professional/business services; 9.5% leisure/hospitality; 5% finance; 4.4% construction; 5.6% other services*

Per-capita income (2005): *$33,116*

STATE FLOWER

Apple blossom

STATE BIRD

Robin

THE WOLVERINE STATE

Michigan's nickname honors the fierce wolverine, once numerous in the state. Its other nickname—the "Great Lakes State"—asserts Michigan's position as the only state that touches four of the five Great Lakes (Superior, Michigan, Huron, and Erie). Michigan's topography consists of plains and low ridges in the south, with gentle uplands in the north. The state is formed by two great peninsulas, the Upper and Lower. The heavily forested Upper Peninsula has snowy winters, receiving 112 inches annually, four times that of the Lower Peninsula. Michigan's principal cities are in the Lower Peninsula, birthplace of the automobile industry. Once dominant in Michigan, automobile manufacturing began declining in the early 1970s, as imports took a major share of the American market. The state has since rebounded to become a national leader in high-tech employment, including information technology, life sciences, and advanced manufacturing.

A Brief History

- Ojibwa, Ottawa, Miami, Potawatomi, and Huron peoples inhabited the area at the time of European contact.
- 17th-century French fur traders and missionaries established a settlement at Sault Ste. Marie, 1668.
- The British took over, 1763, and crushed an uprising led by Ottawa chieftain Pontiac. The Treaty of Paris ceded the area to the United States, 1783, but the British remained until 1796.
- Michigan became a territory, 1805.
- The opening of the Erie Canal, 1825, new land laws, and concessions by the Native Americans brought a flood of settlers.
- Strongly antislavery, Michigan became a state, 1837, and supplied 90,000 soldiers to the Union army in the Civil War.
- In the 20th century, automobile manufacturing was the state's most important industry. Henry Ford launched the Model T car, 1908; the United Auto Workers union was founded, 1935.
- Motown music flourished in Detroit in the 1960s; riots in 1967 dealt the city a heavy blow.
- As the auto industry faltered, Michigan lost 300,000 jobs from 2000 to 2006.

Several Algonquian tribes, including the Chippewa, or Anishnabe (depicted here c. 1821), lived in Michigan in a confederation called the Council of Three Fires.

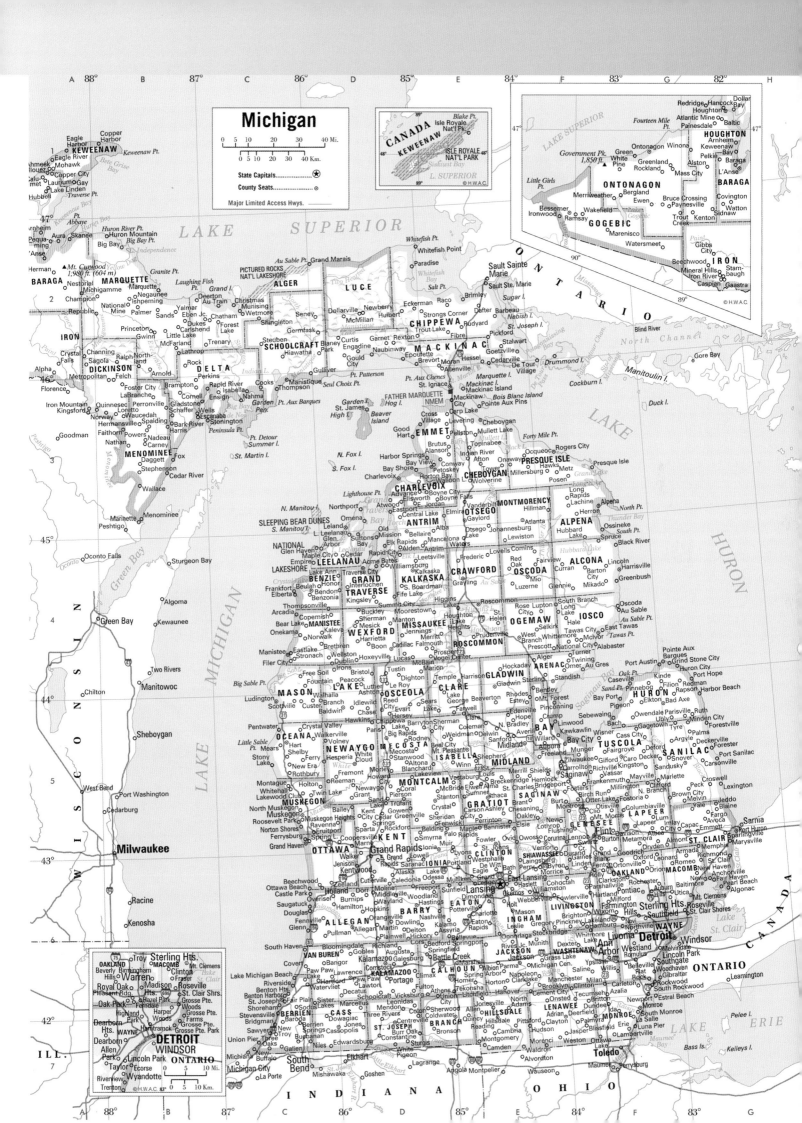

Michigan

FACTS & FIGURES

GEOGRAPHY

Total area: *96,716 sq mi (ranked 11th in size)*

Acres forested: *19.3 million*

CLIMATE

Well-defined seasons tempered by the Great Lakes

STATE TREE

White pine

AVERAGE TEMPERATURE

CITY	JUN	DEC
Alpena	61.3	24.0
Detroit	69.0	29.6
Flint	66.2	26.7
Grand Rapids	67.1	27.6
Houghton Lake	62.2	23.7

FAMOUS MICHIGANDERS

- Francis Ford Coppola (b. 1939), film director
- Thomas Edison (1847–1931), inventor
- Gerald R. Ford (1913–2006), 38th U.S. president
- Henry Ford (1863–1947), founder of Ford Motor Co.
- Aretha Franklin (b. 1942), singer and songwriter
- Charles Lindbergh (1902–74), aviator
- Malcolm X (1925–65), writer and activist

Thomas Edison

ATTRACTIONS

Henry Ford Museum; Greenfield Village, *Dearborn*

Frederick Meijer Gardens and Sculpture Park, *Grand Rapids*

Michigan Space Center, *Jackson*

Tahquamenon (Hiawatha) Falls

DeZwaan Windmill and Tulip Festival, *Holland*

Soo Locks, *Sault Ste. Marie*

Kalamazoo Aviation History Museum; Mackinac Island; Kellogg's Cereal City USA, *Battle Creek*

Museum of African-American History; Motown Historical Museum, *Detroit*

TOPOGRAPHY

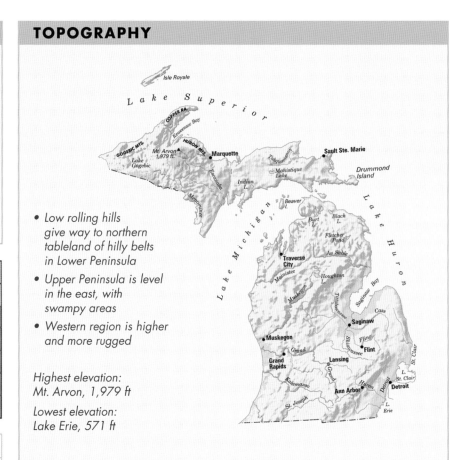

- Low rolling hills give way to northern tableland of hilly belts in Lower Peninsula
- Upper Peninsula is level in the east, with swampy areas
- Western region is higher and more rugged

Highest elevation: Mt. Arvon, 1,979 ft

Lowest elevation: Lake Erie, 571 ft

Ships travel between Lake Superior and the lower Great Lakes through the Soo Locks, in Sault Ste. Marie, Michigan. The Sault Ste. Marie International Bridge between the United States and Canada allows traffic to pass over the locks.

CAPITAL CITY: **DETROIT**

Detroit is Michigan's largest city and the nation's 11th most populous, with 886,000 people in a metro area of 4.38 million. Founded by the French as a trading post in 1701, the settlement occupied a strategic position between Lakes Erie and Huron.

Detroit's history is tied to engineer and entrepreneur Henry Ford, who led the city to be the world's automotive capital. The nickname "Motor City" inspired the term "Motown" for the distinctive soulful music born there.

Detroit's population has been in decline, having lost nearly 7 percent between 2000 and 2005; the city's economic difficulties have been countered by vigorous downtown and riverfront development. Revitalization has been stimulated by major corporate headquarters moving to the city, as well as by the construction of several casinos and hotels, handsome postmodern buildings, as well as two sports stadiums.

Area: 138.8 sq mi

Population (2005): 886,671

Population density: 6,388 per sq mi

Per-capita income: $36,650

The Detroit skyline, featuring General Motors's world headquarters and the Renaissance Center, overlooks the Detroit River.

Lake Superior is the largest freshwater lake in the world by surface area (31,820 square miles) and the third largest freshwater lake by volume (2,900 cubic miles).

In addition to the two Great Lakes surrounding the Upper Peninsula, northern Michigan hosts an astonishing array of waterways, such as 50-foot Bond Falls.

MINNESOTA

L'Etoile du Nord (The star of the north)

Settled: *1805*

Origin of name: *From the Dakota Sioux word meaning "cloudy water" or "sky-tinted water"*

Capital: *St. Paul*

Population (2005): *5,132,799 (ranked 21st in size)*

Population density: *64.5 per sq mi*

ECONOMY

Chief industries: *Agribusiness, forest products, mining, manufacturing, tourism*

Chief manufactured goods: *Food, chemical and paper products, industrial machinery, electric and electronic equipment, computers, printing and publishing, scientific and medical instruments, fabricated metal products, forest products*

Chief crops: *Corn, soybeans, wheat, sugar beets, hay, barley, potatoes, sunflowers*

Commercial fishing (2004): *$187,000*

Chief ports: *Duluth, St. Paul, Minneapolis*

Gross state product (2005): *$233.3 billion*

Employment (May 2006): *15.5% government; 19.1% trade/transportation/utilities; 12.4% manufacturing; 14.3% education/health; 11.4% professional/business services; 9.1% leisure/hospitality; 6.5% finance; 4.8% construction; 6.5% other services*

Per-capita income (2005): *$37,373*

STATE FLOWER

Pink and white lady's slipper

STATE BIRD

Common loon

THE NORTH STAR STATE

As the northernmost of the 48 contiguous states, Minnesota is called the "North Star State." It is also known as the "Gopher State," for its vast prairie lands, which are riddled with gopher holes. Topography ranges from lake-strewn, forested uplands in the north to grasslands in the south. Lake Itasca, located in the northwest, is the source of the Mississippi River, which flows southward to become the state's southeast border; Lake Superior is in the northeast. Iron ore pits in the northeast yield 60 percent of the nation's ore. With fertile farmland in the south and west, Minnesota ranks in the top 10 for agricultural products—a leader in livestock, dairy, corn, soybeans, and wheat. The climate is cool and relatively dry, averaging only 30 inches of rainfall a year. Over 3 million people live in the "Twin Cities" metropolitan area of St. Paul–Minneapolis, making it the country's 16th largest.

A Brief History

- The region was populated by Dakota Sioux when Europeans arrived.
- French fur traders Pierre Radisson and Médard Chouart, Sieur des Groseilliers, explored in the mid-1600s.
- In 1679, Daniel Greysolon, Sieur Duluth, claimed the region for France.
- Ojibwa arrived in the 1700s and warred with the Sioux for over 100 years.
- Britain took the area east of the Mississippi, 1763; the United States gained it after the Revolutionary War and gained the western area in the Louisiana Purchase, 1803.
- The United States built Fort St. Anthony, 1819, and bought Native American lands, 1837, spurring an influx of settlers from the east.
- Minnesota became a territory, 1849, and a state, 1858.
- In response to broken land treaties, the Sioux staged a series of attacks on white settlers, a bloody uprising that led to their being driven from the state.
- Railroad construction after the Civil War spurred the growth of the grain, timber, and iron mining industries.
- The 1959 opening of the St. Lawrence Seaway aided the port of Duluth.

Sioux chief Taoyateduta reluctantly undertook the Dakota War of 1862, a disastrous conflict with the United States.

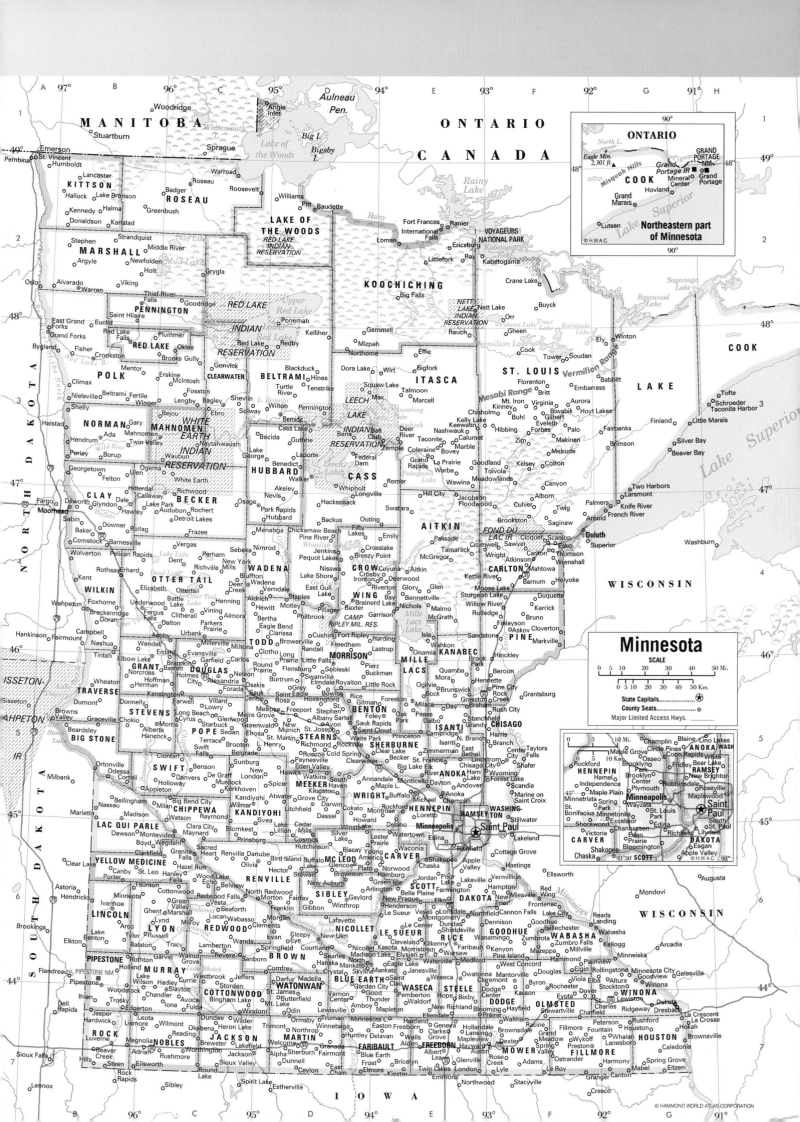

Minnesota

FACTS & FIGURES

GEOGRAPHY

Total area: 86,939 sq mi (ranked 12th in size)

Acres forested: 16.7 million

CLIMATE

Northern part of state lies in the moist Great Lakes storm belt; the western border lies at the edge of the semi-arid Great Plains

STATE TREE

Red pine

AVERAGE TEMPERATURE

CITY	JUN	DEC
Duluth	59.9	14
International Falls	61.6	8.5
Minneapolis–St. Paul	68.4	18.7
Rochester	66.1	17.3
Saint Cloud	65.1	14.4

FAMOUS MINNESOTANS

- Warren Burger (1907–95), U.S. Supreme Court chief justice
- Bob Dylan (b. 1941), folksinger, songwriter
- F. Scott Fitzgerald (1896–1940), author
- Judy Garland (1922–69), singer and actress
- Hubert Humphrey (1911–78), 38th U.S. vice president
- Walter F. Mondale (b. 1928), 42nd U.S. vice president
- Charles Schulz (b. 1922–2000), cartoonist

Charles Schulz

ATTRACTIONS

Minneapolis Institute of Arts; Walker Art Center; Minneapolis Sculpture Garden; Minnehaha Falls (inspiration for Longfellow's "Hiawatha"); Guthrie Theater, *Minneapolis*

St. Paul Winter Carnival; Ordway Theater, *St. Paul*

Voyageurs National Park

Mayo Clinic, *Rochester*

North Shore of Lake Superior

TOPOGRAPHY

- Central hill and lake region covering approximately half the state
- To the northeast, rocky ridges and deep lakes
- To the northwest, flat plains
- To the south, rolling plains and deep river valleys

Highest elevation: Eagle Mt., 2,301 ft

Lowest elevation: Lake Superior, 601 ft

St. Louis River

Split Rock Lighthouse, located on the North Shore of Lake Superior, was in operation between 1910 and 1969; it is now part of the Split Rock Lighthouse State Park.

CAPITAL CITY: **ST. PAUL**

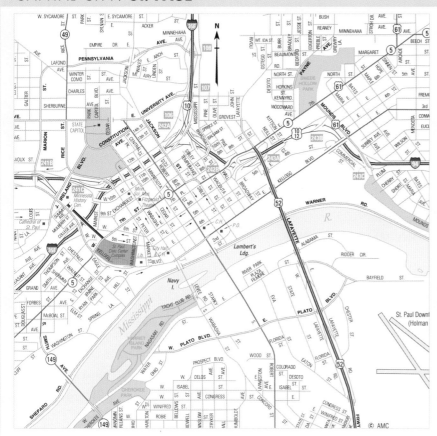

The state's second largest city, with 275,000 residents, St. Paul was founded in the 1840s as "Pig's Eye Landing." It became the capital of the territory in 1849 and was chartered as St. Paul in 1854. The city was on the edge of the frontier for decades, visited by soldiers from nearby Fort Snelling, by native peoples of the reservations, and by railroad-building crews whose companies established headquarters there.

Built at the westernmost boat landing of the Mississippi River, St. Paul is considered "the last city of the East"—although one district is on the river's west bank. The city has a reputation for being proper and traditional, and also "bookish," since it has 11 universities and colleges, 5 other postsecondary institutions, and 3 private prep schools.

Area: 52.8 sq mi

Population (2005): 275,150

Population density: 5,211 per sq mi

Per capita income: $40,915

Less populous than its twin city, Minneapolis, St. Paul is more traditional in culture and architecture.

SPOTLIGHT CITY: **MINNEAPOLIS**

Minneapolis is the "City of Lakes"; in fact, no home is farther than half a mile from a public park with a body of water. It is also called "Mill City," a center for milling lumber and grain. Built on both sides of the Mississippi, Minneapolis has a population of 372,000 and is the main business center between Chicago and Seattle.

As with neighboring St. Paul, it is known for higher education, with 10 universities and colleges. Urban renewal in the 1950s and 1960s razed 40 percent of the downtown, which was rebuilt with a gleaming, modernist skyline of headquarters for shipping, finance, health care, food products, and retailing. In 2005 the city was named "Top Tech City" for its research and development industries, and in 2006 was ranked as one of the "seven cool cities" for young professionals, and as a top-10 "smartest places to live."

Area: 54.9 sq mi

Population (2005): 372,811

Population density: 6,811 per sq mi

Per-capita income: $40,915

Minneapolis adjoins St. Paul, its twin city, and occupies both banks of the Mississippi River.

MISSISSIPPI

FACTS & FIGURES

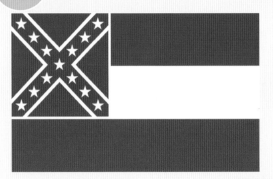

Virtute et Armis (By valor and arms)

Settled: *1716*

Origin of name: *From Chippewa mici zibi, "great river" or "gathering-in of all waters," or from Algonquian messipi*

Capital: *Jackson*

Population (2005): *2,921,088 (ranked 31st in size)*

Population density: *61.9 per sq mi*

ECONOMY

Chief industries: *Warehousing and distribution, services, manufacturing, government, wholesale and retail trade*

Chief manufactured goods: *Chemicals and plastics, food and kindred products, furniture, lumber and wood products, electrical machinery, transportation equipment*

Chief crops: *Cotton, rice, soybeans*

Commercial fishing (2004): *$43.7 million*

Chief ports: *Pascagoula, Vicksburg, Gulfport, Natchez, Greenville*

Gross state product (2005): *$80.2 billion*

Employment (May 2006): *21.4% government; 19.9% trade/transportation/utilities; 15.5% manufacturing; 10.8% education/health; 7.9% professional/business services; 10.3% leisure/hospitality; 4% finance; 4.9% construction; 4.5% other services*

Per-capita income (2005): *$25,318*

STATE FLOWER	STATE BIRD

Magnolia	Mockingbird

THE MAGNOLIA STATE

Mississippi, in the heart of the Deep South, is one of the South Central States. The river after which it is named wends southward along its western border, from the bluffs of the northwest to the Gulf Coastal Plain. At the eastern border is the Black Belt, a prairie region of rich, black soil. Mississippi has a subtropical, humid climate and is mainly rural. Only a fifth of the population lives in the major cities of Jackson and Biloxi-Gulfport. Agriculture is a mainstay of the economy, with approximately 30 percent of all Mississippians working in this sector. The state produces more catfish than anywhere else on the globe. The Yazoo River town of Belzoni (population 2,541) is called the "Catfish Capital of the World."

A Brief History

- Choctaw, Chickasaw, and Natchez peoples were living in the region at the time of European contact.
- Spanish explorer Hernando de Soto visited the area, 1540–41.
- French explorer La Salle traced the Mississippi River from Illinois to its mouth and claimed the entire Mississippi Valley for France, 1682.
- The first settlement was the French Fort Maurepas, 1699, on Biloxi Bay.
- The region became a U.S. territory, 1798, and a state, 1817.
- Slaves on cotton plantations made up 55 percent of the population by 1860.
- Mississippi seceded, 1861.
- During the Civil War, Union forces captured Vicksburg, 1863.
- Mississippi reentered the Union, 1870.
- During the Civil Rights Movement, resistance to desegregation and violence against African Americans made the state a battleground.
- Hurricanes Camille, 1969, and Katrina, 2005, caused substantial damage to the Gulf Coast.
- Since the early 1990s, casino gambling has boosted the economy.

Hernando de Soto, seeking wealth and means of passage across America, was one of the first Europeans to see the Mississippi River.

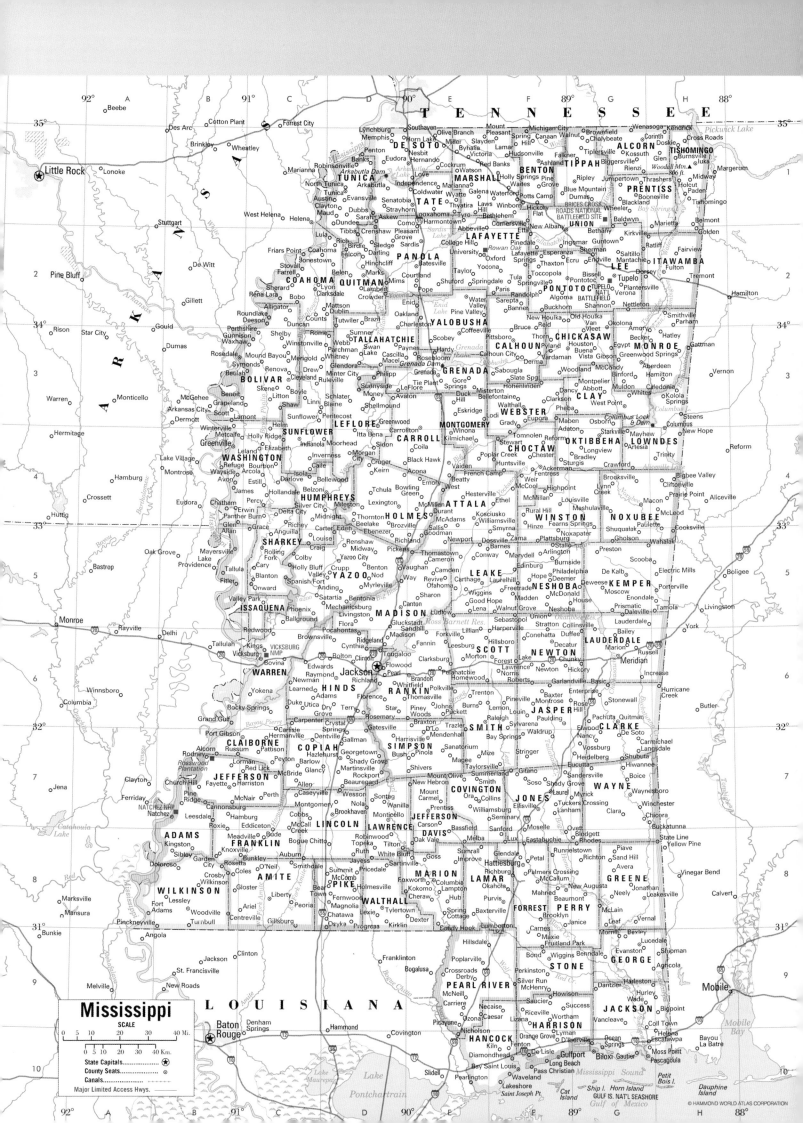

Mississippi

SCALE

0 5 10   20   30   40 Mi.

0 5 10   20   30 40 Km.

State Capitals...................★

County Seats....................◉

Major Limited Access Hwys. ━━━

© HAMMOND WORLD ATLAS CORPORATION

Mississippi

FACTS & FIGURES

GEOGRAPHY

Total area: *48,430 sq mi (ranked 32nd in size)*

Acres forested: *18.6 million*

CLIMATE

Semitropical, with abundant rainfall and long growing season; extreme temperatures unusual

STATE TREE

Magnolia

AVERAGE TEMPERATURE

CITY	JUN	DEC
Jackson	78.5	47.6
Meridian	78.5	48.9
Tupelo	76.9	43.4

FAMOUS MISSISSIPPIANS

- William Faulkner (1897–1962), writer
- Jim Henson (1936–90), puppeteer and director
- Robert Johnson (1911–38), blues singer
- B. B. King (b. 1925), musician
- Elvis Presley (1935–1977), singer
- Leontyne Price (b. 1927), opera singer
- Eudora Welty (1909–2001), writer
- Tennessee Williams (1911–83), playwright

Tennessee Williams

- Oprah Winfrey (b. 1954), talk show host, actress
- Richard Wright (1908–60), writer

ATTRACTIONS

Vicksburg National Military Park and Cemetery

Natchez Trace; Indian mounds; antebellum homes, *Natchez*

Elvis Presley birthplace and museum, *Tupelo*

Smith Robertson Museum; Mynelle Gardens, *Jackson*

Mardi Gras and Shrimp Festival, *Biloxi*

Gulf Islands National Seashore

TOPOGRAPHY

- Low, fertile delta between the Yazoo and Mississippi rivers
- Loess bluffs stretching around delta border
- Sandy gulf coastal terraces followed by piney woods and prairie
- Rugged, high sandy hills in extreme northeast followed by Black Prairie Belt, Pontotoc Ridge, and flatwoods into the north central highlands

Highest elevation: Woodall Mt., 806 ft

Lowest elevation: sea level

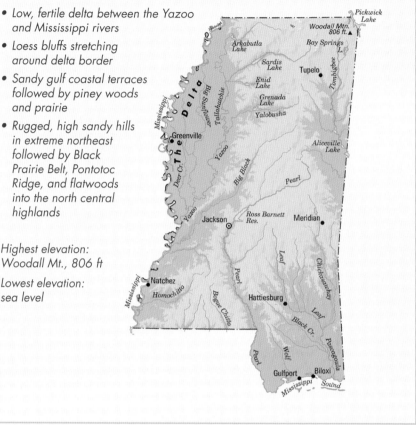

The Mississippi Sound is still traversed regularly by ships, including shrimp fishing boats like these.

CAPITAL CITY: **JACKSON**

The capital's metropolitan area has a population of approximately 530,000, more than one-sixth of the state total. The first white settlement was established by a French-Canadian trader in 1792. With its scenic surroundings on the Pearl River, good water, and proximity to main thoroughfares, Jackson was chosen as the capital in 1821. It was named for Andrew Jackson, hero of the War of 1812, who defended the region against a British invasion.

Economic growth was spurred in the mid-20th century by the development of natural gas fields. The city is home to 10 institutions of higher learning, including Jackson State University, the Mississippi College School of Law, and the University of Mississippi Medical Center. In keeping with the city's musical heritage of gospel, blues, and rhythm and blues, its slogan is, "Jackson, Mississippi: City with a Soul."

Area: 107 sq mi

Population (2000): 184,256

Population density: 1,757 per sq mi

Per-capita income: $25,188

Originally called LeFleur's Bluff, Jackson was renamed in 1822 after Andrew Jackson, who became president in 1829. Today it is the most populous city in Mississippi.

A swamp created by the meeting of Tubby Creek and Wolf River near Ashland, Mississippi. Hardwood swamps like this one are common in Mississippi.

MISSOURI

Salus Populi Suprema Lex Esto
(The welfare of the people shall be the supreme law)

Settled: *1764*

Origin of name: *From the Algonquian for "river of the big canoes"*

Capital: *Jefferson City*

Population (2005): *5,800,310 (ranked 18th in size)*

Population density: *84.2 per sq mi*

ECONOMY

Chief industries: *Agriculture, manufacturing, aerospace, tourism*

Chief manufactured goods: *Transportation equipment, food and related products, electrical and electronic equipment, chemicals*

Chief crops: *Soybeans, corn, wheat, hay*

Gross state product (2005): *$216.1 billion*

Employment (May 2006): *16% government; 19.7% trade/transportation/utilities; 11% manufacturing; 13.5% education/health; 11.7% professional/business services; 10.3% leisure/hospitality; 6% finance; 5.2% construction; 6.5% other services*

Per-capita income (2005): *$31,899*

STATE FLOWER	STATE BIRD

Hawthorn	Bluebird

THE SHOW-ME STATE

Missourians are said to be hard to convince, thus the nickname, the "Show-me State." The most southern of the Grain States, Missouri is also the most populous, as well as the most urban and industrial. Missouri has a warm, humid climate; spring brings tornadoes that often cause considerable damage. The Missouri River borders the northwest, then flows east through the state to join the Mississippi at the eastern border. Fertile plains cover the north and west, with the Ozark Plateau's steep hills in the south. The forested Ozarks attract tourism, an industry important to the state economy. The third largest manufacturing state west of the Mississippi, Missouri is known for heavy industry and food processing. Agriculture is a leading business, with livestock income twice that of crops. The two great metropolitan areas are Kansas City in the west and St. Louis in the east.

A Brief History

- In the 17th century, when French explorers arrived, Algonquian Sauk, Fox, and Illinois, and Siouan Osage, Missouri, Iowa, and Kansa peoples were living in the region.
- French hunters and lead miners established the first settlement, c. 1735, at Ste. Genevieve.

Sent by President Thomas Jefferson, Captain Meriwether Lewis and Second Lieutenant William Clark set out from St. Louis on the first U.S. expedition to the Pacific Coast.

- The territory was ceded to Spain by the French, 1762, then returned to France, 1800, and acquired by the United States in the Louisiana Purchase, 1803.
- Powerful earthquakes rocked New Madrid, 1811–12.
- Missouri became a territory, 1812, and entered the Union as a slave state, 1821.
  - St. Louis became the gateway for pioneers heading West. Though Missouri remained with the Union, pro- and anti-slavery forces battled there during the Civil War.
- In the late 19th century, railroad building and the cattle trade made Kansas City a boomtown.
- The most notable Missourian of the 20th century, Harry S. Truman, was U.S. president, 1945–53.

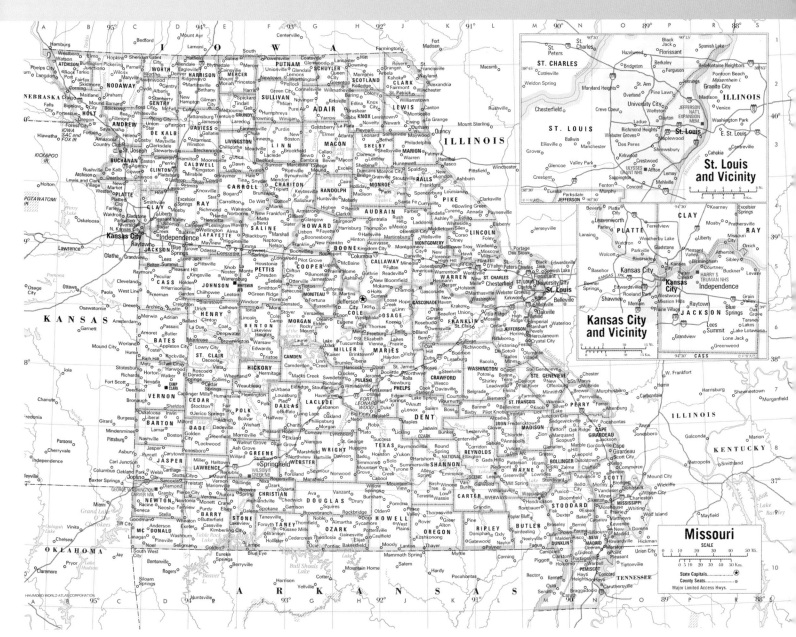

Established in 1935, Squaw Creek National Wildlife Refuge in northwestern Missouri plays host to many species of animals and birds, including bald eagles and snow geese.

Missouri

FACTS & FIGURES

GEOGRAPHY

Total area: 69,704 sq mi (ranked 21st in size)

Acres forested: 14 million

CLIMATE

Continental, susceptible to cold Canadian air, moist, warm gulf air, and drier southwest air

STATE TREE

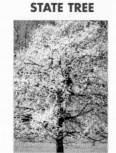

Dogwood

AVERAGE TEMPERATURE

CITY	JUN	DEC
Columbia	72.7	32.0
Kansas City	73.6	31.3
St. Louis	75.6	33.9
Springfield	73.4	35.7

FAMOUS MISSOURIANS

- Thomas Hart Benton (1889–1975), painter
- Yogi Berra (b. 1925), baseball Hall-of-Famer
- Walt Disney (1901–1966), animator
- T. S. Eliot (1888–1965), poet
- Edwin Hubble (1889–1953), astronomer
- Jesse James (1847–82), outlaw
- Reinhold Niebuhr (1892–1971), theologian
- Harry S. Truman (1884–1972), 33rd U.S. president

T. S. Eliot

ATTRACTIONS

Silver Dollar City, *Branson*

Mark Twain Area, *Hannibal*

Pony Express Museum, *St. Joseph*

Harry S. Truman Library, *Independence*

Gateway Arch, *St. Louis*

Lake of the Ozarks; Churchill Memorial, Fulton State Capitol, *Jefferson City*

TOPOGRAPHY

- Rolling hills, open, fertile plains, and well-watered prairie north of the Missouri River
- Rough and hilly land with deep, narrow valleys south of the river
- Alluvial plain in the southeast; low elevation in the west

Highest elevation: Taum Sauk Mt., 1,772 ft

Lowest elevation: Saint Francis River, 230 ft

CAPITAL CITY: **JEFFERSON CITY**

Located nearly in the center of the state, Jefferson City (named after the 3rd president) is overlooked by the capitol building, which stands on a high bluff near the Missouri River.

SPOTLIGHT CITY: **ST. LOUIS**

Founded in 1764 as a French trading post near the confluence of the Mississippi and Missouri rivers, St. Louis is called the "Gateway to the West." In the 19th century the city was a starting point for westward-bound wagon trains. Commemorating this heritage is the gleaming Gateway Arch, visible many miles from the city.

St. Louis is widely known for brewing beer, but its cultural heritage also includes the St. Louis Symphony, founded in 1880 and the second oldest in the United States. Greater St. Louis is the 18th largest metro area, with 2.79 million people, and encompassing communities in Illinois, across the Mississippi. Revitalization resulting from downtown renovations and new construction gave St. Louis a net population gain of more than 5,500 between 2000 and 2006, the first such gain since 1950.

Area: 61.9 sq mi

Population (2005): 344,362

Population density: 5,563 per sq mi

Per-capita income: $34,735

The Gateway Arch, part of the Jefferson National Expansion Memorial, commemorates President Thomas Jefferson's vision of the spread of democracy over the continent.

Nearly a mile long and 130 feet deep, the Grand Gulf, in Thayer, Missouri's Grand Gulf State Park, is sometimes referred to as Missouri's "Little Grand Canyon."

MONTANA

Oro y Plata (Gold and silver)

Settled: *1809*

Origin of name: *From the Latin or Spanish for "mountainous"*

Capital: *Helena*

Population (2005): *935,670 (ranked 44th in size)*

Population density: *6.4 per sq mi*

ECONOMY

Chief industries: *Agriculture, timber, mining, tourism, oil and gas*

Chief manufactured goods: *Food products, wood and paper products, primary metals, printing and publishing, petroleum and coal products*

Chief crops: *Wheat, barley, sugar beets, hay, oats*

Employment (May 2006):
20.8% government;
20.7% trade/transportation/utilities;
4.5% manufacturing;
13.4% education/health;
8.3% professional/business services;
12.8% leisure/hospitality;
5.1% finance;
7% construction;
5.7% other services

Per-capita income (2005): *$29,387*

STATE FLOWER

Bitterroot

STATE BIRD

Western meadowlark

THE TREASURE STATE

The northernmost of the Mountain States, Montana is the fourth largest state. Western Montana is covered by the Northern Rockies; the eastern region is plains and prairie. Montana's waters supply great river systems: the Snake and Columbia, flowing westward, and the Missouri, which joins the Mississippi to flow south. The climate is harsh, with cold winters, especially in the storm-prone Rockies, and daily temperatures that can vary in extremes. The nickname "Treasure State" reflects the importance of precious metals and gems, which have been mined in Montana since the Gold Rush of 1852. Montana sapphires are the most valuable jewel found in the United States. Agriculture is chiefly wheat—the state is one of the country's largest producers—and cattle. Lumber production is a major industry. Montana has more government-owned wilderness areas than any other state, attracting hunters after big game, such as moose, elk, and bear.

A Brief History

- Cheyenne, Blackfoot, Crow, Assiniboine, Salish (Flatheads), Kootenai, and Kalispel peoples lived in the region before Europeans arrived.
- French explorers visited the area, 1742.
- The United States acquired the region through the Louisiana Purchase, 1803.
- Lewis and Clark explored, 1805–06.
- Fur traders and missionaries established posts in the early 19th century.
- Gold was discovered, 1862.
- Montana became a territory, 1864.
- General George Custer was defeated at the Battle of Little Bighorn, 1876.
- Chief Joseph and the Nez Perce tribe surrendered, 1877.
- Mining activity and the coming of the Northern Pacific Railway, 1883, brought population growth.
- Montana became a state, 1889.
- Copper wealth from the Butte pits resulted in the turn of the century "War of Copper Kings."
- During the first half of the 20th century, the Anaconda Copper firm wielded enormous political influence.

Mining towns sprouted quickly after the discovery of gold and copper in the late 19th century.

Glacier National Park, with two mountain ranges, hundreds of lakes, and thousands of species of flora and fauna, is both a Biosphere Reserve and a World Heritage site.

Montana

FACTS & FIGURES

Geography

Total area: 147,042 sq mi
(ranked 4th in size)

Acres forested: 23.3 million

CLIMATE

Colder, continental climate
with low humidity

STATE TREE

Ponderosa pine

AVERAGE TEMPERATURE

CITY	JUN	DEC
Billings	65.2	26.1
Glasgow	64.4	15.6
Great Falls	60.0	24.3

FAMOUS MONTANANS

- Dana Carvey (b. 1955), comedian
- Gary Cooper (1901–61), actor
- Chet Huntley (1911–74), newsman
- Mike Mansfield (1903–2001), U.S. senator
- Brent Musburger (b. 1939), sportscaster
- Jeannette Rankin (1880–1973), 1st female member of Congress
- Charles M. Russell (1864–1926), artist
- Lester Thurow (b. 1938), economist

Mike Mansfield

ATTRACTIONS

Glacier National Park

Yellowstone National Park

Museum of the Rockies, *Bozeman*

Museum of the Plains Indian, *near Browning*

Little Bighorn Battlefield National Monument

Custer National Cemetery

Flathead Lake, *Helena*

Lewis and Clark Caverns State Park, *near Whitehall*

Lewis and Clark Interpretive Center, *Great Falls*

TOPOGRAPHY

- Rocky Mountains in western third of the state
- Eastern two-thirds gently rolling northern Great Plains

Highest elevation:
Granite Peak, 12,799 ft

Lowest elevation:
Kootenai River, 1,800 ft

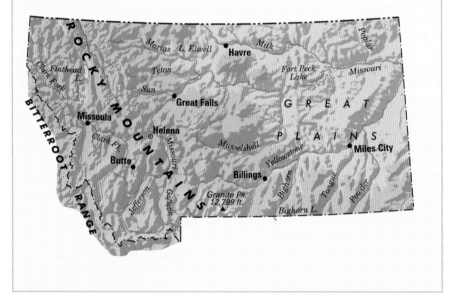

The Mission Mountain range is studded with lakes fed from ubiquitous snowfields.

CAPITAL CITY: **HELENA**

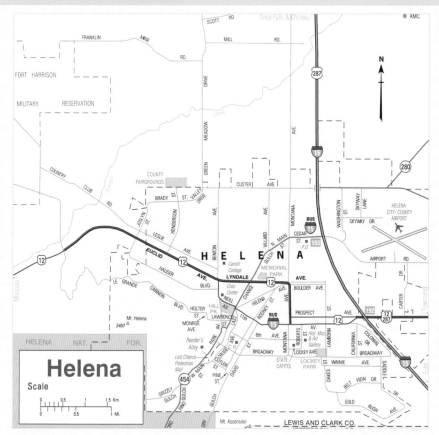

Helena

Scale

Settled after the discovery of gold along Last Chance Creek, Helena was first named Crabtown, for local miner John Crab, who found the gold. The more elegant name of Helena is derived from Saint Helena, Minnesota, the hometown of another miner.

Gold was key to Helena's prosperity, as more than $3.6 billion was taken from Last Chance Gulch over 20 years. In 1888, Helena had 50 millionaires, more than any town in the world. Today, the city's blocks and streets are irregular, first shaped by paths twisting around claims and along the gold creek. Helena became capital of Montana Territory in 1875, and the state capital upon admission to the union in 1889. The metropolitan area has a population of 67,600 and is close to national wilderness areas, state parks, the Missouri River, and mountain lakes.

Area: 14 sq mi

Population (2000): 25,780

Population density: 1,840 per sq mi

Per-capita income: $20,020

Helena, which sprang up with the discovery of gold in Last Chance Gulch, quickly became immensely wealthy.

Lake McDonald, the largest lake in Glacier National Park, is 10 miles long, 1 mile wide, and 472 feet deep.

Montana

Consisting of 1,584 square miles and crossed by over 700 miles of hiking trails, Glacier National Park draws almost 2 million visitors a year.
Top left: Swiftcurrent Lake. Bottom left: Rock Creek. Right: Emerald Lake.

NEBRASKA

Equality before the law

Settled: *1847*

Origin of name: *From Omaha or Otos Indian word meaning "broad water" or "flat river," describing the Platte River*

Capital: *Lincoln*

Population (2005): *1,758,787 (ranked 38th in size)*

Population density: *22.9 per sq mi*

ECONOMY

Chief industries: *Agriculture, manufacturing*

Chief manufactured goods: *Processed foods, industrial machinery, printed materials, electric and electronic equipment, primary and fabricated metal products, transportation equipment*

Chief crops: *Corn, sorghum, soybeans, hay, wheat, dry beans, oats, potatoes, sugar beets*

Chief ports: *Omaha, Sioux City, Brownville, Blair, Plattsmouth, Nebraska City*

Gross state product (2005): *$70.3 billion*

Employment (May 2006): *17.4% government; 21.1% trade/transportation/utilities; 10.8% manufacturing; 13.8% education/health; 10.4% professional/business services; 8.7% leisure/hospitality; 6.9% finance; 4.9% construction; 5.9% other services*

Per-capita income (2005): *$33,616*

STATE FLOWER	STATE BIRD

Goldenrod	Western meadowlark

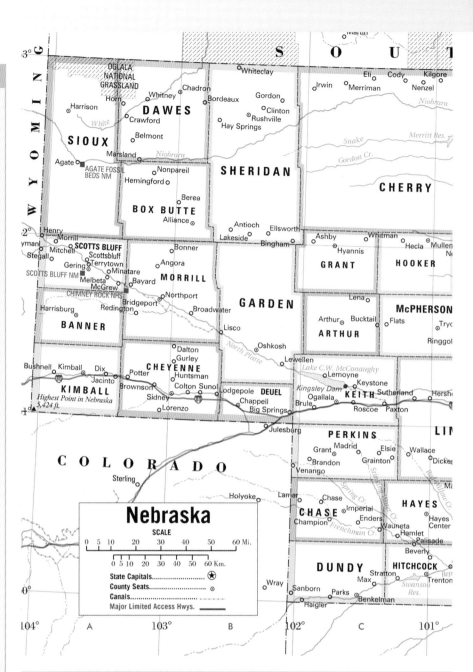

Nebraska

SCALE

0 5 10 20 30 40 50 60 Mi.

0 5 10 20 30 40 50 60 Km.

State Capitals............................ ⊛
County Seats............................. ○
Canals.......................................
Major Limited Access Hwys. ───

THE CORNHUSKER STATE

Nebraska, one of the country's greatest food producers, lies in the heart of the country's grain-growing region, with more than 90 percent of its land devoted to agriculture. The state's major crops are corn, soybeans, oats, and sorghum. A leader in agribusiness, Nebraska is dominant in beef cattle and hogs; livestock accounts for more than half its agricultural income. The state has also become a major telemarketing center. In Omaha, the Missouri River, which forms the state's eastern border, meets the Platte River, which flows across the state from west to east. The Great Plains cover much of Nebraska, except for the eastern region of fertile lowlands along the Missouri, where most of the corn is grown. Rich soil and warm, moist summer air from the south make the area agriculturally productive. Weather moves quickly across the plains, however, bringing sudden changes in temperature and powerful storms; the state is located in Tornado Alley.

A Brief History

- When Europeans first arrived, Pawnee, Ponca, Omaha, and Oto peoples were living in the region.
- Spanish and French explorers and fur traders visited the area before it was acquired in the Louisiana Purchase, 1803.
- Lewis and Clark passed through, 1804–06.
- The first permanent settlement was Bellevue, 1823, near present-day Omaha.
- The 1834 Indian Intercourse Act declared Nebraska Indian country, but Native Americans were eventually forced to move to reservations.
- Nebraska became a territory, 1854, and a state, 1867.
- Many Civil War veterans settled under free-land terms of the 1862 Homestead Act; struggles followed between homesteaders and ranchers.
- Nebraskan investor Warren Buffett announced in 2006 he would give most of his $44 billion fortune to charity.

North of the Platte River, settlers found fertile, hilly land, ideal for growing corn.

Sioux leader Chief Hollow Horn Bear

Nebraska

FACTS & FIGURES

GEOGRAPHY

Total area: *77,354 sq mi* (ranked 16th in size)

Acres forested: *0.9 million*

CLIMATE

Continental semiarid

STATE TREE

Cottonwood

CITY	JUN	DEC
AVERAGE TEMPERATURE		
Grand Island	71.1	25.6
Lincoln	72.7	26.5
Omaha	71.5	26.2
Scotts Bluff	67.2	25.7
Valentine	67.6	23.6

FAMOUS NEBRASKANS

- Fred Astaire (1899–1987), dancer
- Marlon Brando (1924–2004), actor
- William Jennings Bryan (1860–1925), lawyer and politician
- Warren Buffett (b. 1930), investor and philanthropist
- Willa Cather (1873–1947), writer

Marlon Brando

- Loren Eiseley (1907–77), naturalist and writer
- Darryl Zanuck (1902–79), film producer and director

ATTRACTIONS

Ashfall Fossil Beds; Strategic Air Command Museum, *Ashland*

Scotts Bluff National Monument, *near Gering*

Stuhr Museum of the Prairie Pioneer, *Grand Island*

Pioneer Village, *Minden*

Arbor Lodge State Park, *Nebraska City*

Henry Doorly Zoo; Joslyn Art Museum; Boys Town, *Omaha*

Oregon Trail landmarks

Chimney Rock National Historic Site, *near Bayard*

Fort Robinson State Park, *near Crawford*

TOPOGRAPHY

- *Till Plains of the central lowland in the eastern third rising to the Great Plains and hill country of the north central and northwest*

Highest elevation: Panorama Point, 5,424 ft

Lowest elevation: Missouri River, 840 ft

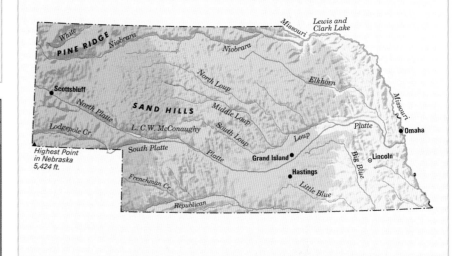

The mushroomlike formations at Toadstool National Park in the Oglala National Grassland were formed by ancient rivers that once flowed from the Rockies to the west and the Black Hills to the north.

CAPITAL CITY: **LINCOLN**

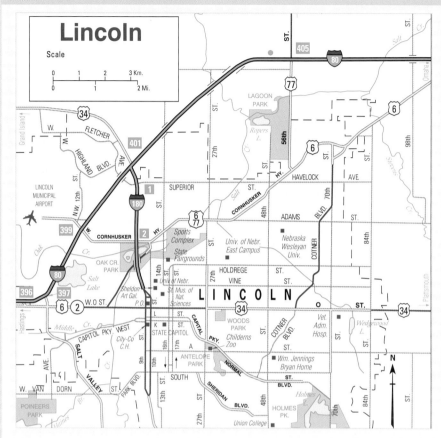

Lincoln, originally named Lancaster, was established in the 1850s. Just after the Civil War, when Nebraska Territory was preparing for admission as a state, the name was changed to Lincoln, honoring the wartime president.

There is little suburban development outside the city limits. Although the Lincoln metropolitan area is the state's second most populous, it includes only 40,000 people outside the city limits, for a total of 266,000. The major employers are the state government and the University of Nebraska–Lincoln.

The state capitol, a 34-story skyscraper with a golden dome, is visible for miles around; by law no other structure may exceed it in height. Lincoln is the home of the National Roller Skate Museum, the Pioneer Telephone Museum, and the residence of statesman and orator William Jennings Bryan.

Area: 74.6 sq mi

Population (2005): 239,213

Population density: 3,207 per sq mi

Per-capita income: $32,749

The airport in Lincoln is one of a number of designated emergency landing sites for the NASA Space Shuttle.

SPOTLIGHT CITY: **OMAHA**

The Omaha metro area has a population of more than 820,000. In a region traditionally devoted to agriculture, Omaha is a hub for part of neighboring Iowa, including Council Bluffs, across the Missouri River. Regional agribusiness depends on Omaha's meat-packing operations, grain storage depots, and transportation facilities—river, rail, and highway.

Telecommunications and information-processing are also leading businesses in Omaha, which has been ranked as one of the top 10 "high-tech havens" in the country.

Once the territorial capital, Omaha remains the region's leading metropolis, rich in culture. Important institutions include the Jocelyn Art Museum and Durham Western Heritage Museum, as well as performing arts centers and a minor league baseball club. The *Omaha World-Herald* is the largest employee-owned newspaper in the country.

Area: 115.7 sq mi

Population (2005): 414,521

Population density: 3,583 per sq mi

Per-capita income: $36,124

Omaha, situated at the confluence of the Missouri and Platte rivers, has been an important place for trade and travel for centuries.

NEVADA

All for our country

Settled: *1850*

Origin of Name: *Spanish for "snow-clad"*

Capital: *Carson City*

Population (2005): *2,414,807* (ranked 35th in size)

Population density: *22 per sq mi*

ECONOMY

Chief industries: *Gaming, tourism, mining, manufacturing, government, retailing, warehousing, trucking*

Chief manufactured goods: *Food products, plastics, chemicals, aerospace products, lawn and garden irrigation equipment, seismic and machinery-monitoring devices*

Chief crops: *Hay, alfalfa seed, potatoes, onions, garlic, barley, wheat*

Gross state product (2005): *$110.5 billion*

Employment (May 2006): *11.8% government; 17.4% trade/transportation/utilities; 3.8% manufacturing; 6.8% education/health; 12.2% professional/business services; 26.3% leisure/hospitality; 5.3% finance; 11.5% construction; 4.1% other services*

Per-capita income (2005): *$35,883*

STATE FLOWER	STATE BIRD

Sagebrush	Mountain bluebird

THE SILVER STATE

Nevada is sometimes called the "Sagebrush State," after the sturdy plant found on its deserts whose blossom is the state flower. Rich silver mines, which brought settlers and prospectors to Nevada in the 19th century, earned the state its more common nickname. In the 20th century, gaming and tourism surpassed gold and silver mining as the leading industries. Las Vegas, in the southern part of the state, and Reno, in the west, are famous centers of legalized gambling. Rugged, snow-capped mountain ranges occupy much of the state, but the largest topographical feature is the east central region's Great Basin desert plain. Nevada is the driest state in the country, averaging less than 7 inches of rain a year. With little moisture in the air, days are hot and nights cold year-round. Most rivers are dry, running only after a rain. Lake Mead, formed by the Hoover Dam on the Colorado River, is the largest body of water in the state.

A Brief History

- Shoshone, Paiute, Bannock, and Washoe peoples lived in the area at the time of European contact.
- Nevada was first explored by Spaniards, 1776; fur traders Peter Skene Ogden and Jedediah Smith each explored the area in the 1820s.
- The United States acquired the region at the end of the Mexican War, 1848.
- A trading post at Mormon Station, now Genoa, was established, 1850.
- Discovery of the Comstock Lode, rich in gold and silver, 1859, spurred a population boom.
- Nevada became a territory, 1861, and a state, 1864.
- Hoover Dam was built, 1931–36.
- A surge in resort casino construction after World War II made Las Vegas one of the top tourist destinations.
- An influx of Hispanics and Asians, attracted by service and construction jobs, helped make Nevada the fastest growing state from 1990 to 2005.

The discovery of gold in the late 19th century resulted in massive population growth, but today the town of Gold Hill and similar Nevada communities are virtually ghost towns.

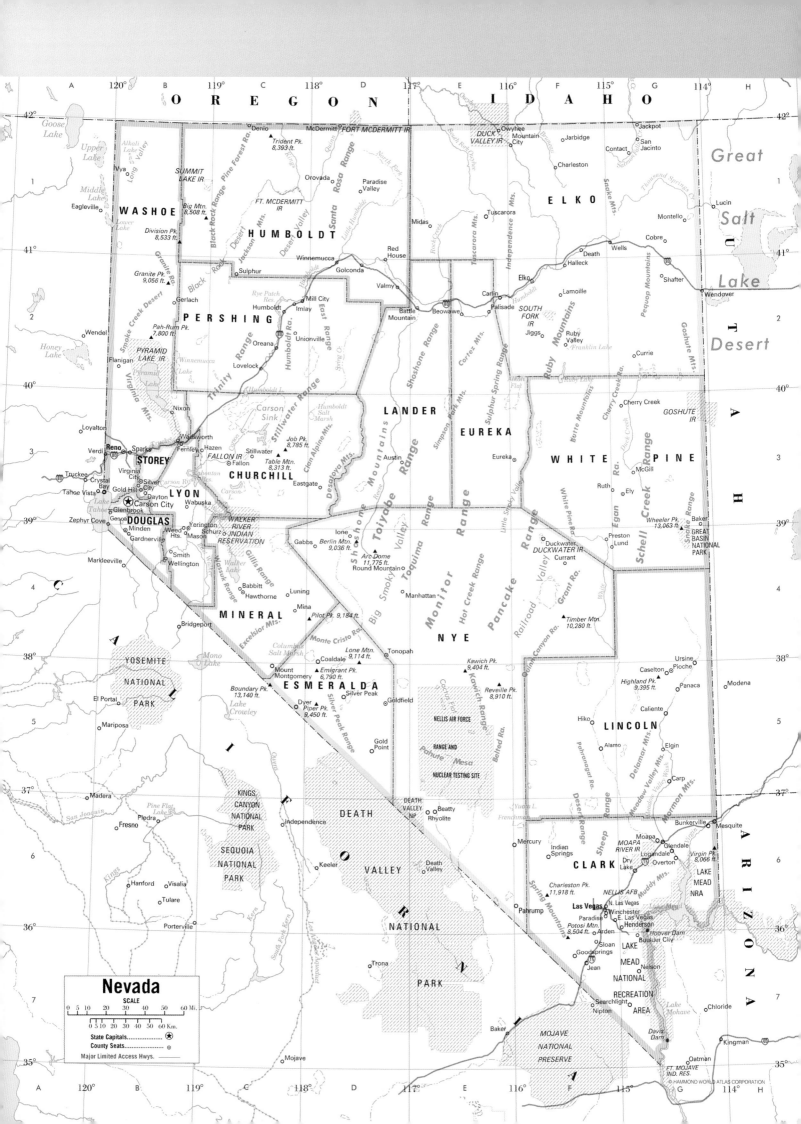

Nevada

SCALE

0 5 10   20   30   40   50   60 Mi.

0 5 10 20 30 40 50 60 Km.

State Capitals.............. ★
County Seats.............. ◉
Major Limited Access Hwys. ——

Nevada

FACTS & FIGURES

GEOGRAPHY

Total area:
110,561 sq mi
(ranked 7th in size)

Acres forested:
10.2 million

CLIMATE

Semi-arid and arid

STATE TREE

Singleleaf pinyon pine

AVERAGE TEMPERATURE

CITY	JUN	DEC
Elko	61.7	26
Ely	59.9	25.8
Las Vegas	85.6	47.0
Reno	64.7	33.6
Winnemucca	64.3	29.6

FAMOUS NEVADANS

- Andre Agassi (b. 1970), tennis player
- Walter Van Tilburg Clark (1909–71), writer
- George Ferris (1859–96), inventor
- Sarah Winnemucca Hopkins (1841–91), writer
- Paul Laxalt (b. 1922), U.S. senator
- Dat So La Lee (1829–1925), artist

Sarah Winnemucca Hopkins

ATTRACTIONS

Hoover Dam, *near Boulder City*

Great Basin National Park, *near Ely*

Lamoille Canyon

Lost City Museum, *Overton*

Pyramid Lake, *near Sparks*

Valley of Fire State Park

Virginia City

Red Rock Canyon; Liberace Museum; Las Vegas Strip, *Las Vegas*

Lake Mead, *southeast of Las Vegas*

TOPOGRAPHY

- Rugged north–south mountain ranges
- Southern area is within the Mojave Desert

Highest elevation:
Boundary Peak, 13,140 ft

Lowest elevation:
Colorado River at southern tip of state, 479 ft

Mojave Desert

CAPITAL CITY: **CARSON CITY**

The Paul Laxalt Building was built 30 years after Carson City (named after American frontiersman Christopher "Kit" Carson) was founded in 1858, during the booming mining years.

SPOTLIGHT CITY: **LAS VEGAS**

Las Vegas, located in the arid Mojave Desert near the Colorado River, is the largest city in Nevada, and the largest American city founded in the 20th century. The city's name is Spanish for "meadows," because of its original pastures, which were watered by artesian wells.

Las Vegas was founded in 1905. Within two decades after its incorporation in 1911, it had approved legalized gambling. This step coincided with the construction of nearby Hoover Dam on the Colorado, which—along with gambling—spurred tourism. As organized crime gained influence over casinos on the famous Las Vegas Strip, Las Vegas acquired the name "Sin City."

By the turn of the 21st century Las Vegas was redeveloping its downtown and attracting other industries, such as light manufacturing, finance, and service enterprises. Affordable real estate brought an influx of homebuyers, and the city's population grew by almost 14 percent between 2000 and 2005.

Area: 113.3 sq mi

Population (2005): 545,147

Population density: 4,812 per sq mi

Per-capita income: $32,963

Known around the world for its immense casinos, Las Vegas has been called the "Entertainment Capital of the World."

SPOTLIGHT CITY: **RENO**

Reno was established in 1868 at a newly built bridge across the Truckee River that opened the way for settlers and gold miners passing through the high desert of western Nevada Territory.

Reno's metro area (pop. 409,000) is the second largest in Nevada, after Las Vegas (pop. 1.82 million). Reno is known as the home of copper-riveted Levi's jeans, created in 1871 by tailor Jacob Davis. Tourism developed with the legalization of gambling in the 1930s. The city also became a destination because of the quick-divorce laws that brought couples from all over the country to untie the knot. Before the 1960s Reno was considered the national gaming capital, but it was surpassed by Las Vegas. Reno has undergone a 21st-century housing boom that has made real estate skyrocket.

Area: 69.1 sq mi

Population (2005): 203,550

Population density: 2,946 per sq mi

Per-capita income: $39,430

The establishment of casinos following the legalization of gambling in 1931 gave Reno a boost in popularity and importance.

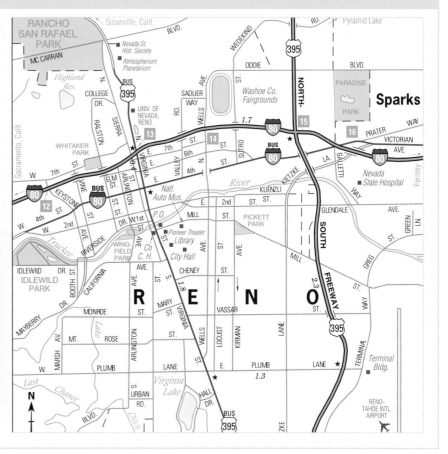

NEW HAMPSHIRE

Live free or die

Settled: *1623*

Origin of name: *Named by Captain John Mason, after his home county in England*

Capital: *Concord*

Population (2005): *1,309,940 (ranked 41st in size)*

Population density: *146.1 per sq mi*

ECONOMY

Chief industries: *Tourism, manufacturing, agriculture, trade, mining*

Chief manufactured goods: *Machinery, electrical and electronic products, plastics, fabricated metal products*

Chief crops: *Dairy products, nursery and greenhouse products, hay, vegetables, fruit, maple syrup and sugar products*

Commercial fishing (2004): *$8.8 million*

Chief ports: *Portsmouth, Hampton, Rye*

Gross state product (2005): *$55.7 billion*

Employment (May 2006): *14.3% government; 21.9% trade/transportation/utilities; 11.9% manufacturing; 15.7% education/health; 9.5% professional/business services; 10% leisure/hospitals; 6.3% finance; 5% construction; 5.2% other services*

Per-capita income (2005): *$38,408*

STATE FLOWER	STATE BIRD

Purple lilac	Purple finch

THE GRANITE STATE

The mountains of this New England state have thin, stony soil, making agriculture difficult, but the granite and marble they produce have been used in buildings in many American cities. Part of the Appalachian range, the White Mountains cover a quarter of the state. Mount Washington is the Northeast's highest peak at 6,288 feet. Timber is also harvested from New Hampshire's mountains, which have cold winters and cool summers. In the southeast, near the ocean, the landscape becomes rolling and gentle, the climate milder. Tourism is the leading industry, followed by manufacturing and agriculture. Tourists are attracted by New Hampshire's scenic countryside, many lakes, and snowy winters. Southern New Hampshire is close to the Boston metropolitan area and has many commuters. New Hampshire experienced a surge in population growth—as much as 23 percent—in the last two decades of the 20th century.

A Brief History

- Algonquian-speaking peoples, including the Pennacook, were living in the region when Europeans arrived.
- The first explorers to visit the area were England's Martin Pring, 1603, and France's Samuel de Champlain, 1605.
- The first settlement was Odiorne's Point (now port of Rye), 1623.
- Before the American Revolution, New Hampshire residents raided a British fort at Portsmouth, 1774, and drove the royal governor out, 1775.
- New Hampshire was the first colony to adopt its own constitution, 1776.
- After statehood, 1788, New Hampshire became a textile manufacturing center.
- The mill towns declined in the first half of the 20th century, but tourism and high-technology industries, lured by low taxes, have revived the economy since the 1960s.

A young girl in front of the Manchester textile factory where she works, in 1909.

New Hampshire

FACTS & FIGURES

GEOGRAPHY

Total area: *9,350 sq mi* (ranked 46th in size)

Acres forested: *4.8 million*

CLIMATE

Highly varied, due to its nearness to high mountains and ocean

STATE TREE

White birch

AVERAGE TEMPERATURE

CITY	JUN	DEC
Concord	64.9	25.9
Mt. Washington	44.4	10.1

FAMOUS NEW HAMPSHIRITES

Alan Shepard

- Salmon P. Chase (1809–73), politician and jurist
- Ralph Adams Cram (1863–1942), architect
- Mary Baker Eddy (1821–1910), founder of Christian Science Church
- Daniel Chester French (1850–1931), sculptor
- Robert Frost (1874–1963), poet
- Horace Greeley (1811–72), newspaper editor and politician
- Sarah Buell Hale (1788–1879), writer
- Franklin Pierce (1804–69), 14th U.S. president
- Augustus Saint-Gaudens (1848–1907), sculptor
- Alan Shepard (1923–98), astronaut
- David H. Souter (b. 1939), U.S. Supreme Court justice
- Daniel Webster (1782–1852), U.S. senator and secretary of state

ATTRACTIONS

Mt. Washington, *White Mountains*

Lake Winnipesaukee

White Mountain National Forest

Crawford, Franconia, Pinkham notches, *White Mountain region*

Aerial tramway, *Cannon Mountain*

Saint-Gaudens National Historic Site, *Cornish*

Mount Monadnock, *near Jaffrey*

TOPOGRAPHY

- Low, rolling coast followed by countless hills and mountains rising out of a central plateau

Highest elevation: Mt. Washington, 6,288 ft

Lowest elevation: sea level

Hampton Beach, New Hampshire

CAPITAL CITY: **CONCORD**

Concord was connected to Boston by the Middlesex Canal, which opened in 1802. The growth of the railroads later in the 19th century eventually eclipsed the canal in popularity and usefulness.

Once hunted virtually to extinction, moose have recovered in New Hampshire, as well as in much of the rest of New England, from a low point of about 15 animals in the mid-18th century to 7,000 or more.

The White Mountains, composed largely of granite, are some of the most rugged mountains in New England.

Echo Lake sits at the base of the sheer, 700-foot-high Cathedral Ledge, both popular destinations in Echo Lake State Park, near Conway.

NEW JERSEY

Liberty and prosperity

Settled: *1617*

Origin of name: *After the Isle of Jersey in England*

Capital: *Trenton*

Population (2005): *8,717,925 (ranked 10th in size)*

Population density: *1,175.3 per sq mi*

ECONOMY

Chief industries: *Pharmaceuticals/drugs, telecommunications, biotechnology, printing and publishing*

Chief manufactured goods: *Chemicals, electronic equipment, food*

Chief crops: *Nursery/greenhouse, tomatoes, blueberries, peaches, peppers, cranberries, soybeans*

Commercial fishing (2004): *$139.4 million*

Chief ports: *Newark, Elizabeth, Hoboken, Camden*

Gross state product (2005): *$430.8 billion*

Employment (May 2006): *16% government; 21.5% trade/transportation/utilities; 7.8% manufacturing; 14% education/health; 14.7% professional/business services; 8.5% leisure/hospitality; 6.9% finance; 4.2% construction; 6.2% other services*

Per-capita income (2005): *$43,771*

STATE FLOWER

Purple violet

STATE BIRD

Eastern goldfinch

THE GARDEN STATE

With 1,175 people per square mile, New Jersey is the most densely populated state in the country's most densely populated region. Most of the population is concentrated in the northeast metropolitan area, however, while the western and southern regions are mainly open, rolling countryside. New Jersey is called the "Garden State," because agriculture is so important to the economy, especially tomatoes, blueberries, and peaches. The topography is divided between the Atlantic Coastal Plain in the south and hills in the north. The climate is moderate because of New Jersey's long coastline, with white beaches that contribute to tourism, the second leading industry after manufacturing.

A Brief History

- The Lenni Lenape (Delaware) peoples were living in the region when the first European explorers arrived, Giovanni da Verrazzano, 1524, and Henry Hudson, 1609.
- The first permanent European settlement was Dutch, at Bergen (now Jersey City), 1660.
- Britain took New Netherland, 1664, giving the area between the Delaware and Hudson rivers to Lord John Berkeley and Sir George Carteret.
- New Jersey was the scene of major Revolutionary War battles: Trenton, 1776; Princeton, 1777; and Monmouth, 1778.
- New Jersey was the third state to ratify the Constitution, 1787, and the first to approve the Bill of Rights, 1789.
- Vice President Aaron Burr fatally shot Alexander Hamilton in a duel in Weehawken, 1804.
- The building of canals and railroads in the 19th century led to the growth of cities and industries.
- The 20th century arrival of large numbers of African Americans, Italians, Irish, European Jews, Puerto Ricans, Asian Indians, and other groups made New Jersey one of the most diverse states in the country.
- Construction of resort casinos, beginning in the late 1970s, revitalized tourism in Atlantic City.

Victory over the Hessians at the Battle of Trenton (December 26, 1776) gave George Washington's Continental Army and the Continental Congress renewed spirit and resolve.

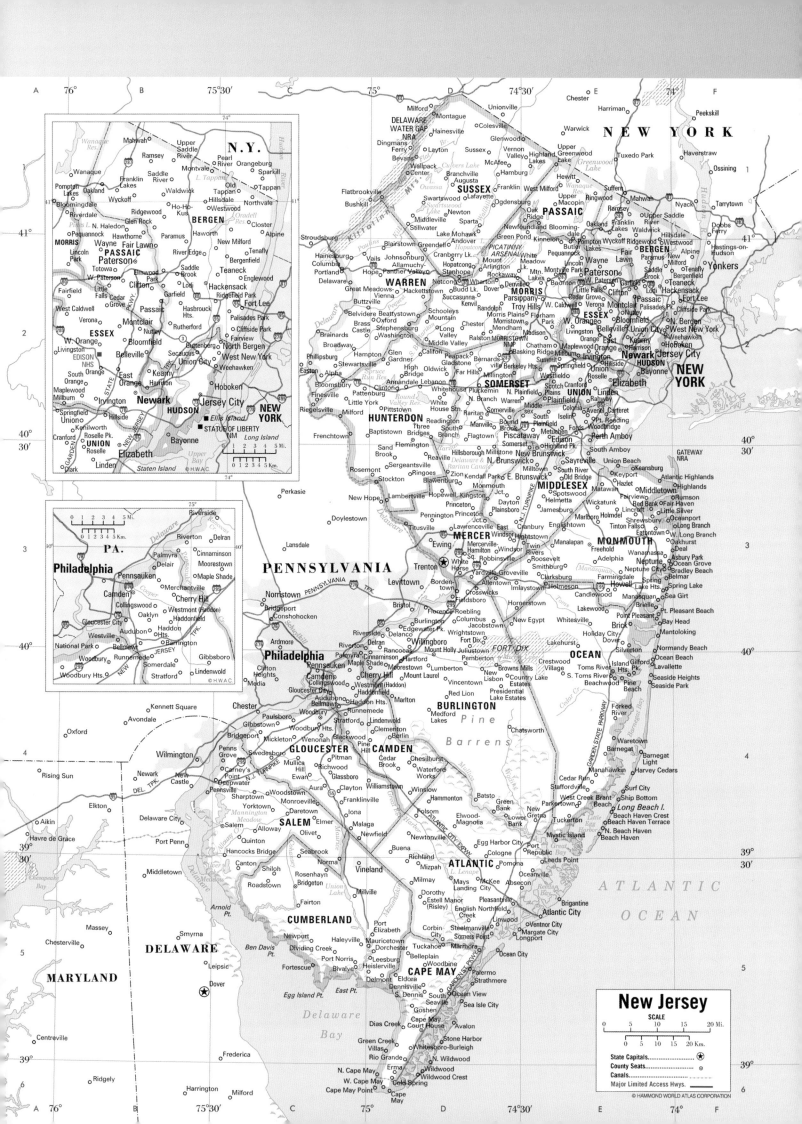

New Jersey

TOPOGRAPHY

- Appalachian Valley in the northwest
  also has highest elevation, 1,801 ft
- Appalachian Highlands, flat-topped
  northeast-southwest mountain ranges
- Piedmont Plateau, low plains broken
  by high ridges (Palisades) rising
  400–500 ft
- Coastal Plain, covering three-fifths
  of state in southeast, rises from sea
  level to gentle slopes

Highest elevation: High Point, 1,801 ft

Lowest elevation: sea level

New Jersey Shore

CAPITAL CITY: **TRENTON**

Named for William Trent, an early settler and prominent landowner in the area, Trenton has been the official state capital since 1790. Philadelphia and New York City are both within commuting distance by train.

Since its incorporation in 1854, Atlantic City has been a tourist destination. The famous boardwalk, which at one time stretched for 7 miles, and gigantic turn-of-the-century hotels gave way in the late 20th century to casinos, when the city made an effort to reverse a period of economic decline.

SPOTLIGHT CITY: **NEWARK**

New Jersey's largest city, Newark was founded in the late 1600s and is the third-oldest major city in the nation. Situated across the Hudson River from Manhattan, Newark's metropolitan area has a population of 2.1 million.

In colonial days, Newark was known for its beer brewing, cider, and leather tanneries. By the 19th century, Newark manufactured 90 percent of the nation's leather goods and was nicknamed the "Brick City," for its thriving brick-making industry.

Newark prospered until the mid-20th century, when its housing stock began to age, and it lost both businesses and people to the Sun Belt. Urban renewal projects destroyed many neighborhoods, and the city became notorious for its poverty and crime.

Newark underwent a renaissance in the 1990s, with a new performing arts center and sports complexes, and revitalization of the downtown.

Area: 23.8 sq mi

Population (2005): 280,666

Population density:
11,793 per sq mi

Per-capita income: $43,277

One of the oldest cities in America and the largest in New Jersey, Newark has one of the most diverse populations in the nation.

NEW MEXICO

NM FACTS & FIGURES

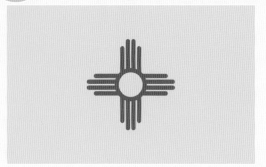

Crescit Eundo (It grows as it goes)

Settled: *1605*

Origin of name: *Named after Mexico by Spaniards in the 16th century*

Capital: *Santa Fe*

Population (2005): *1,928,384* *(ranked 36th in size)*

Population density: *15.9 per sq mi*

ECONOMY

Chief industries: *Government, services, trade*

Chief manufactured goods: *Foods, machinery, apparel, lumber, printing, transportation equipment, electronics, semiconductors*

Chief crops: *Hay, onions, chiles, greenhouse nursery, pecans, cotton*

Gross state product (2005): *$69.3 billion*

Employment (May 2006): *24.9% government; 17% trade/transportation/utilities; 14.4% manufacturing; 13.2% education/health; 11.3% professional/business services; 10.3% leisure/hospitality; 4.3% finance; 7% construction; 5.3% other services*

Per-capita income (2005): *$27,644*

STATE FLOWER

Yucca

STATE BIRD

Roadrunner

THE LAND OF ENCHANTMENT

The southernmost of the Mountain States, New Mexico is divided by the Rio Grande, which flows through the heart of the state. The Rocky Mountains in the north give rise to the headwaters of the river. The Great Plains, whose elevation averages 4,000 feet, lie in the east. Northwest is mesa, canyon, and butte country, where forested mountains rise to 10,000 feet. The southwest is basin and range country, a semiarid desert divided by low mountains. The climate is generally one of warm days and cool nights, with little rainfall, except in the mountains. New Mexico leads the country in uranium mining and ranks in the top 10 in natural gas production. Tourism is another major source of jobs in the state nick-named the "Land of Enchantment" for its sublime beauty.

A Brief History

- The region was home to Sandia, Clovis, Folsom, Mogollon, and Anasazi cultures, followed by the Pueblo people (Anasazi descendants), and then nomadic Navajo and Apache.
- Franciscan Marcos de Niza and a for-mer black slave, Estevanico, explored the area, 1539, seeking gold; Francisco Vázquez de Coronado followed, 1540.
- First settlements were near San Juan Pueblo, 1598, and at Santa Fe, 1610.
- Settlers traded and fought with the Apache, Comanche, and Navajo.
- Trade began on the Santa Fe Trail to Missouri, 1821.
- After the Mexican War began, General Stephen Kearny took Santa Fe with-out firing a shot, 1846.
- All Hispanic New Mexicans and Pueblo became U.S. citizens by terms of the 1848 treaty ending the war.
- New Mexico became a territory, 1850, but did not attain statehood until 1912.
- Pancho Villa raided Columbus, 1916, and U.S. troops were sent to the area.
- The world's first atomic bomb was exploded at a test site near Alamogordo, 1945.
- An underground nuclear waste deposi-tory opened near Carlsbad, 1999.

The Spanish mission at Jemez State Monument, built between 1621 and 1625 near an ancient pueblo, is a haunting reminder of Catholic Spain's ill-fated interest in America's Southwest.

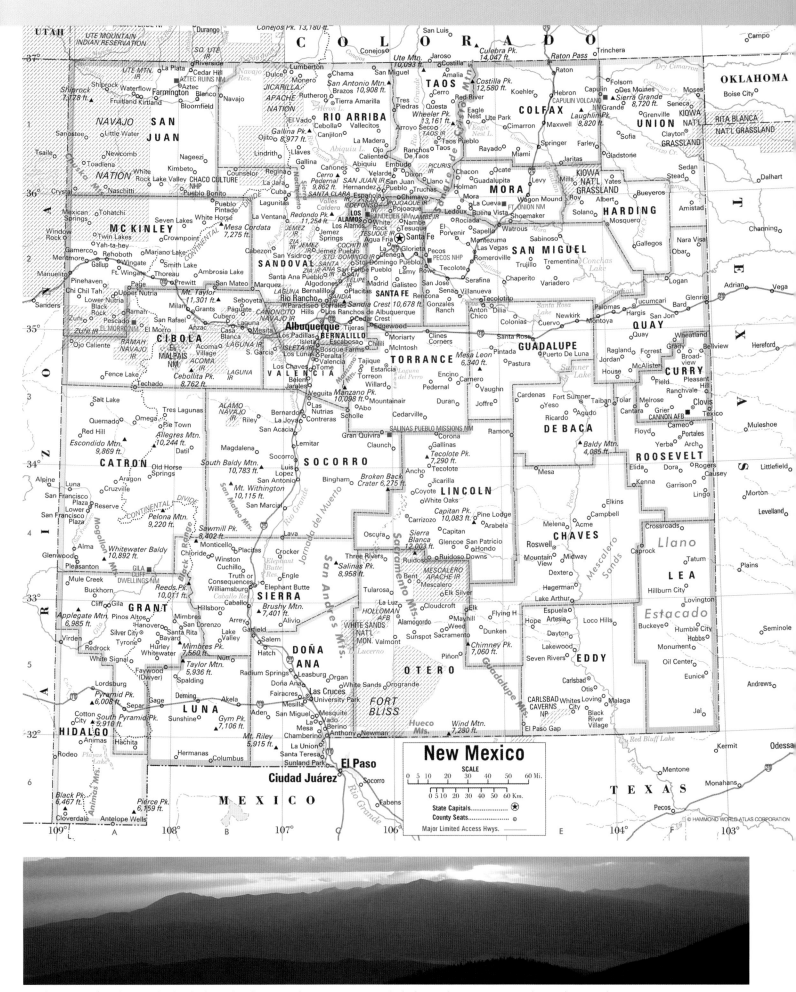

Standing 13,161 feet above sea level, Wheeler Peak in the Sangre de Cristo Mountains is the highest peak in New Mexico and a popular tourist destination.

New Mexico

FACTS & FIGURES

GEOGRAPHY

Total area: 121,589 sq mi (ranked 5th in size)

Acres forested: 16.7 million

CLIMATE

Dry, with temperatures rising or falling 5° F with every 1,000 ft elevation

STATE TREE

Pinyon

AVERAGE TEMPERATURE

CITY	JUN	DEC
Albuquerque	74.8	36.1
Clayton	69.9	34.8
Roswell	78.0	40.7

FAMOUS NEW MEXICANS

- Ben Abruzzo (1930–85), hot air balloonist
- Jeff Bezos (b. 1964), founder of Amazon
- Billy (the Kid) Bonney (1859–81), outlaw
- Kit Carson (1809–68), frontiersman
- Bob Foster (b. 1938), boxing champion
- Peter Hurd (1904–84), artist
- Tony Hillerman (b. 1925), writer
- Nancy Lopez (b. 1957), golfer
- Bill Mauldin (1921–2003), cartoonist
- Georgia O'Keeffe (1887–1986), artist

Georgia O'Keeffe

ATTRACTIONS

Carlsbad Caverns National Park, *near Carlsbad*

Santa Fe, oldest capital in the United States

White Sands National Monument, *near Alamogordo*

Chaco Culture National Historical Park, *near Farmington*

Acoma Pueblo, the "sky city" built atop a 357-ft mesa, *west of Albuquerque*

Taos

Ute Lake State Park, *near Logan*

TOPOGRAPHY

- Eastern third, Great Plains
- Central third, Rocky Mts. (elevation of 85 percent of the state is over 4,000 ft)
- Western third, high plateau

Highest elevation: Wheeler Peak, 13,161 ft

Lowest elevation: Red Bluff Reservoir, 2,842 ft

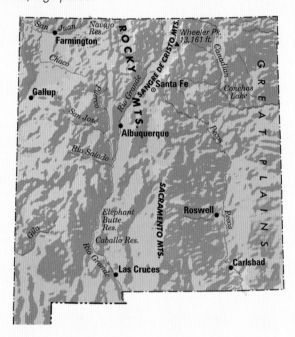

CAPITAL CITY: **SANTA FE**

At an elevation of 7,000 feet, Santa Fe is the highest state capital in the United States; founded in 1610, it is also the nation's oldest state capital. Originally it was the capital of a province of New Spain.

SPOTLIGHT CITY: **ALBUQUERQUE**

Sited on the Rio Grande, Albuquerque was founded in 1706 as a Spanish colonial outpost. The largest city in New Mexico, Albuquerque has a metropolitan population of 816,000.

The metro area, with its scenic surroundings, Kirtland Air Force Base, nuclear weapons research labs, and the University of New Mexico, has grown twice as fast as the city, which grew 10.2 percent between 2000 and 2005. The metro area is expected to pass 1 million by 2020. Rancho Rio, part of the metro area, is one of the fastest growing cities in the country.

Albuquerque's climate is dry and sunny, with short winters. Tourists are attracted by both the fine weather and many arts and cultural institutions. Albuquerque annually plays host to the world's largest gathering of hot-air balloonists. The city also holds a Native American powwow, with 3,000 dancers and musicians from 500 tribes.

Area: 180.6 sq mi

Population (2005): 494,236

Population density: 2,737 per sq mi

Per-capita income: $29,453

Albuquerque still retains Spanish influences from its early days, despite its rapid expansion in the 20th century.

Cattle forage near the Rio Grande. Snowfall varies statewide, between 3 and 300 inches.

The Rio Chama flows from the San Juan Mountains in Colorado into the Rio Grande.

New Mexico

The dunes of White Sands National Monument, in south-central New Mexico, cover 275 square miles. They are composed of gypsum, a common mineral rarely found in sand form.

A national monument since 1907, the Gila Cliff Dwellings are exceptionally well-preserved homes of the Mogollon culture and date to the late 13th or 14th century.

Magnificent stalactites hang in Carlsbad Caverns National Park, which includes 113 of the 300 known caves below the Chihuahuan Desert and Guadalupe Mountains.

The sun burnishes the red rock formations of the Jemez Mountains, a volcanic range dominating northern central New Mexico and the southernmost tip of the Rocky Mountains.

NEW YORK

Excelsior (Ever upward)

Settled: *1614*

Origin of name: *Named for the Duke of York and Albany*

Capital: *Albany*

Population (2005): *19,254,630*

Population density: *407.8 per sq mi*

ECONOMY

Chief industries: *Manufacturing, finance, tourism communications, transportation, services*

Principal manufactured goods: *Books and periodicals, clothing and apparel, pharmaceuticals, machinery, instruments, toys and sporting goods, electronic equipment, automotive and aircraft components*

Chief crops: *Apples, grapes, strawberries, cherries, pears, onions, potatoes, cabbage, sweet corn, green beans, cauliflower, field corn, hay, wheat, oats, dry beans*

Commercial fishing (2004): *$46.4 million*

Chief ports: *New York, Buffalo, Albany*

Gross state product (2005): *$963.5 billion*

Employment (May 2006): *17.5% government; 17.4% trade/transportation/utilities; 6.5% manufacturing; 18.3% education/health; 12.7% professional/business services; 8% leisure/hospitality; 8.4% finance; 3.9% construction; 7.9% other services*

Per-capita income (2004): *$38,228*

STATE FLOWER

Rose

STATE BIRD

Bluebird

Located high in the Adirondack Mountains, serene Lake Placid is appropriately named.

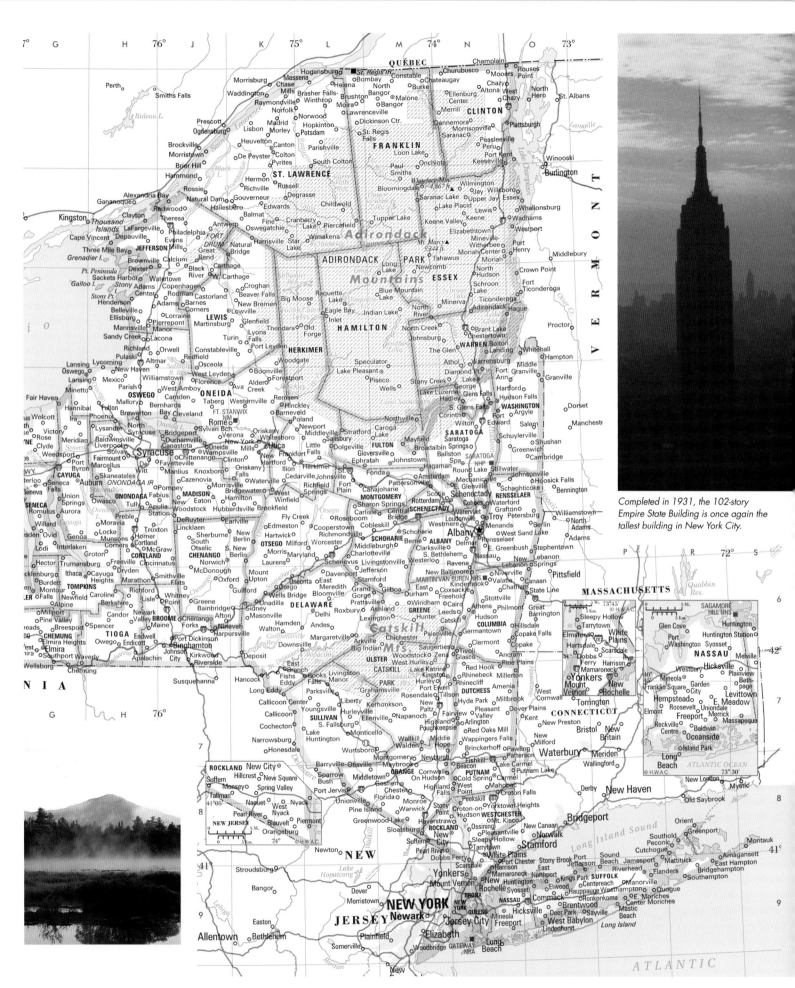

Completed in 1931, the 102-story Empire State Building is once again the tallest building in New York City.

New York

FACTS & FIGURES

GEOGRAPHY

Total area: *54,556 sq mi (ranked 27th in size)*

Acres forested: *18.4 million*

CLIMATE

Variable; the southeast region moderated by the ocean

STATE TREE

Sugar maple

AVERAGE TEMPERATURE

CITY	JUN	DEC
Albany	66.3	28
Buffalo	65.8	29.8
New York City	71.2	37.3
Rochester	65.8	29.4

FAMOUS NEW YORKERS

- James Baldwin (1924–97), writer
- Aaron Copland (1900–90), composer
- Lou Gehrig (1903–41), baseball player
- Ruth Bader Ginsburg (b. 1933), U.S. Supreme Court justice
- Stephen Jay Gould (1941–2002), scientist
- Henry and William James (1843–1916, 1842–1910), writers
- Michael Jordan (b. 1963), basketball player
- Colin Powell (b. 1937), U.S. secretary of state
- John D. and Nelson Rockefeller (1839–1937, 1908–79), philanthropists
- Edith Wharton (1862–1937), writer

Edith Wharton

ATTRACTIONS

Adirondack and Catskill Mts.

Finger Lakes; Lake Placid

Niagara Falls

Saratoga Springs

Philipsburg Manor; Sunnyside (Washington Irving's home); the Dutch Church of Sleepy Hollow, *near Tarrytown*

Fenimore House; National Baseball Hall of Fame and Museum, *Cooperstown*

Fort Ticonderoga, *overlooking Lake Champlain*

THE EMPIRE STATE

New York is the third most populous state, with 19.3 million residents. It acquired the nickname "Empire State" in the 19th century, when New York was the country's unchallenged commercial and business leader. New York City is still a major international center for business and finance. The state stretches from New England in the east to Lake Erie in the west, and north from the Atlantic to Canada. Much of New York is rolling country, while in the north are the rugged Adirondack Mountains. Southern New York's climate is moderate, influenced by the sea and by the Hudson River Valley. In the Adirondacks and the west, winters are harsh and snowy. Manufacturing (of products ranging from steel to apparel) and agriculture are leading industries, as is tourism. New York City, the greatest tourist attraction, and natural wonder Niagara Falls draw visitors from all over the world.

A Brief History

- When Europeans arrived, Algonquians including the Mohegan, Wappinger, and Lenni Lenape inhabited the region, as did the Iroquoian Mohawk, Oneida, Onondaga, Cayuga, and Seneca tribes, the League of the Five Nations.
- Giovanni da Verrazzano entered New York harbor, 1524.
- In 1609, Henry Hudson and Samuel de Champlain explored the river and lake later named for them.
- The first permanent settlement was Dutch, near present-day Albany, 1624.
- New Amsterdam was settled, 1626, at the southern tip of Manhattan; the British seized New Netherland, 1664.
- Key battles of the American Revolution included Saratoga, 1777.
- In the 19th century, New York City emerged as a great center for trade, finance, and the arts, and as a haven for millions of immigrants.
- Completion of the Erie Canal, 1825, made the state a gateway to the West.
- The first women's rights convention was held in Seneca Falls, 1848.
- Although the state backed the Union in the Civil War, the military draft, 1863, triggered three days of riots in New York City.
- Industry declined in the 20th century, and California and Texas surpassed New York in population.
- A terrorist attack on September 11, 2001, destroyed New York City's World Trade Center.

As Henry Hudson sailed up the Hudson River, he traded for food and supplies with Algonquian, Iroquois, and other Indian tribes.

TOPOGRAPHY

- Highest and most rugged mountains in the northeast Adirondack upland
- St. Lawrence–Champlain lowlands extend from Lake Ontario northeast
- Hudson–Mohawk lowlands follow the river valleys north and west, 10–30 mi wide
- Atlantic Coastal Plain in the southeast

- Appalachian Highlands cover half the state westward from the Hudson Valley, including the Catskill Mts. and Finger Lakes
- Plateau of Erie–Ontario lowlands

Highest elevation: Mt. Marcy, 5,344 ft

Lowest elevation: sea level

The mighty Hudson River runs for more than 300 miles and has been a crucial waterway in New York since the 17th century.

American Falls, 70–100 feet high, is one of Niagara Falls's three waterfalls, at the border of New York and Canada.

CAPITAL CITY: ALBANY

Albany, the capital of New York State, stands on the west bank of the Hudson River. Centrally located for the Northeast and southeastern Canada, Albany has long been a commercial hub—for the fur trade in the early 1600s, and in modern times for the distribution of goods and products.

The fourth oldest city in the nation, Albany is part of the Capital District metro area, which includes the cities of Schenectady and Troy and has 851,000 people. In 2005, Forbes magazine ranked the Capital District as the third best place in the country to live, and named Albany a "Top IQ Campus" and one of its "150 Places to Live Rich."

Along with a number of private schools, the city has the State University of New York at Albany, Albany Law School, the Albany College of Pharmacy, and Albany Medical School.

Area: 22 sq mi

Population (2005): 95,993

Population density: 5,488 per sq mi

Per-capita income: $34,025

The second-oldest state capital in the United States, Albany sprawls on the site of the Dutch settlement of Fort Orange (built in 1624).

New York

One of the world's greatest international centers of finance, media, law, and business, New York City is also a leader in culture and the arts and is home to the United Nations.

New York is the most populous city in the United States, with almost as many people as the next three cities combined (Los Angeles, Chicago, and Houston). The consolidated metro area, encompassing parts of New Jersey and Connecticut, has more than 18 million people.

At the mouth of the Hudson River, New York has one of the world's finest harbors, a reason Dutch traders estab-lished the town—as New Amsterdam—in the early 1600s. For all its commercial importance, New York is also a major tourist destination, with such popular attractions as Broadway, the Empire State Building, and the Statue of Liberty.

New York is also an international city, with more than one-third of its population foreign born.

Area: 303.3 sq mi

Population (2004): 8,143,197

Population density: 2,199 per sq mi

Per-capita income: $28,114

Punctuated with enormous skyscrapers, New York City's Manhattan skyline is a familiar and emblematic sight.

Midtown Manhattan's Times Square. It is best known for its New Year's Eve celebrations but is busy year-round.

SPOTLIGHT CITY: **ROCHESTER**

Situated on the Genesee River in western New York, Rochester has a metro area population of 1.04 million, the third largest in the state.

In 1803, the site was chosen because of three cataracts on the Genesee that promised ample water power for mills and industry. First nicknamed "The Young Lion of the West," Rochester had earned the name "Flour City" by 1838, when it was the world's largest flour producer.

Home to Eastman Kodak and to the Institute of Optics at the University of Rochester, the city also has a number of leading imaging and optical science

businesses and considers itself the "world capital of imaging." Education is the leading industry, including the Eastman School of Music and the suburban Rochester Institute of Technology. The university is the city's largest employer.

Rochester has been ranked in the top 10 of the country's "most livable" cities.

Area: 35.8 sq mi

Population (2004): 212,481

Population density: 5,935 per sq mi

Per-capita income: $31,057

Named after one of its founders, Colonel Nathaniel Rochester, the city of Rochester straddles the Genesee River.

The Catskill Mountain region, which is an eroded plateau rather than true mountains, is known for the beauty of its forests and rivers.

Contained within the 6.1-million-acre Adirondack State Park in northeastern New York, the Adirondack Mountains showcase peaks up to 4,000 feet high, thousands of lakes, and idyllic scenery.

NORTH CAROLINA

NC **FACTS & FIGURES**

Esse Quam Videri (To be rather than to seem)

Settled: *1650*

Origin of name: *After King Charles I of England*

Capital: *Raleigh*

Population (2005): *8,683,242 (ranked 11th in size)*

Population density: *178.3 per sq mi*

ECONOMY

Chief industries: *Manufacturing, agriculture, tourism*

Chief manufactured goods: *Food products, textiles, industrial machinery and equipment, electrical and electronic equipment, furniture, tobacco products, apparel*

Chief crops: *Tobacco, cotton, soybeans, corn, food grains, wheat, peanuts, sweet potatoes*

Commercial fishing (2004): *$77.1 million*

Chief ports: *Morehead City, Wilmington*

Gross state product (2005): *$344.6 billion*

Employment (May 2006): *17.3% government; 18.3% trade/transportation/utilities; 14% manufacturing; 12% education/health; 11.3% professional/business services; 9.3% leisure/hospitality; 5.1% finance; 6% construction; 6.4% other services*

Per-capita income (2005): *$30,553*

STATE FLOWER	STATE BIRD

Dogwood	Cardinal

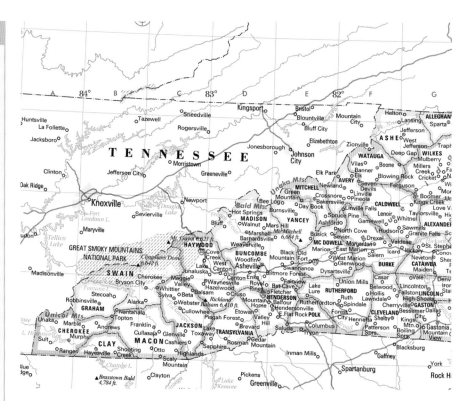

The Blue Ridge Mountains, so called for their bluish tinge when viewed from a distance, provide stunning views. They run north, along the western border of North Carolina, as far as Pennsylvania.

THE TAR HEEL STATE

North Carolina, the northernmost of the South Atlantic States, rises from sea level in the east, to the gently rolling hills of the central Piedmont region, to the Appalachian Mountains in the west, which contain the highest peak east of the Mississippi, Mount Mitchell, at 6,684 feet. The rural coastal plain, where tobacco, cotton, and soybeans are major crops, is sheltered by the Outer Banks, a chain of barrier islands off the coast, where the Wright brothers made their famous flight at Kitty Hawk. The coastal climate is warm and humid, while the mountain weather is cool, much like that of New England, although not as cold in winter. Tropical storms and hurricanes regularly hit North Carolina. Only Florida and Louisiana are struck more often. North Carolina's economy is diverse, and its population is growing steadily, having increased by 10 percent between 2000 and 2006. Manufacturing, agriculture, and tourism are the leading industries. The nickname "Tar Heel State" derives from the pitch and tar used in the colonial era to build and maintain sailing ships.

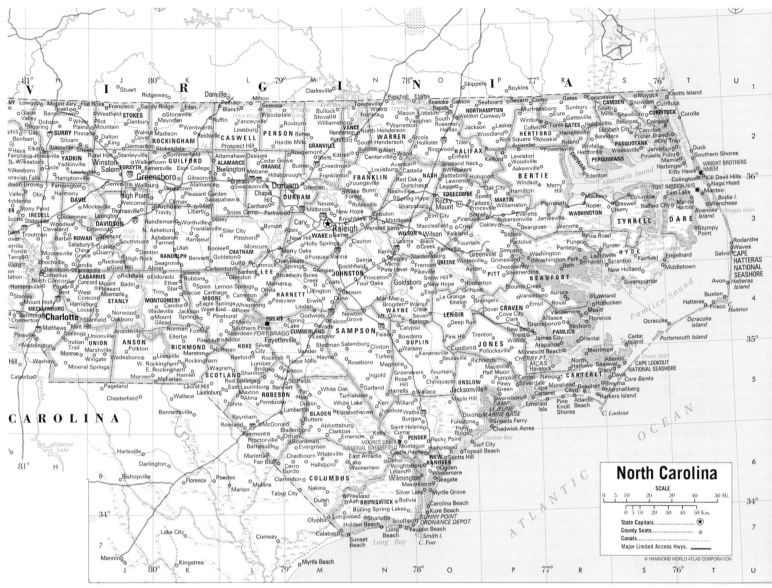

North Carolina

SCALE

0 5 10 20 30 40 50 Mi.

0 5 10 20 30 40 50 Km.

State Capitals.............................★

County Seats.............................◉

Canals..................................

Major Limited Access Hwys.

© HAMMOND WORLD ATLAS CORPORATION

A Brief History

- Algonquian, Siouan, and Iroquoian peoples lived in the region at the time of European contact.
- The colonists left by Sir Walter Raleigh on Roanoke Island, 1584–87, disappeared without a trace.
- Permanent settlers came from Virginia in the mid-17th century.
- The province's congress was the first to vote for independence, 1776.
- In the Revolutionary War, Cornwallis's forces were thwarted, 1780.
- The state ratified the Constitution, 1789, only after Congress passed the Bill of Rights.
- North Carolina, with slaves one-third of the population, seceded from the Union, 1861, and provided more troops to the Confederacy than any other state; it was readmitted, 1868.
- The Wright brothers made the first airplane flight at Kitty Hawk, 1903.
- Sit-ins at segregated Greensboro lunch counters, 1960, drew national attention to the Civil Rights Movement.
- Long reliant on tobacco, textiles, and wood products, North Carolina has prospered since the 1960s from advanced technologies (in Raleigh–Durham–Chapel Hill) and banking.

Sir Walter Raleigh, founder of the "Lost Colony."

North Carolina

FACTS & FIGURES

GEOGRAPHY

Total area: 53,819 sq mi (ranked 28th in size)

Acres forested: 19.3 million

CLIMATE

Subtropical in southeast, medium-continental in mountain region; tempered by the Gulf Stream and the mountains in west

STATE TREE

Pine

AVERAGE TEMPERATURE

CITY	JUN	DEC
Asheville	69.2	39.0
Cape Hatteras	74.8	50.0
Charlotte	76.5	44.4
Raleigh	74.7	43.0
Wilmington	77.0	48.9

FAMOUS NORTH CAROLINIANS

- David Brinkley (1920–2003), newsman
- John Coltrane (1926–67), saxophonist
- Richard J. Gatling (1818–1903), inventor
- Andrew Jackson (1767–1845), 7th U.S. president
- Andrew Johnson (1808–75), 17th U.S. president
- Edward R. Murrow (1908–65), newsman
- Arnold Palmer (b. 1929), golfer
- James K. Polk (1795–1849), 11th U.S. president
- Thomas Wolfe (1900–38), writer

Thomas Wolfe

ATTRACTIONS

Cape Hatteras National Seashore

Great Smoky Mts.

Guilford Courthouse and Moore's Creek parks

Fort Raleigh, *Roanoke Island*

Wright Brothers National Memorial, *Kitty Hawk*

Battleship *North Carolina, Wilmington*

North Carolina Zoo, *Asheboro*

North Carolina Symphony; North Carolina Museum, *Raleigh*

Carl Sandburg Home, *Hendersonville*

Biltmore House and Gardens, *Asheville*

TOPOGRAPHY

- Coastal plain and tidewater extending to the fall line of the rivers
- Piedmont Plateau of gentle to rugged hills
- Southern Appalachian Mts. contain the Blue Ridge and Great Smoky Mts.

Highest elevation: Mt. Mitchell, 6,684 ft

Lowest elevation: sea level

Blue Ridge Mountains

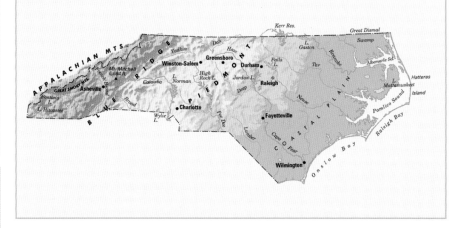

The Great Smoky Mountains, part of the Appalachian Mountain range, straddle the border between North Carolina and Tennessee and contain the popular Great Smoky Mountains National Park.

CAPITAL CITY: **RALEIGH**

The capital of North Carolina, Raleigh is the second most populous city in the state and part of the three-city "Research Triangle," known for its universities and high-tech company headquarters. The other cities—Durham and Chapel Hill—have a combined population with Raleigh of 1.56 million.

Established in 1792, the city was named for English adventurer Sir Walter Raleigh, who sponsored American colonization in the late 1500s. In the heart of farm country over its first 150 years, the city grew slowly until the 1960s, when IBM opened major operations and an interstate highway was constructed.

Local attractions include the North Carolina Museum of Art, the North Carolina Museum of Natural Sciences, the Harley Davidson Bikes Museum, and major centers for the performing arts. Raleigh is also home to the state's symphony, opera company, and ballet company, as well as the National Hockey League's Carolina Hurricanes.

Area: 114.6 sq mi

Population (2005): 341,530

Population density: 2,980 per sq mi

Per-capita income: $34,498

Named after Sir Walter Raleigh, founder of an early failed settlement, Raleigh was built to be the state capital in 1792.

SPOTLIGHT CITY: **CHARLOTTE**

Charlotte is the most populous city in North Carolina, and the 20th largest in the country. Nicknamed the "Queen City" for Queen Charlotte, the wife of King George III, Charlotte is also called the "Hornet's Nest," for its opposition to the British during the Revolutionary War. Residents are "Charlotteans."

The city was founded in 1755 by family of future 11th president James K. Polk (1845–49). In the early 19th century, Charlotte became famous for minting gold: North Carolina was the nation's largest producer of gold

until the California discovery of 1848. The Mint Museum of Art is in the original Charlotte Mint building.

Once a major railroad hub and a center for cotton processing, Charlotte is now a leader in financial services. The metropolitan area is home to 1.58 million people.

Area: 242.3 sq mi

Population (2005): 610,949

Population density: 2,521 per sq mi

Per-capita income: $34,816

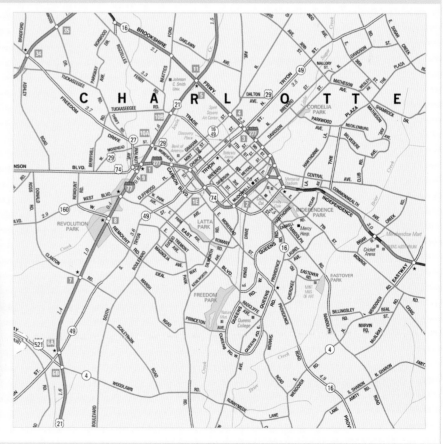

Charlotte has become a major banking center since the 1970s. Bank of America's headquarters, a skyscraper designed by Cesar Pelli, is a recent addition to the city's skyline.

NORTH DAKOTA

Liberty and union, now and forever, one and inseparable

Settled: *1780*

Origin of name: *From the Sioux word meaning "friend" or "ally"*

Capital: *Bismarck*

Population (2005): *636,677 (ranked 48th in size)*

Population density: *9.2 per sq mi*

ECONOMY

Chief industries: *Agriculture, mining, tourism, manufacturing, telecommunications, energy, food processing*

Chief manufactured goods: *Farm equipment, processed foods, fabricated metal, high-tech electronics*

Chief crops: *Spring wheat, durum, barley, flaxseed, oats, potatoes, dry edible beans, honey, soybeans, sugar beets, sunflowers, hay*

Gross state product (2005): *$24.2 billion*

Employment (May 2006): *22% government; 21.5% trade/transportation/utilities; 7.3% manufacturing; 13.9% education/health; 7.7% professional/business services; 9.2% leisure/hospitality; 5.4% finance; 5.4% construction; 6.4% other services*

Per-capita income (2005): *$31,395*

STATE FLOWER

Wild prairie rose

STATE BIRD

Western meadowlark

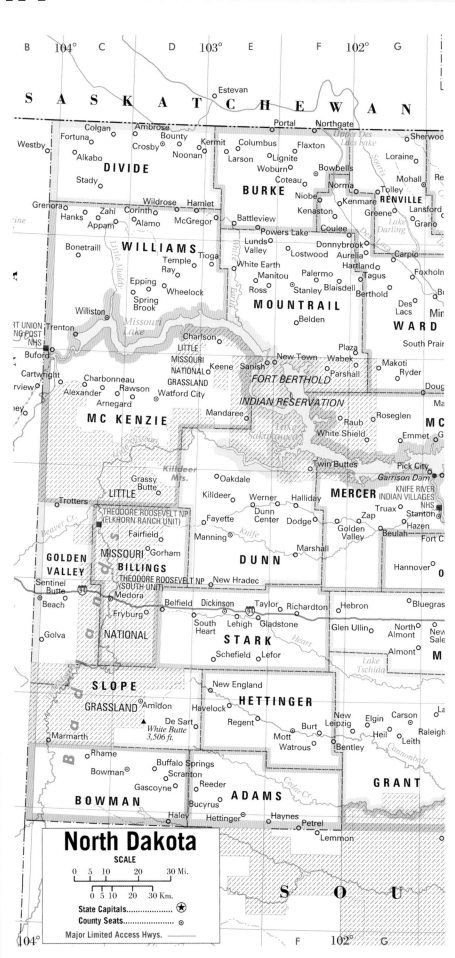

North Dakota

FACTS & FIGURES

Geography

Total area: *70,700 sq mi (ranked 19th in size)*

Acres forested: *0.7 million*

CLIMATE

Continental, with a wide range of temperature and moderate rainfall

STATE TREE

American elm

AVERAGE TEMPERATURE

CITY	JUN	DEC
Bismarck	64.7	15.2
Fargo	66.0	12.5
Grand Forks	65.2	11.3
Williston	63.7	13.0

FAMOUS NORTH DAKOTANS

- Maxwell Anderson (1888–1959), playwright
- John Bernard Flannagan (1895–1942), sculptor
- Phil Jackson (b. 1945), basketball coach
- Louis L'Amour (1908–88), writer
- Peggy Lee (1920–2002), singer
- Eric Sevareid (1912–92), journalist
- Vilhjalmur Stefansson (1879–1962), explorer

Peggy Lee

ATTRACTIONS

North Dakota Heritage Center, *Bismarck*

Bonanzaville, *Fargo*

Fort Union Trading Post National Historic Site, *near Williston*

Lake Sakakawea; Knife River Indian Villages National Historic Site, *near Bismarck*

International Peace Garden, *north of Dunseith*

Theodore Roosevelt National Park, including Elkhorn Ranch, *Badlands*

Fort Abraham Lincoln State Park and Museum, *near Mandan*

Dakota Dinosaur Museum, *Dickinson*

THE PEACE GARDEN STATE

The International Peace Garden, which straddles the boundary between North Dakota and Canada, was established in 1932 to honor peace between the neighboring countries. In 1957, North Dakota formally adopted "Peace Garden State" as its nickname. The northernmost of the Great Plains States, also known as the Grain States, North Dakota is mainly agricultural, although it also produces coal and oil. Livestock ranches are numerous in the hilly west; in the east are the farms of the fertile lowlands along the Red River. Two-thirds of the agricultural income comes from crops, mainly wheat, barley, and flaxseed. The Missouri River, which flows through the western part of the state, is dammed in the northwest to create Lake Sakakawea, the third largest manmade lake in the country. As with many Plains states, the climate is one of extremes, from cold, blizzard-prone winters to dry summers. North Dakota receives only 16 inches of precipitation annually.

A Brief History

- At the time of European contact, the Ojibwa, Yanktonai and Teton Sioux, Mandan, Arikara, and Hidatsa peoples lived in the region.
- Pierre Gaultier de Varennes, Sieur de La Vérendrye, the first French fur trader in the area, 1738, was followed by the English in the late 18th century.
- Lewis and Clark built Fort Mandan, near present-day Washburn, 1804–05, and wintered there.
- The first permanent settlement was established at Pembina, 1812.
- Missouri River steamboats reached the area, 1832.
- Dakota Territory was organized, 1861.
- The first railroad arrived, 1872.
- Many settlers came west to farm, 1870s–80s, leading to statehood, 1889.
- The predominantly agricultural state had a 6.5 percent drop in population between 1930 and 2005.

Built in 1827 by the American Fur Company, Fort Union was a primary trading point between white settlers and Assiniboin Indians for four decades. Lithograph, c. 1855.

TOPOGRAPHY

- Central lowland in the east comprises the flat Red River Valley and the Rolling Drift Prairie
- Missouri Plateau of the Great Plains in the west

Highest elevation:
White Butte, 3,506 ft

Lowest elevation:
Red River, 750 ft

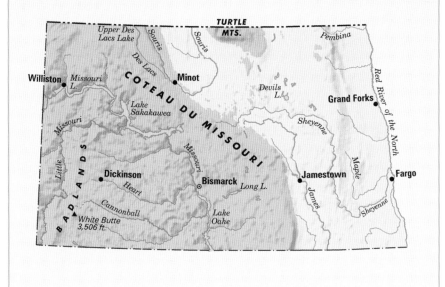

Theodore Roosevelt National Park comprises three distinct regions of badlands, all located in the Little Missouri National Grassland.

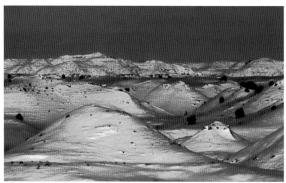

Glowing blue under a layer of snow, the badlands draw visitors even during the cold winter nights.

CAPITAL CITY: BISMARCK

Founded in 1872, Bismarck is the capital of North Dakota and the second most populous city after Fargo. Across the Missouri River is Mandan. The total population of the Bismarck–Mandan metropolitan area is 100,000. Originally named Edwinton after a railroad executive, the city was renamed in 1873 in honor of German chancellor Otto von Bismarck in hope of attracting German immigrants.

On the Great Plains, the city has warm, humid summers, and long, cold winters. The state government is the largest single employer.

Bismarck is unusual in that its downtown, rather than a suburban mall, is still the region's main shopping district. Near downtown is the historic Cathedral District, named for the Cathedral of the Holy Spirit, an Art Deco church built in the early 20th century. The city has a large, attractive park system, much of it along the banks of the Missouri River.

Area: 27 sq mi

Population (2000): 55,532

Population density: 2,065 per sq mi

Per-capita income: $31,692

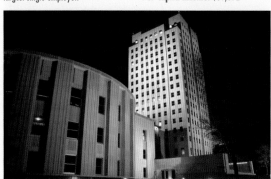

Founded in 1872, Bismarck was the capital of the Dakota Territory before the state of North Dakota joined the Union in 1889.

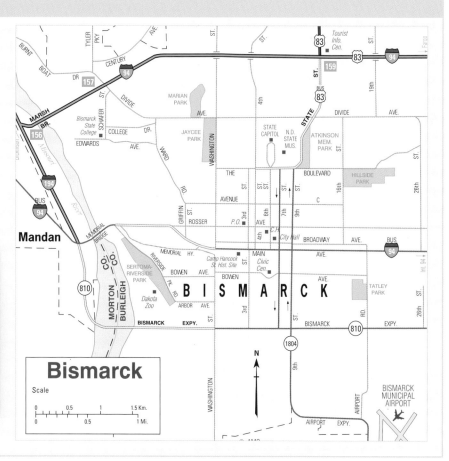

OHIO

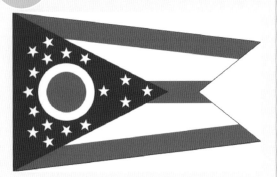

With God, all things are possible

Settled: *1788*

Origin of name: *Iroquois word meaning "good river" or "fine river"*

Capital: *Columbus*

Population (2005): *11,464,042 (ranked 7th in size)*

Population density: *280 per sq mi*

ECONOMY

Chief industries: *Manufacturing, trade, services*

Chief manufactured goods: *Transportation equipment, machinery, primary and fabricated metal products*

Chief crops: *Corn, hay, winter wheat, oats, soybeans*

Commercial fishing (2004): *$2.9 million*

Chief ports: *Toledo, Conneaut, Cleveland, Ashtabula*

Gross state product (2005): *$442.4 billion*

Employment (May 2006): *14.9% government; 18.9% trade/transportation/utilities; 14.7% manufacturing; 14.1% education/health; 11.9% professional/business services; 9.6% leisure/hospitality; 5.7% finance; 4.4% construction; 5.7% other services*

Per-capita income (2005): *$32,478*

STATE FLOWER

Scarlet carnation

STATE BIRD

Cardinal

THE BUCKEYE STATE

Nicknamed for its state tree, the Buckeye chestnut, Ohio is a Great Lakes State, with shoreline on Lake Erie. The Ohio River forms the state's southern border. Much of Ohio's topography is gentle, rolling plain, from the Allegheny Plateau in the east to the Lake Erie plains that extend south and west. The land is generally fertile, supporting farming; the eastern regions are rich in mineral deposits. Ohio's economy depends on crops, particularly corn. The state is a leader in both manufacturing and mining, especially of coal, natural gas, and limestone. The climate is humid, with hot summers and cold winters; as much as 50 inches of snow can fall annually near Lake Erie. Ohio, which has the distinction of being within a day's drive of 50 percent of North America's population, is crisscrossed by the country's 10th largest network of highways.

A Brief History

- Paleoindians hunted in the area about 11,000 years ago; the Adena and Hopewell cultures followed.
- Wyandot, Delaware, Miami, and Shawnee peoples sparsely occupied the area when the first Europeans arrived.
- La Salle visited the region, 1669.
- France claimed the area, 1682, but ceded it to Britain, 1763.
- Ohio became part of the Northwest Territory, 1787.
- The first permanent settlement was at Marietta, 1788. Cincinnati was also founded in 1788; Cleveland, 1796.
- Indian warfare abated with the Treaty of Greenville, 1795.
- Ohio became a state, 1803.
- In the War of 1812, Oliver Hazard Perry's victory on Lake Erie and William Henry Harrison's invasion of Canada, 1813, ended British incursions.
- Columbus, founded 1812, became the state capital, 1816.
- Ohioans aided the Underground Railroad, helping runaway slaves.
- The state became an industrial, as well as agricultural, powerhouse in the 20th century.
- Manufacturing jobs dropped by 21 percent from 1998 to 2006.

Burial mounds and other ancient monuments in Hopewell Culture National Historical Park are visible remnants of the Hopewell culture (active between 200 BCE and 500 CE).

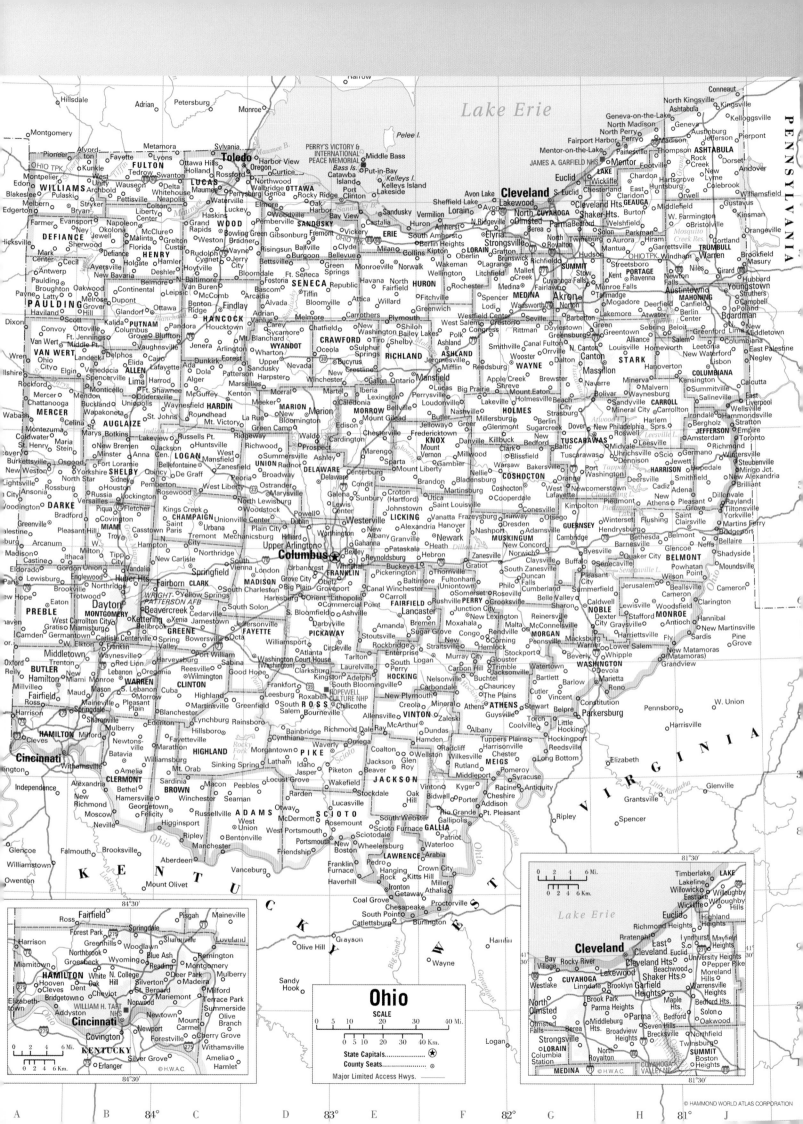

Ohio

SCALE

```
0   5   10      20      30      40 Mi.
0  5  10   20   30   40 Km.
```

State Capitals.............................★
County Seats.............................o
Major Limited Access Hwys. ———

© HAMMOND WORLD ATLAS CORPORATION

Ohio

FACTS & FIGURES

GEOGRAPHY

Total area: *44,825 sq mi* (ranked 34th in size)

Acres forested: *7.9 million*

CLIMATE

Temperate but variable; weather subject to much precipitation

STATE TREE

Buckeye chestnut

AVERAGE TEMPERATURE

CITY	JUN	DEC
Cleveland	67.5	31.1
Columbus	71.2	33.5
Dayton	70.2	31.4
Toledo	68.8	29.2

FAMOUS OHIOANS

- Sherwood Anderson (1876–1941), writer
- Neil Armstrong (b. 1930), astronaut
- George Bellows (1882–1925), painter
- George Custer (1839–76), general
- Clarence Darrow (1857–1938), lawyer
- Clark Gable (1901–60), actor
- John Glenn (b. 1921), astronaut
- Jesse Owens (1913–80), Olympic runner
- Eddie Rickenbacker (1890–1973), World War I fighter ace
- William Sherman (1820–91), Civil War general
- Steven Spielberg (b. 1946), director

George Bellows

ATTRACTIONS

Mound City Group, in Hopewell Culture National Historical Park, *near Chillicothe*

Neil Armstrong Air and Space Museum, *Wapakoneta*

Air Force Museum, *Dayton*

Lake Erie Islands; Cedar Point amusement park, *Sandusky*

Amish Region, *Tuscarawas/Holmes counties*

German Village, *Columbus*

Rock and Roll Hall of Fame and Museum, *Cleveland*

TOPOGRAPHY

- Generally rolling plain
- Allegheny Plateau in east
- Lake Erie plains extend southward
- Central plains in the west

Highest elevation: Campbell Hill, 1,549 ft

Lowest elevation: Ohio River, 455 ft

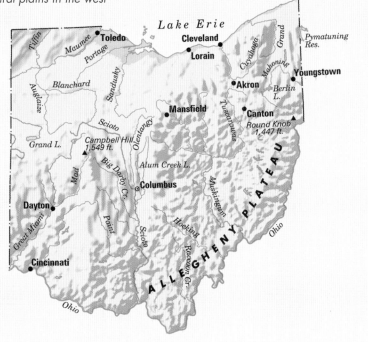

CAPITAL CITY: **COLUMBUS**

The capital city since 1816, Columbus is located at the confluence of the Scioto and Olentangy rivers.

SPOTLIGHT CITY: **CINCINNATI**

Cincinnati is Ohio's third largest city, after Cleveland and Columbus, but it is the second-largest metro area. With 2.1 million people, Greater Cincinnati grew 4.7 percent between 2000 and 2006 and is predicted to pass the Cleveland metropolitan area in population by the end of the decade.

Founded on the Ohio River in 1788 by veterans of the Revolutionary War, the settlement was named after the honorary Society of the Cincinnati, made up of former officers. Cincinnati was a Roman commander who returned from war to resume farming.

By the early 19th century, Cincinnati was considered the first inland city of the United States. It was nicknamed the "City of Seven Hills" for its early landscape. The city is unique for being designed around Fountain Square, which is overlooked by tall buildings, including the 49-story Art Deco Carew Tower, Cincinnati's tallest building.

Area: 78 sq mi

Population (2005): 308,728

Population density: 3,958 per sq mi

Per-capita income: $34,368

The Great American Ballpark, sited by the Ohio River, is a recent addition to the Cincinnati skyline.

SPOTLIGHT CITY: **CLEVELAND**

Cleveland stands on the shores of Lake Erie, at the mouth of the Cuyahoga River in northeastern Ohio. The city is the second largest in Ohio, after the capital, Columbus, but Greater Cleveland is the largest metro area, with 2.25 million people.

Cleveland was founded in 1796. With the building of canals and railroads in the 19th century the city became a national leader in heavy manufacturing. After an industrial decline in the mid-20th century, Cleveland turned to service businesses, finance, and health care.

In 2005, Cleveland was ranked with Pittsburgh as the nation's two most

livable cities. That same year, Cleveland was named the best city in the continental United States for business meetings.

One nickname, "Forest City," may derive from a 19th-century description of Cleveland rising in the wilderness, or from the vision of a 19th-century mayor, who encouraged the wholesale planting of fruit trees.

Area: 77.6 sq mi

Population (2005): 452,208

Population density: 5,827 per sq mi

Per-capita income: $34,264

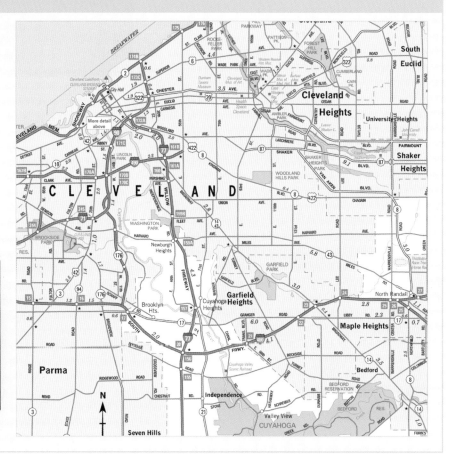

Rapid growth in the 19th century due to its pivotal location on the nation's waterways made Cleveland a prosperous, populous city.

OKLAHOMA

FACTS & FIGURES

OKLAHOMA

Labor Omnia Vincit (Labor conquers all things)

Settled: *1889*

Origin of name: *Choctaw word meaning "red man"*

Capital: *Oklahoma City*

Population (2005): *3,547,884 (ranked 28th in size)*

Population density: *51.7 per sq mi*

ECONOMY

Chief industries: *Manufacturing, mineral and energy exploration and production, agriculture, services*

Chief manufactured goods: *Nonelectrical machinery, transportation equipment, food products, fabricated metal products*

Chief crops: *Wheat, cotton, hay, peanuts, grain sorghum, soybeans, corn, pecans*

Chief ports: *Catoosa, Muskogee*

Gross state product (2005): *$120.5 billion*

Employment (May 2006): *20.9% government; 18.3% trade/transportation/utilities; 9.5% manufacturing; 12% education/health; 11.3% professional/business services; 8.9% leisure/hospitality; 5.4% finance; 4.5% construction; 6.7% other services*

Per-capita income (2005): *$29,330*

STATE FLOWER

Mistletoe

STATE BIRD

Scissor-tailed flycatcher

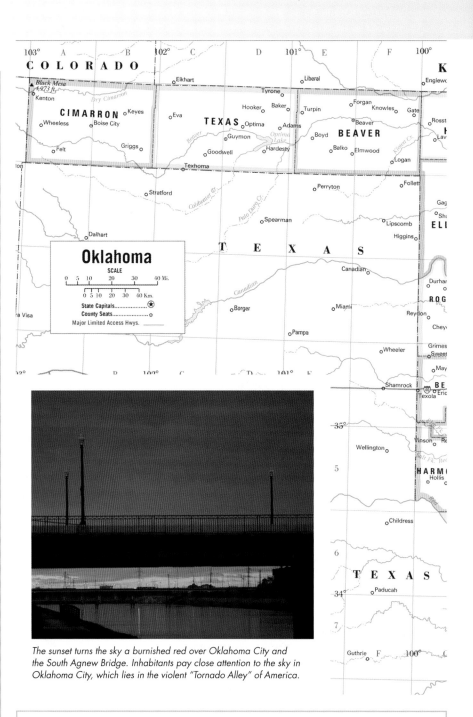

The sunset turns the sky a burnished red over Oklahoma City and the South Agnew Bridge. Inhabitants pay close attention to the sky in Oklahoma City, which lies in the violent "Tornado Alley" of America.

THE SOONER STATE

Oklahoma first won fame when it was opened for homesteaders in 1889. In the subsequent land rush, those who slipped in ahead of schedule were called "Sooners." The state's topography slopes upward from east to west, rising from 400 feet above sea level to nearly 5,000 feet. The southeast is hilly, cut by the Arkansas River Valley, with a number of reservoirs interrupting the river's flow. The climate is temperate, humid in the east and dry in the west, as the southern humid belt merges with colder northern air. Manufacturing and production of oil and natural gas lead the economy. Coal, once the primary mineral, has diminished in importance in favor of oil and gas. Nearly 80 percent of Oklahoma is farmland, with most of the agricultural income from livestock. The main crops are winter wheat, sorghum, and cotton.

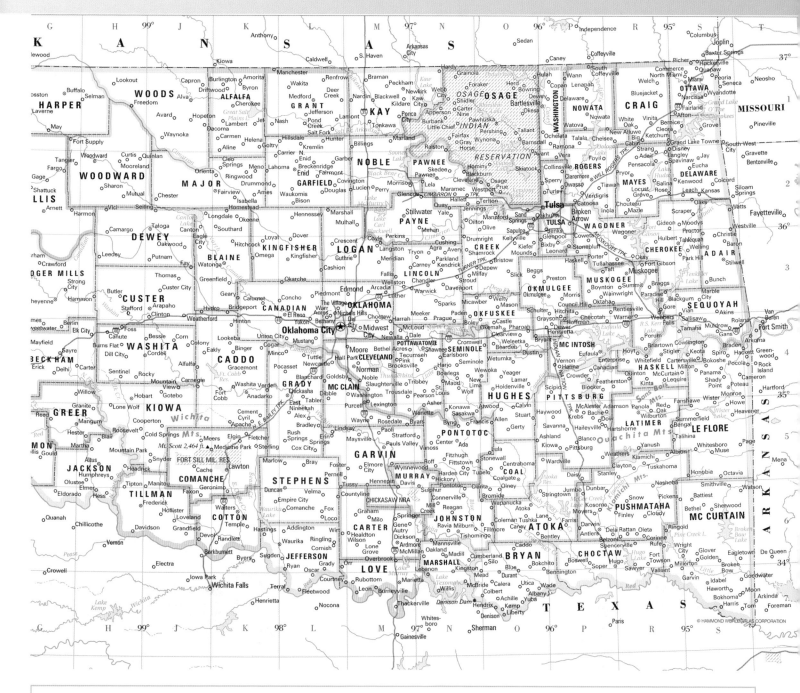

A Brief History

- Few Native Americans inhabited the region when the Spanish explorer Francisco Vázquez de Coronado arrived, 1541; in the 16th and 17th centuries, French traders visited.
- Part of the Louisiana Purchase, 1803, Oklahoma was first called Indian Country, and from 1834 until 1907, Indian Territory.
- It became home to the "Five Civilized Tribes"—Cherokee, Choctaw, Chickasaw, Creek, and Seminole—after the forced removal of Indians from the eastern United States, 1828–46. The land was also used by Comanche, Osage, and other Plains Indians.

- The Indian Appropriation Act of 1899 opened the "Unassigned Lands" of Oklahoma to settlement by land runs.
- Statehood was achieved, 1907.
- In the early 20th century, oil finds brought wealth to the Tulsa area; the Greenwood section of the city, then known as the "Negro Wall Street," was devastated by a white mob, 1921.
- Depression and drought drove many "Okies" from the Dust Bowl to California in the 1930s.
- A truck bomb in Oklahoma City, 1995, destroyed a federal office building, killing 168 people; Timothy McVeigh was executed for the crime, 2001.

As white settlers pressed westward, land was opened for home-steading by "runs" and lottery. The first run was in 1889; the most famous and largest land run, in 1893, was to the Cherokee Outlet, on the Kansas border.

Oklahoma

FACTS & FIGURES

GEOGRAPHY

Total area: *69,898 sq mi (ranked 20th in size)*

Acres forested: *7.7 million*

CLIMATE

Temperate; southern humid belt merging with colder northern continental; humid eastern and dry western zones

STATE TREE

Redbud

AVERAGE TEMPERATURE

CITY	JUN	DEC
Oklahoma City	76.8	39.5
Tulsa	78.0	39.7

FAMOUS OKLAHOMANS

- Troy Aikman (b. 1966), football player
- Gene Autry (1907–98), singer
- Johnny Bench (b. 1947), baseball player
- Walter Cronkite (b. 1916), newsman
- John Hope Franklin (b. 1915), historian
- Geronimo (1829–1909), Apache leader
- Woody Guthrie (1912–67), singer
- Jeane Kirkpatrick (1926–2006), ambassador to the UN
- Mickey Mantle (1931–95), baseball player
- Will Rogers (1879–1935), actor
- Sam Snead (1912–2002), golfer
- Maria Tallchief (b. 1925), ballerina
- Jim Thorpe (1888–1953), Olympic athlete

Jim Thorpe

ATTRACTIONS

Cherokee Heritage Center, *Tahlequah*

Oklahoma City National Memorial

National Cowboy Hall of Fame and Remington Park Race Track, *Oklahoma City*

Fort Gibson Stockade, *near Muskogee*

Ouachita National Forest

Wichita Mts. Wildlife Refuge, *Lawton*

Woolaroc Museum and Wildlife Preserve, *Bartlesville*

Sequoyah's Home Site, *near Sallisaw*

Philbrook Museum of Art and Gilcrease Museum, *Tulsa*

TOPOGRAPHY

- High plains predominate in the west, hills and small mountains in the east
- East central region is dominated by the Arkansas River basin, and the south by the Red River plains

Highest elevation: Black Mesa, 4,973 ft

Lowest elevation: Little River, 289 ft

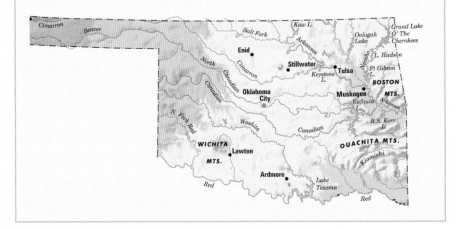

Glittering selenite crystals give the Glass Mountains, a series of low mesas in north central Oklahoma, south of the Cimarron River, their striking appearance.

CAPITAL CITY: **OKLAHOMA CITY**

Oklahoma's capital and most populous city, Oklahoma City was founded by the 1889 land run that opened the state to white settlement. A tent city of 10,000 land-seekers appeared on the first day.

Stockyards were the major industry until the discovery of oil brought new prosperity in the early 20th century. After World War II the city became a crossroads in the interstate highway system. The development of Tinker Air Force Base was also an economic boost. Oklahoma City earned unwanted prominence in 1995 with the bombing of a federal office building that cost many lives.

The city's institutes of higher learning include Oklahoma City University and the University of Oklahoma. A notable attraction is the Myriad Botanical Gardens, an urban park, with its Crystal Bridge designed by I.M. Pei. Other features are the National Cowboy and Western Heritage Museum and the Kirkpatrick Air and Space Museum.

Area: 607 sq mi

Population (2005): 531,324

Population density: 875 per sq mi

Per-capita income: $30,449

Founded in 1889 during the first of five Oklahoma land runs, Oklahoma City has been the state capital since 1910.

SPOTLIGHT CITY: **TULSA**

Tulsa was settled in 1836 by the Creek nation, one of the "Five Civilized Tribes," which had been forced by the federal government off its lands in the South. Oklahoma was designated Indian Territory until late in the century, when it was opened to white settlers. The city was established in 1882.

Located in northeast Oklahoma, Tulsa has a metro population of almost 900,000. Tulsa, on the Arkansas River, has the farthest inland river port in the country. The economy of Tulsa and the surrounding region, once a major center of the oil industry, has lately come to depend more on aviation and high-tech industry.

The city is Oklahoma's cultural center, with two world-class art museums and full-time opera and ballet companies. Tulsa has a number of early 20th-century Art Deco buildings. Formerly the "Oil Capital of the World," Tulsa now claims to be "America's Most Beautiful City."

Area: 182.6 sq mi

Population (2005): 382,457

Population density: 2,095 per sq mi

Per-capita income: $32,150

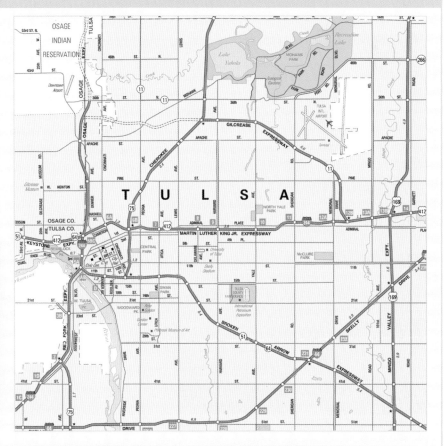

The 76-foot-tall "Golden Driller" overlooks the entrance to the Tulsa Expo Center, in tribute to the economic asset of the state's oil fields.

OREGON

FACTS & FIGURES

She flies with her own wings

Settled: *1810*

Origin of name: *Possibly from the French name for the Wisconsin River, "Ouaricon-sint"*

Capital: *Salem*

Population (2005): *3,641,056 (ranked 27th in size)*

Population density: *37.9 per sq mi*

ECONOMY

Chief industries: *Manufacturing, services, trade, finance, insurance, real estate, government, construction*

Chief manufactured goods: *Electronics and semiconductors, lumber and wood products, metals, transportation equipment, processed food, paper*

Chief crops: *Greenhouse, hay, wheat, grass seed, potatoes, onions, Christmas trees, pears, mint*

Commercial fishing (2004): *$101.1 million*

Chief ports: *Portland, Astoria, Coos Bay*

Gross state product (2005): *$145.4 billion*

Employment (May 2006): *17.2% government; 19.5% trade/transportation/utilities; 12.2% manufacturing; 12.2% education/health; 11.2% professional/business services; 9.7% leisure/hospitals; 6.2% finance; 5.8% construction; 5.5% other services*

Per-capita income (2005): *$32,103*

STATE FLOWER	STATE BIRD

Oregon grape	Western meadowlark

THE BEAVER STATE

Sixteenth-century adventurers and traders penetrated the Oregon wilderness for the valuable beaver pelts that earned the state its nickname. The forests and mountains and long Pacific seacoast attracted permanent white settlers in the 1830s. At least 30 million acres of forest still covers half the state. The Cascade Range, with 10,000-foot peaks, runs north to south, dividing the coast from the inland plateau, which extends east to the Idaho border. Most of the population lives in the Willamette Valley between the Cascades and the Pacific Coast Range. Heavy rains fall along the coast, especially in winter, but the Cascades block the arid eastern regions, which receive about 12 inches of precipitation annually. Agriculture and lumbering are economic leaders; Oregon produces one-sixth of the nation's Douglas fir lumber. Nickel mining is also important, while manufacturing—including wood products, electronics, and computer components—is the main industry. Tourism is growing in importance to Oregon's economy.

A Brief History

- More than 100 Native American tribes inhabited the area at the time of European contact, including the Chinook, Yakima, Cayuse, Modoc, and Nez Perce.
- Captain Robert Gray sighted and sailed into the Columbia River, 1792.
- Lewis and Clark, traveling overland, wintered at the mouth of the Columbia River, 1805–06.
- Fur traders sent by John Jacob Astor established the Astoria trading post in the Columbia River region, 1811.
- Settlers arrived in the Williamette Valley, 1834.
- In 1843, the first large wave of settlers arrived via the Oregon Trail.
- Oregon became a territory, 1848, and a state, 1859.
- Early in the 20th century, the "Oregon System"—political reforms including initiative, referendum, recall, direct primary, and women's suffrage—was adopted.
- Originally dominated by forest products, the economy diversified after World War II, with high-tech firms clustering in the "Silicon Forest" area around Portland.

Thousands of Oregon settlers traveled over 2,000 miles by wagon in the mid-19th century.

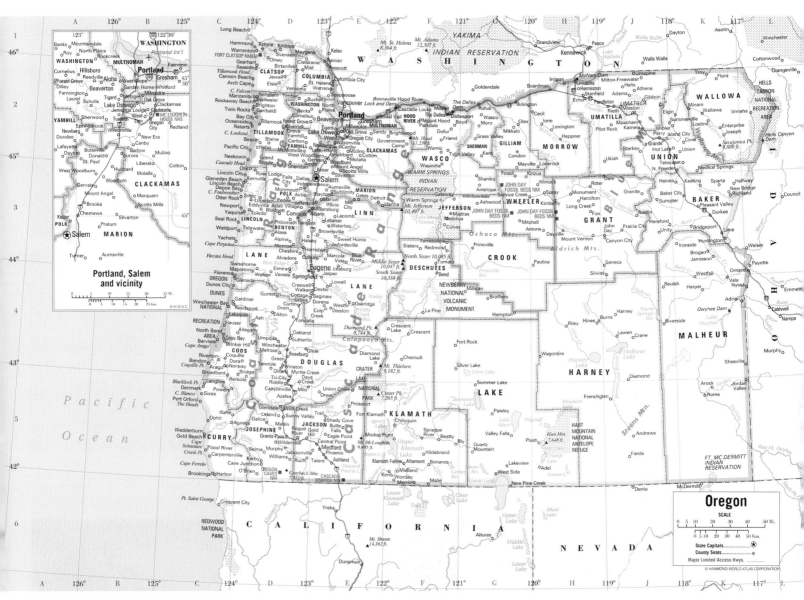

Portland, Salem and vicinity

Cannon Beach is one of many beautiful beaches studding over 350 miles of Oregon's coast. Known for its forested landscape, Oregon draws tourists throughout the year.

Oregon

FACTS & FIGURES

GEOGRAPHY

Total area: 98,381 sq mi
(ranked 9th in size)

Acres forested: 29.7 million

CLIMATE

Coastal mild and humid
climate; continental dryness
and extreme temperatures in
the interior

STATE TREE

Douglas fir

AVERAGE TEMPERATURE

CITY	JUN	DEC
Eugene	60.2	39.5
Portland	62.7	40.2
Salem	61.2	40.2

FAMOUS OREGONIANS

- Ernest Bloch (1880–
  1959), composer
- Chief Joseph
  (1840–1904),
  Nez Perce leader
- Ken Kesey (1935–2001),
  writer
- Ursula K. Le Guin
  (b. 1929), writer
- Linus Pauling
  (1901–94), scientist
- Steve Prefontaine
  (1951–75), runner
- John Reed (1887–1920),
  journalist
- Alberto Salazar
  (b. 1958), runner
- Mary Decker Slaney
  (b. 1958), runner
- William Simon U'Ren
  (1859–1949), lawyer
  and reformer

Ken Kesey

ATTRACTIONS

John Day Fossil Beds National Monument,
near Kimberly

Columbia River Gorge

Timberline Lodge, Mt. Hood National Forest

Crater Lake National Park

Oregon Dunes National Recreation Area

Fort Clatsop National Memorial, *near Astoria*

Oregon Caves National Monument, *Cave Junction*

Oregon Museum of Science and Industry, *Portland*

Shakespearean Festival, *Ashland*

High Desert Museum, *Bend*

TOPOGRAPHY

- Coast Ranges of rugged mountains
- Fertile Willamette River Valley to
  east and south
- Cascade Mountain Range of
  volcanic peaks east of the valley
- Plateau east of Cascades,
  remaining two-thirds of state

Highest elevation:
Mt. Hood, 11,239 ft

Lowest elevation:
sea level

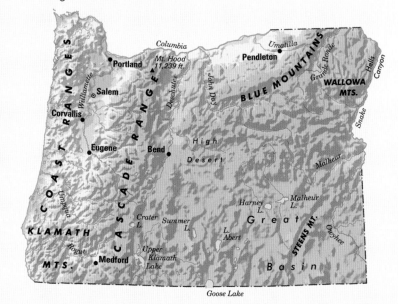

CAPITAL CITY: **SALEM**

In tribute to the pioneers who trekked thousands of miles to settle Oregon in the 19th century, the state
capitol is topped with the 8-ton, gold-plated Oregon Pioneer statue.

SPOTLIGHT CITY: **PORTLAND**

Portland, Oregon's largest city, stands at the confluence of the Columbia and Willamette rivers. Portland is known as the "City of Roses" because of its many rose gardens, which thrive in the mild and humid climate. The city is also known for its large number of microbreweries.

When Portland was established in 1843, a co-founder from Portland, Maine, won a coin toss and the right to name the city. Portland was chartered in 1851.

A busy seaport, Portland was once notorious as a city where men risked being abducted and forced to work on ships headed to China. The underground network of "Shanghai Tunnels" used to transfer the captives is now a popular tourist attraction.

Portland is famed for its cultural and educational institutions as well as for its environmentalism. The city has beautiful vistas and an extensive park system: Forest Park, with 5,000 acres, is one of the largest "wilderness parks" within a city's limits.

Area: 134.3 sq mi

Population (2005): 533,427

Population density: 3,972 per sq mi

Per-capita income: $33,875

Portland, Oregon's most populous city, sits below Mount Hood.

Famous for the clarity of its crystal blue waters, Crater Lake is the deepest lake in the United States. Occupying a bowl-shaped caldera, it is the highlight of Crater Lake National Park.

PENNSYLVANIA

Virtue, liberty, and independence

Settled: *1682*

Origin of name: *Named after William Penn*

Capital: *Harrisburg*

Population (2005): *12,429,616* (ranked 6th in size)

Population density: *277.3 per sq mi*

ECONOMY

Chief industries: *Agribusiness, manufacturing, health care, travel and tourism, depository institutions, biotechnology, printing and publishing, research and consulting, trucking and warehousing, transportation by air, engineering and management, legal services*

Chief manufactured goods: *Fabricated metal products, industrial machinery and equipment, transportation equipment, rubber and plastics, chemicals and pharmaceuticals, electronic equipment, lumber and wood products, stone, clay, and glass products*

Chief crops: *Corn, hay, mushrooms, apples, potatoes, winter wheat, oats, vegetables, tobacco, grapes, peaches*

Commercial fishing (2004): *$65,000*

Chief ports: *Philadelphia, Pittsburgh, Erie*

Gross state product (2005): *$487.2 billion*

Employment (May 2006): *13.2% government; 19.5% trade/transportation/utilities; 11.6% manufacturing; 18.2% education/health; 11.6% professional/business services; 8.7% leisure/hospitality; 5.8% finance; 4.5% construction; 6.4% other services*

Per-capita income (2005): *$34,897*

STATE FLOWER   STATE BIRD

Mountain laurel   Ruffed grouse

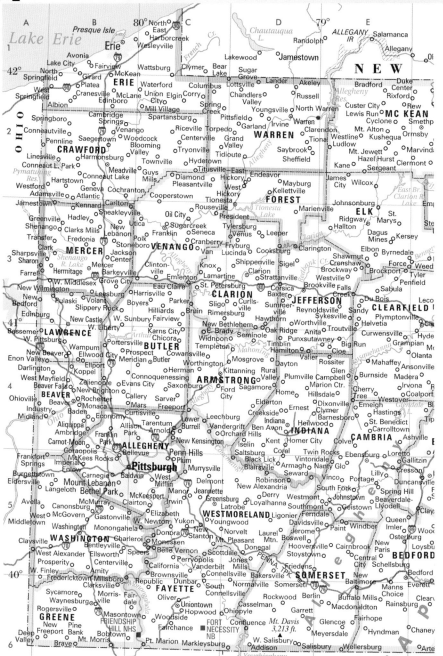

THE KEYSTONE STATE

Pennsylvania earned its nickname for its central, or "keystone," political and economic importance in the early 1800s. The Appalachian Mountains cut a diagonal swath across the state, from the southwest to the northeast, while the Piedmont Plateau is a fertile corner of farmland in the southeast. The Delaware River forms the state's eastern border. The climate varies from the hot summers of the lowlands of the Delaware to the snowy winters and cooler summers in the west. Philadelphia in the southeast and Pittsburgh in the southwest are major manufacturing centers. The state has long ranked in the top 10 for manufacturing products from steel to pharmaceuticals, but its chief industry is agribusiness. Coal mining is also important. Since the mid-1700s, Pennsylvania has been known as a leader in coal production.

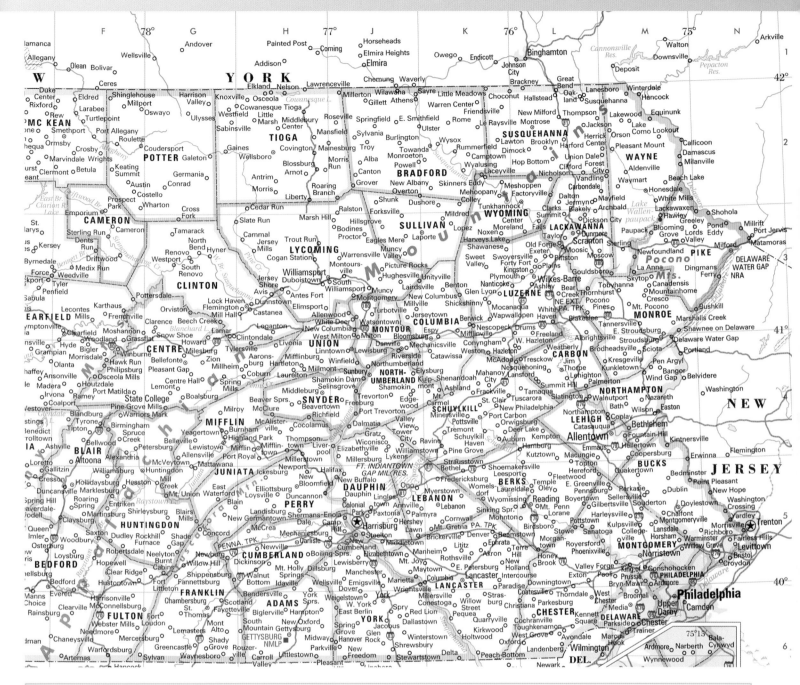

William Penn was renowned for his fair dealings and equitable treaties with Native Americans.

Pennsylvania

FACTS & FIGURES

GEOGRAPHY

Total area: 46,055 sq mi (ranked 33rd in size)

Acres forested: 16.9 million

CLIMATE

Continental with wide fluctuations in seasonal temperatures

STATE TREE

Eastern hemlock

AVERAGE TEMPERATURE

CITY	JUN	DEC
Allentown	68.5	32.0
Harrisburg	70.7	34.8
Philadelphia	72.3	37.4
Pittsburgh	68.4	32.5

FAMOUS PENNSYLVANIANS

- Marian Anderson (1897–1993), opera singer
- James Buchanan (1791–1868), 15th U.S. president
- Bill Cosby (b. 1937), comedian
- Thomas Eakins (1844–1916), painter
- Robert Fulton (1765–1815), inventor
- Martha Graham (1894–1991), dancer and choreographer
- George C. Marshall (1880–1959), U.S. Army general
- Margaret Mead (1901–78), cultural anthropologist
- Andrew W. Mellon (1855–1937), banker
- John Updike (b. 1932), writer

Bill Cosby

ATTRACTIONS

Independence Hall; Franklin Institute Science Museum; Philadelphia Museum of Art, *Philadelphia*

Valley Forge National Historic Park

Gettysburg National Military Park

Pennsylvania Dutch Country

Hershey

Duquesne Incline; Carnegie Institute; Heinz Hall, *Pittsburgh*

Pocono Mts

Allegheny National Forest

Presque Isle State Park

Fallingwater, *Mill Run*

TOPOGRAPHY

- Allegheny Mts. run southwest to northeast, with Piedmont and coast plain in the southeast triangle
- Allegheny Front a diagonal spine across the state's center
- North and west rugged plateau falls to Lake Erie lowland

Highest elevation: Mt. Davis, 3,213 ft

Lowest elevation: Delaware River, sea level

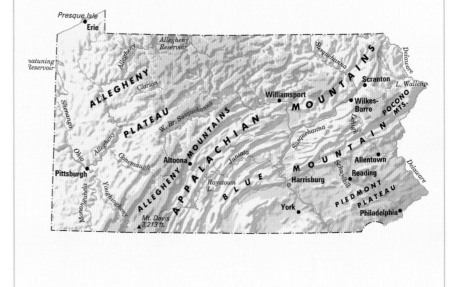

CAPITAL CITY: **HARRISBURG**

Named state capital in 1812, Harrisburg is crowned by its magnificent capitol building, constructed in 1906.

The site of the crucial Civil War Battle of Gettysburg, fought from July 1 to July 3, 1863, is now devoted to memorials.

The construction of Kinzua Dam in 1965 for flood control created the Allegheny Reservoir, displacing the last of the Seneca Indians.

Pennsylvania is known for its acres of rolling farmland, although in recent years, with the high demand for land and high cost of farming, as farms are being sold, rural counties are becoming more suburban.

SPOTLIGHT CITY: **PHILADELPHIA**

"The City of Brotherly Love" is the most populous city in Pennsylvania and the fifth largest in the nation. Founded by Quakers in 1682, Philadelphia was the British Empire's second-largest colonial city in the 18th century.

Philadelphia is steeped in history of the Revolutionary era, when the city was the seat of government for the Continental Congress. Its many historical sites include the Liberty Bell and Independence Hall, where the Declaration of Independence was signed in 1776.

The city was a leading corporate and manufacturing center through the 20th century, though a shortage of good housing brought about "white flight," as the middle class moved out. By the end of the century, however, Philadelphia was recovering, with city-center redevelopment, new investment, increased tourism, and the arrival of new service-based businesses.

Area: 135.1 sq mi

Population (2004): 1,470,151

Population density: 10,882 per sq mi

Per-capita income: $37,059

Known as the City of Brotherly Love, Philadelphia is the largest city in Pennsylvania and once served as the nation's capital.

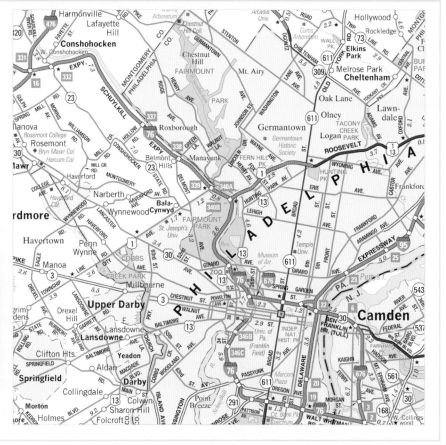

RHODE ISLAND

Hope

Settled: *1636*

Origin of name: *Perhaps named Roode Eylandt for its red clay by Dutch explorer Adriaen Block*

Capital: *Providence*

Population (2005): *1,076,189 (ranked 43rd in size)*

Population density: *1,029.9 per sq mi*

ECONOMY

Chief industries: *Services, manufacturing*

Chief manufactured goods: *Costume jewelry, toys, machinery, textiles, electronics*

Chief crops: *Nursery products, turf and vegetable production*

Chief ports: *Providence, Quonset Point, Newport*

Commercial fishing (2004): *$71.1 million*

Gross state product (2005): *$43.8 billion*

Employment (May 2006): *13.3% government; 16% trade/transportation/utilities; 10.7% manufacturing; 19.6% education/health; 11.5% professional/business services; 10.3% leisure/hospitality; 7.2% finance; 4.7% construction; 6.6% other services*

Per-capita income (2005): *$36,153*

STATE FLOWER	STATE BIRD

Violet	Rhode Island Red chicken

THE OCEAN STATE

The smallest state, Rhode Island has been called "Little Rhody," but its official nickname is the "Ocean State" for its beaches and long coastline along Narragansett Bay. The bay reaches inland as far as Providence and is sprinkled with 30 islands. Two of Rhode Island's earliest settlements, Portsmouth and Newport, were made on Aquidneck Island, where colonists came seeking religious freedom. Off the southern coast, where Rhode Island Sound meets the Atlantic Ocean, is Block Island, named for Dutch explorer Adriaen Block. The state was a pioneer in the American Industrial Revolution of the late 18th and early 19th century, harnessing waterpower to operate cotton mills and factories. The economic boom brought waves of immigrant workers. A leading 19th-century textile producer, Rhode Island suffered economically in the 20th century with the decline in industry. In the 21st century the major industries have become health care, tourism, and education.

A Brief History

- When Europeans first arrived, Narragansett, Niantic, Nipmuc, and Wampanoag peoples lived in the region.
- Giovanni da Verrazano visited the area, 1524.
- The first permanent settlement was founded at Providence, 1636, by Roger Williams, who was exiled from the Massachusetts Bay Colony; Anne Hutchinson, also exiled, settled Portsmouth, 1638.
- Quaker and Jewish immigrants seeking freedom of worship began arriving, 1650s–60s.
- The colonists broke the power of the Narragansett in the Great Swamp Fight, 1675, the decisive battle in King Philip's War.
- The colony was the first to formally renounce all allegiance to King George III, May 4, 1776.
- Initially opposed to joining the Union, Rhode Island was the last of the 13 colonies to ratify the Constitution, 1790.
- Trade, textiles, and metal goods dominated the 19th-century economy; Newport became a fashionable resort after the Civil War.
- Immigration, from Ireland, Portugal, Italy, French Canada, and recently Latin America, has given Rhode Island the highest proportion of Catholics of any state, 64 percent in 2006.

Roger Williams, Rhode Island Colony's co-founder, insisted on fair dealings with Native Americans and on freedom of religious worship.

Rhode Island

FACTS & FIGURES

GEOGRAPHY

Total area:
1,545 sq mi
(ranked 50th in size)

Acres forested:
0.4 million

CLIMATE

Changeable; humid
summers, cold winters

STATE TREE

Red maple

AVERAGE TEMPERATURE		
CITY	JUN	DEC
Providence	67.6	33.8

FAMOUS RHODE ISLANDERS

- Ambrose Burnside (1824–81), Civil War Union Army general
- George M. Cohan (1878–1942), composer
- Bill Conti (b. 1942), composer
- Nathanael Greene (1742–86), Revolutionary War general
- Matthew C. and Oliver Hazard Perry (1794–1858, 1785–1819), naval commanders
- Gilbert Stuart (1755–1828), painter

Gilbert Stuart

- Meredith Vieira (b. 1953), newscaster
- James Woods (b. 1947), actor

ATTRACTIONS

Newport mansions

Yacht races, including Newport to Bermuda

Block Island

Touro Synagogue, oldest in the United States, *Newport*

First Baptist Church in America, *Providence*

Slater Mill Historic Site, *Pawtucket*

Gilbert Stuart birthplace, *Saunderstown*

Watch Hill, *Westerly*

TOPOGRAPHY

- Eastern lowlands of Narragansett Basin
- Western uplands of flat and rolling hills

Highest elevation:
Jerimoth Hill, 812 ft

Lowest elevation:
sea level

New England's largest suspension bridge, the Claiborne Pell Newport Bridge spans 1,601 feet between Rhode (also still called by its original name, Aquidneck) and Conanicut islands.

Block Island, south of mainland Rhode Island, regularly hosts sailing races around its perimeter.

CAPITAL CITY: **PROVIDENCE**

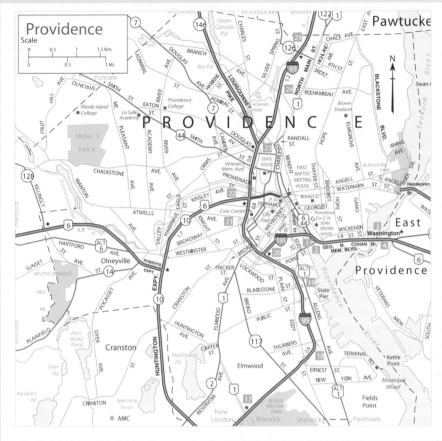

Providence is the capital of Rhode Island and the second-largest city in New England after Boston. Founded in 1636 by religious exiles from Massachusetts Bay Colony, Providence has been called both the "Divine City" and the "Beehive of Industry." Its tradition of religious freedom was a cornerstone for growth as persecuted groups settled in Rhode Island over the years. By the 1800s, Providence was a leader in the production of silverware, jewelry, and textiles.

The Great Depression of the 1930s brought about an economic decline that was worsened by the devastating New England Hurricane of 1938.

In the 1970s, the investment of more than $600 million in development funds began a downtown renaissance. New housing, malls, parks, and renewed access to the water helped stimulate construction of condominiums, hotels, and offices and revitalized the city.

Area: 20.5 sq mi

Population (2005): 176,862

Population density: 9,401 per sq mi

Per-capita income (2005): $20,333

One of the nation's oldest cities, Providence was founded by Roger Williams in 1636 after his exile from Massachusetts Bay Colony.

One of the "summer cottages" of Newport's Gilded Age, the Isaac Bell House is an excellent example of the rustic Shingle Style houses that became popular in the Northeast in the late 19th century.

During the late 19th century, Newport became a fashionable retreat for America's elite, who built enormous "cottages" on the shore.

Despite being the smallest state in the nation, Rhode Island has 400 miles of shoreline. Newport and other coastal towns are popular among the nautically inclined.

SOUTH CAROLINA

Dum Spiro Spero (While I breathe, I hope)

Settled: *1623*

Origin of name: *From Carolus, Latin name for Charles, after King Charles I*

Capital: *Columbia*

Population (2005): *4,255,083 (ranked 25th in size)*

Population density: *141.3 per sq mi*

ECONOMY

Chief industries: *Tourism, agriculture, manufacturing*

Chief manufactured goods: *Textiles, chemicals and allied products, machinery and fabricated metal products, apparel and related products*

Chief crops: *Tobacco, cotton, soybeans, corn, wheat, peaches, tomatoes*

Chief ports: *Charleston, Georgetown, Port Royal*

Commercial fishing (2004): *$18.5 million*

Gross state product (2005): *$139.8 billion*

Employment (May 2006): *17.7% government; 19.3% trade/transportation/utilities; 13.5% manufacturing; 10% education/health; 10.9% professional/business services; 11.% leisure/hospitality; 5.3% finance; 6.5% construction; 6.6% other services*

Per-capita income (2005): *$28,352*

STATE FLOWER   STATE BIRD

Yellow jessamine   Carolina wren

THE PALMETTO STATE

This southeastern state takes its nickname from the palmetto trees that grow along its 190-mile shoreline, on the Atlantic Coastal Plain. The coast has many salt marshes and estuaries, as well as the unusual "Carolina bays," oval-shaped inlets that might have been formed by a prehistoric meteor strike. South Carolina is part of the East's Intercoastal Waterway for shipping. The Sea Islands barrier reef shelters the coast from the ocean. Inland, the Piedmont Plateau of low hills, which have been widely reforested, rises to meet the Blue Ridge Mountains in the northwest. The Savannah River forms the state's southern border. South Carolina's climate is warm and humid, with 46 inches of precipitation annually. Tourism is steadily increasing, while industrial products such as textiles, chemicals, and machinery, and agricultural products such as tobacco, poultry, and cattle remain important to the economy.

A Brief History

- When 16th-century Spanish and French explorers first arrived, Cherokee, Catawba, and Muskogean peoples lived in the area.
- The first English colonists settled near the Ashley River, 1670, and moved to the site of Charleston, 1680.
- The colonists seized the government, 1775, and the royal governor fled.
- The British took Charleston, 1780, but were defeated at Kings Mountain that same year, and at Cowpens, 1781.
- Slaves, whose labor the economy relied on, made up 57 percent of the population in 1860, when South Carolina seceded from the Union.
- Confederate troops fired on U.S. troops at Fort Sumter, in Charleston Harbor, 1861, launching the Civil War.
- South Carolina was readmitted to the Union, 1868.
- Formerly dependent on textiles, the state has attracted new industries by courting foreign investment.
- Strom Thurmond served 48 years in the Senate (1955–2003), till age 100.

At Fort Moultrie National Monument tourists can visit all periods of the fort's history, from its defensive action in the Revolution to its role in starting the Civil War to its last active days in World War II.

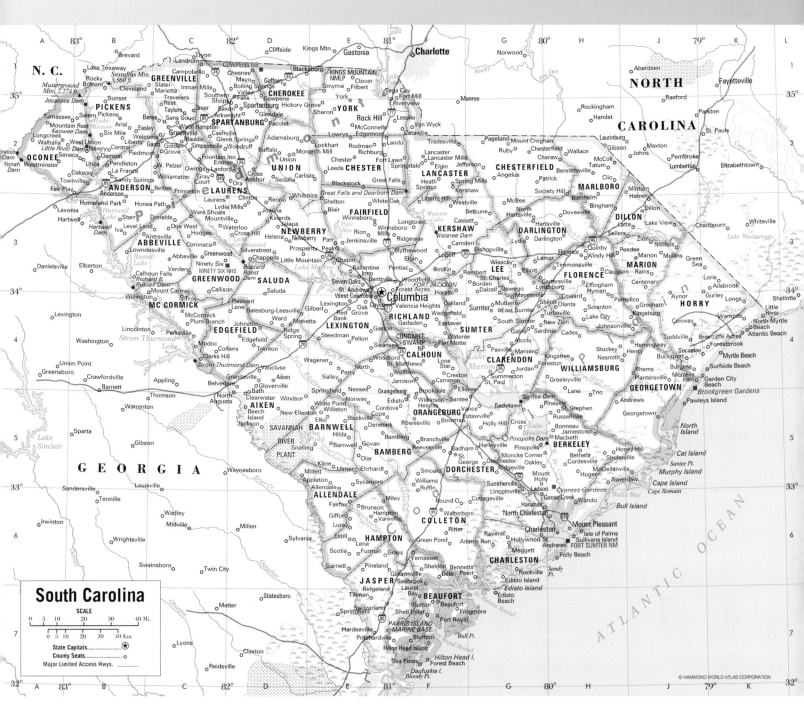

South Carolina

SCALE

| 0 | 5 | 10 | 20 | 30 | 40 Mi. |

| 0 | 5 | 10 | 20 | 30 | 40 Km. |

State Capitals.....................★

County Seats.....................◎

Major Limited Access Hwys._____

© HAMMOND WORLD ATLAS CORPORATION

The Isle of Palms, one of many barrier islands between the Atlantic Ocean and the mainland, has beautiful beaches but bears the brunt of dangerous hurricanes.

South Carolina

FACTS & FIGURES

GEOGRAPHY

Total area:
32,020 sq mi
(ranked 40th in size)

Acres forested:
12.5 million

CLIMATE:

Humid subtropical

STATE TREE

Cabbage palmetto

AVERAGE TEMPERATURE

CITY	JUN	DEC
Charleston	78.2	50.5
Columbia	78.5	47.0
Greenville/Spartanburg	74.7	43.5

FAMOUS PEOPLE

- Charles Bolden
  (b. 1946), astronaut
- John C. Calhoun
  (1782–1850),
  7th U.S. vice president
- Joe Fraizer (b. 1944),
  boxing champion
- Jesse Jackson (b. 1941),
  politician and Civil
  Rights activist
- "Shoeless" Joe Jackson
  (1888–1951),
  baseball player
- James Longstreet
  (1821–1904),
  Confederate general
- Ronald McNair
  (b. 1950), astronaut

"Shoeless" Joe Jackson

- John Rutledge
  (1739–1800), U.S.
  Supreme Court justice
- Thomas Sumter
  (1734–1832),
  Revolutionary War
  lieutenant colonel
- Strom Thurmond
  (1902–2003),
  U.S. senator

ATTRACTIONS

Charleston

Fort Sumter National Monument,
Charleston Harbor

Magnolia Plantation; Cypress Gardens; Middleton
Place; Drayton Hall, *near Charleston*

Myrtle Beach

Hilton Head Island

Andrew Jackson State Park and Museum,
Lancaster

South Carolina State Museum; Riverbanks Zoo,
Columbia

TOPOGRAPHY

- Blue Ridge region in northwest has highest peaks
- Piedmont lies between the mountains and the fall line
- Coastal plain covers two-thirds of the state

Highest elevation:
Sassafras Mt., 3,560 ft

Lowest elevation:
sea level

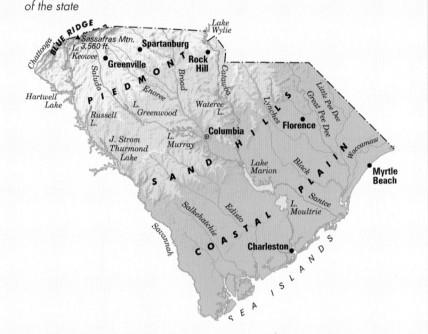

CAPITAL CITY: **COLUMBIA**

Located in the geographic center of the state, Columbia was chosen to be the capital in 1786.

In the 1670s, English colonists established Charles Towne, named after King Charles II. A century later, this port city was one of the largest towns in the new United States.

Today, Charleston is the state's second most populous city after Columbia, the capital. The metro region has 603,000 people, also second to the capital metro area. Warm weather and traditional Southern hospitality have helped make Charleston a major tourist destination. Experts in etiquette have named it the nation's "best-mannered city."

Pastel-colored houses and trees hung with Spanish moss contribute to the city's elegant appearance. Its elegance and graciousness are matched, however, by a robust commercial scene—for example, Charleston has the second largest container port on the East Coast. Biotechnology and medical research are important businesses in the central downtown, and the Medical University of South Carolina is one of the city's leading employers.

Area: 178.1 sq mi

Population (2005): 118,270

Population density: 996.5 per sq mi

Per-capita income: $30,339

Beautiful antebellum homes adorn Charleston's tree-lined avenues.

Located on Johns Island just southwest of Charleston, the Angel Oak is a Southern live oak, estimated to be about 1,400 years old.

The snowy egret, a type of heron, lives year-round along the coast of South Carolina, while northern birds migrate inland in winter.

SOUTH DAKOTA

FACTS & FIGURES

Under God, the people rule

Settled: *1856*

Origin of name: *Sioux for "friend" or "ally"*

Capital: *Pierre*

Population (2005): *775,933*
(ranked 46th in size)

Population density: *10.2 per sq mi*

ECONOMY

Chief industries: *Agriculture, services, manufacturing*

Chief manufactured goods: *Food and kindred products, machinery, electric and electronic equipment*

Chief crops: *Corn, soybeans, oats, wheat, sunflowers, sorghum*

Gross state product (2005): *$31.1 billion*

Employment (May 2006): *9.2% government; 20% trade/transportation/utilities; 10.3% manufacturing; 14.6% education/health; 6.3% professional/business services; 10.9% leisure/hospitality; 7.2% finance; 5.6% construction; 5.7% other services*

Per-capita income (2005): *$31,614*

STATE FLOWER	STATE BIRD

Pasqueflower	Ring-necked pheasant

THE COYOTE STATE

South Dakota, which lies in the middle of the Great Plains, is one of the Grain States, producing corn, soybeans, oats, and wheat. Central and northern South Dakota have the most productive croplands, but 90 percent of the state is devoted to agriculture. Its eastern region, known as the Prairie Plains, produces livestock, mainly cattle and hogs. In the hilly west, mining is the main industry. The largest single source of gold in the United States is South Dakota's Homestake Mine. The Black Hills, the highest mountains east of the Rockies, rise out of the plains in the west. It was there that in 1925 a sculptor and historian chose Mount Rushmore for what was to be a massive monument to the first 150 years of United States history. The 60-foot-high likenesses of George Washington, Thomas Jefferson, Abraham Lincoln, and Theodore Roosevelt—carved out of the granite mountainside—attract 2 million visitors a year.

A Brief History

- Paleoindians hunted in the region at least 11,500 years ago.
- At the time of first European contact, Mandan, Hidatsa, Arikara, and Sioux lived in the area.
- The French Vérendrye brothers explored the region, 1742–43.
- The United States acquired the area in the Louisiana Purchase, 1803; the Lewis and Clark expedition passed through, 1804–06.
- In 1817 a trading post was opened at Fort Pierre, which later became the site of the first European settlement in South Dakota.
- Dakota Territory was established by Congress, 1861.
- Gold was discovered, 1874, in the Black Hills on Sioux land; the "Great Dakota Boom" began in 1879.
- Conflicts with the Sioux led to the Great Sioux Agreement, 1889, which established reservations and opened up more land for white settlement.
- South Dakota became a state, 1889.
- The massacre of Native American families at Wounded Knee, 1890, ended Sioux resistance.
- Major economic activities include agribusiness and, since the 1980s, credit card services.

Bison herds were decimated by hunting in the 19th century as settlers poured into the West.

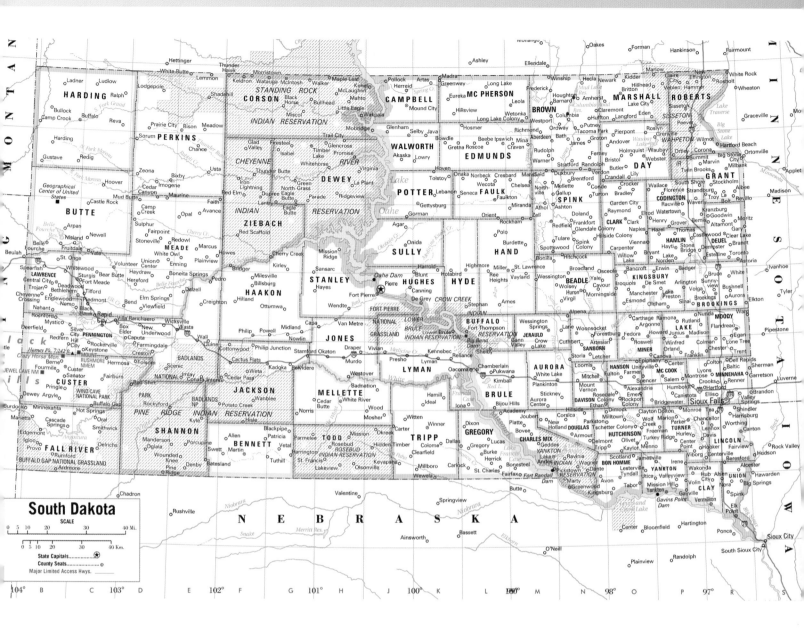

Although admitted to the Union in 1889, South Dakota has remained largely rural, with one of the lowest population densities in the nation and acres of untouched landscape.

South Dakota

FACTS & FIGURES

GEOGRAPHY

Total area: *77,116 sq mi* (ranked 17th in size)

Acres forested: *1.6 million*

CLIMATE:

Characterized by extremes of temperature, persistent winds, low precipitation and humidity

STATE TREE

Black Hills spruce

AVERAGE TEMPERATURE

CITY	JUN	DEC
Rapid City	64.6	24.7
Sioux Falls	67.5	18.3

FAMOUS SOUTH DAKOTANS

- Sparky Anderson (b. 1934), baseball player
- Black Elk (1863–1950), medicine man of the Lakota
- Tom Brokaw (b. 1940), television journalist
- Crazy Horse (1840–77), Lakota war leader
- Myron Floren (1919–2005), accordionist
- Ernest O. Lawrence (1901–58), physicist
- George McGovern (b. 1922), U.S. senator
- Billy Mills (b. 1938), runner
- Allen Neuharth (b. 1924), founder of *U.S.A. Today*
- Sitting Bull (1831–1890), Lakota chief

Sitting Bull

ATTRACTIONS

Mt. Rushmore National Memorial; Crazy Horse Memorial, *Black Hills*

Needles Highway; Custer State Park, *Custer*

Deadwood, 1876 Gold Rush town

Jewel Cave National Monument; Wind Cave National Park; Badlands National Park, *near Rapid City*

Great Lakes of South Dakota

Fort Sisseton, *near Lake City*

Great Plains Zoo and Delbridge Museum, *Sioux Falls*

Corn Palace, *Mitchell*

TOPOGRAPHY

- *Prairie plains in the east*
- *Rolling hills of the Great Plains in the west*
- *The Black Hills, rising 3,500 ft, in the southwest corner*

Highest elevation:
Harney Peak, 7,242 ft

Lowest elevation:
Big Stone Lake, 966 ft

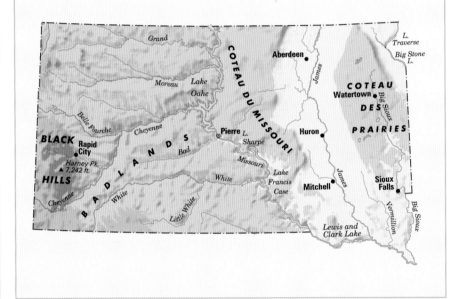

CAPITAL CITY: PIERRE

State capital since 1889, Pierre is located on the banks of the Missouri River in Hughes County.

Mount Rushmore National Memorial, with the carved faces of presidents Washington, Jefferson, Theodore Roosevelt, and Lincoln, stands 5,725 feet high.

The badlands of South Dakota lie between the Black Hills to the west and the Great Plains to the north and east. Some flat-topped buttes rise to 600 feet high.

TENNESSEE

FACTS & FIGURES

Agriculture and commerce

Settled: *1757*

Origin of name: *From Tanasi, Cherokee villages on the Little Tennessee River*

Capital: *Nashville*

Population (2005): *5,962,959 (ranked 16th in size)*

Population density: *144.7 per sq mi*

ECONOMY

Chief industries: *Manufacturing, trade, services, tourism, finance, insurance, real estate*

Chief manufactured goods: *Chemicals, food, transportation equipment, industrial machinery and equipment, fabricated metal products, rubber/plastic products, paper and allied products, printing and publishing*

Chief crops: *Tobacco, cotton, lint, soybeans, grain, corn*

Chief ports: *Memphis, Nashville, Chattanooga, Knoxville*

Gross state product (2005): *$226.5 billion*

Employment (May 2006): *15.2% government; 21.7% trade/transportation/utilities; 14.6% manufacturing; 12.1% education/health; 11.2% professional/business services; 9.9% leisure/hospitality; 5.2% finance; 4.5% construction; 5.5% other services*

Per-capita income (2005): *$30,952*

STATE FLOWER	STATE BIRD

Iris	Mockingbird

THE VOLUNTEER STATE

This South Central State is 400 miles wide, stretching from eastern Tennessee's mountain ranges—including the Appalachians and Great Smoky Mountains—and the Cumberland Plateau to a strip of Mississippi River bottomland in the west. Its nickname, "Volunteer State," came from the War of 1812, when Tennessee fighting men hurried down the Mississippi River to help defend New Orleans. The Mississippi historically has been the key commercial artery for Tennesseans. The Tennessee River loops its way through the state, its dams creating hydroelectric plants and reservoirs. Cheap electricity from the system has stimulated the state's industrial growth. As manufacturing has continued to grow, surpassing agriculture in economic importance, the state's population has become increasingly urban. The major population centers are Nashville, the capital, which lies in the middle of the state in the Nashville Basin, and Memphis, Tennessee's largest city, on a bluff overlooking the Mississippi, in the southwest corner of the state.

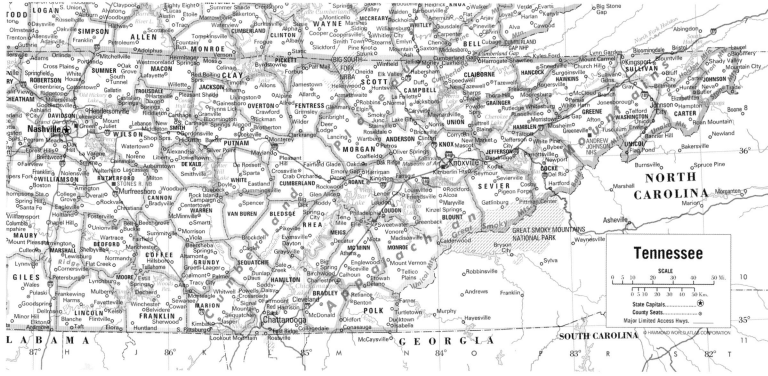

A Brief History

- Inhabited for at least 20,000 years, the region was home to Creek and Yuchi peoples when the first Europeans arrived; the Cherokee arrived in the early 18th century.
- Spanish explorers visited the area, 1540.
- English traders crossed the Great Smoky Mountains from the east; France's Jacques Marquette and Louis Jolliet sailed down the Mississippi in the west, 1673.
- Virginians established a permanent settlement on the Watauga River, 1769.
- After the American Revolution, in which Tennesseans fought in several eastern campaigns, the region became a territory, 1790, and a state, 1796.
- Slavery was widespread in western Tennessee, where cotton was the main crop, but much less common in the east.
- The state seceded, 1861, and saw many Civil War engagements; some 187,000 Tennesseans fought for the Confederacy and 51,000 for the Union.
- Tennessee was readmitted in 1866; it was the only former

Confederate state not to have a postwar military government.
- The famous Scopes trial, 1925, questioned the teaching of evolution in public schools.
- In the 1930s, the Tennessee Valley Authority, a federal program, brought electric power to rural areas.
- Nashville became the capital of country music, while Memphis fostered the blues and, with Elvis Presley in the 1950s, rock and roll.
- Martin Luther King Jr. was assassinated in Memphis, 1968.
- Since the 1970s, auto plants have become major employers, as has Federal Express.

Preserved 19th-century log cabins, built by early European settlers, are now a major attraction in the Great Smoky Mountains National Park.

Cataract Falls is one of the many waterfalls and cascades that are found on every river and stream in the Great Smoky Mountains, where rainfall is abundant.

Tennessee

FACTS & FIGURES

GEOGRAPHY

Total area: 42,143 sq mi (ranked 36th in size)

Acres forested: 14.4 million

CLIMATE:

Humid continental to the north; humid subtropical to the south

STATE TREE

Tulip tree

AVERAGE TEMPERATURE

CITY	JUN	DEC
Memphis	78.7	43.3
Nashville	75.1	40.5

FAMOUS TENNESSEANS

- Davy Crockett (1786–1836), folk hero
- David Farragut (1801–70), Civil War naval commander
- Aretha Franklin (b. 1942), singer
- Al Gore Jr. (b. 1948), 45th vice president
- Cordell Hull (1871–1955), U.S. senator and secretary of state
- Andrew Jackson (1767–1845), 7th U.S. president
- Andrew Johnson (1808–75), 17th U.S. president
- James Polk (1795–1849), 11th U.S. president
- Bessie Smith (1894–1937), singer

Andrew Jackson

ATTRACTIONS

Reelfoot Lake, *northwest Tennessee*

Lookout Mountain; Tennessee Aquarium, *Chattanooga*

Fall Creek Falls, *Pikeville*

Great Smoky Mts. National Park

Lost Sea, *Sweetwater*

Cherokee National Forest

Cumberland Gap National Historical Park

Andrew Jackson's home, *near Nashville*

American Museum of Science and Energy, *Oak Ridge*

Parthenon; Grand Ole Opry; Opryland, *Nashville*

Graceland, Elvis Presley's home, *Memphis*

Alex Haley Home and Museum, *Henning*

TOPOGRAPHY

- Rugged country in the east
- The Great Smoky Mts. of the Unakas
- Low ridges of the Appalachian Valley
- The flat Cumberland Plateau
- Slightly rolling terrain and knobs of the Interior Low Plateau, the largest region
- Eastern Gulf Coastal Plain to the west, laced with streams
- Mississippi Alluvial Plain, a narrow strip of swamp and floodplain in the extreme west

Highest elevation: Clingman's Dome, 6,643 ft

Lowest elevation: Mississippi River, 178 ft

Clingman's Dome in Great Smoky Mountains National Park

Running along the northern edge of the Great Smoky Mountains National Park, the Foothills Parkway provides stunning views of mountain peaks and valleys.

Born along the banks of the Mississippi, Memphis has always been dependent on the mighty river for trade, travel, and water.

Tens of thousands of cattle farms make ample use of Tennessee's rich pastures.

CAPITAL CITY: **NASHVILLE**

Nashville calls itself "Music City U.S.A." The famous Grand Ole Opry has operated in the city since 1925, and a dynamic music-industry community is active in writing, performing, and recording popular songs.

Founded on the Cumberland River in 1779 as Fort Nashborough, the city and port prospered, eventually becoming a manufacturing and railroad center. Nashville suffered greatly during the Civil War but recovered its commercial position as a major industrial city soon after the conflict.

Nashville is Tennessee's second most populous city after Memphis. Since the 1970s, the city has grown rapidly. An economic boom in the 1990s encouraged new construction and renovation downtown. Nashville is the crossroads for three interstates.

Major new sports facilities and performing arts venues have promoted economic growth in the city, which at the end of the 1990s became home to both NFL and NHL teams.

Area: 473.3 sq mi

Population (2005): 549,110

Population density: 1,160 per sq mi

Per-capita income: $34,904

Founded in 1779 and named the capital of Tennessee in 1843, Nashville is now a thriving hub for the music, publishing, and transportation industries.

SPOTLIGHT CITY: **MEMPHIS**

A leading Mississippi River port, Memphis is Tennessee's largest city and the Southeast's second largest, after Jacksonville, Florida.

In the 1680s French explorers built Fort Prudhomme, the first European settlement in the area. The city was incorporated in 1826, named after the ancient Egyptian city on the Nile. As a river and railroad town, Memphis thrived through the 19th century, with cotton and hardwood lumber among its main commercial commodities. As late as the mid-20th century it was still the world's largest market for mules.

Memphis was the scene of major events during the Civil Rights Movement in the 1960s. It was here in 1968 that Dr. Martin Luther King Jr. was assassinated.

The city is known for its food and for its rich musical heritage, especially the unique blues and jazz that developed here.

Area: 279.3 sq mi

Population (2005): 672,277

Population density: 2,407 per sq mi

Per-capita income: $32,741

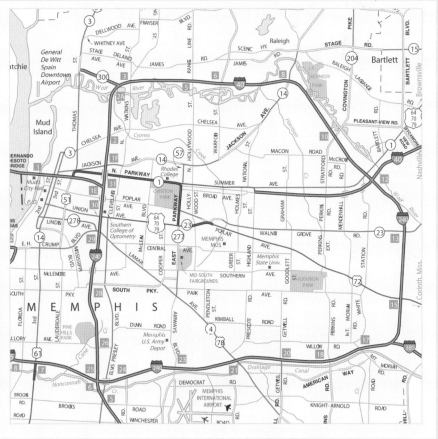

Memphis, the largest city in Tennessee, sprawls on the eastern bank of the Mississippi River, which has been central to its development.

TEXAS

Friendship

Settled: *1686*

Origin of name: *Variant of word used by Caddo and other Indians, meaning "friends" or "allies"*

Capital: *Austin*

Population (2005): *22,859,968 (ranked 2nd in size)*

Population density: *87.3 per sq mi*

ECONOMY

Chief industries: *Manufacturing, trade, oil and gas extraction, services*

Chief manufactured goods: *Industrial machinery and equipment, foods, electrical and electronic products, chemicals and allied products, apparel*

Chief crops: *Cotton, grains (wheat), sorghum grain, vegetables, citrus and other fruits, greenhouse/nursery, pecans, peanuts*

Chief ports: *Houston, Galveston, Brownsville, Beaumont, Port Arthur, Corpus Christi*

Commercial fishing (2004): *$166.2 million*

Gross state product (2005): *$982.4 billion*

Employment (May 2006): *17.3% government; 20.2% trade/transportation/utilities; 9% manufacturing; 12.2% education/health; 12.1% professional/business services; 9.4% leisure/hospitality; 6.3% finance; 6% construction; 5.7% other services*

Per-capita income (2005): *$32,462*

STATE FLOWER	STATE BIRD

Bluebonnet	Mockingbird

THE LONE STAR STATE

Taking its nickname from the single-starred flag of the 1836 Republic of Texas, this Oil State is the largest of the 48 contiguous states. Its southern border, formed by the course of the Rio Grande, separates the state from Mexico. Two-thirds of the population lives in urban areas such as Houston–Galveston and Dallas–Fort Worth. The state's landscape consists mainly of westward-rising plains. The climate in the interior is dry, with cold winters; it is more humid and warm along the Gulf Coast, where tropical storms and hurricanes are common. As is common in other Oil States, Texas also has natural gas. After California, Texas is the largest manufacturing state in the West. Petroleum refining, industrial equipment, electronics—especially for the aerospace industry—and food are chief industries. Texas leads the nation in beef and sheep production, with five times as much land devoted to livestock as to its major crops, which are cotton, sorghum, rice, citrus fruits, peanuts, and vegetables.

A Brief History

- Coahuiltecan, Karankawa, Caddo, Jumano, and Tonkawa peoples were in the area when the first Europeans arrived; later, Apache, Comanche, Cherokee, and Wichita arrived.
- Early Spanish explorers included Alonso Álvarez de Pineda, 1519; Cabeza de Vaca, shipwrecked near Galveston along with a former slave, Estevanico, 1528; and Coronado, 1541. Spaniards made the first settlement at Ysleta, near El Paso, 1682.
- Americans moved into the land in the early 19th century.
- Mexico, of which Texas was part, won independence from Spain, 1821.
- Texans rebelled, 1836, losing to Santa Anna at the Alamo, but winning under Sam Houston at San Jacinto.
- The Republic of Texas functioned as a nation, 1836–45, with Houston as president, until admitted to the Union.
- With a slave population of 30 percent, Texas seceded from the Union, 1861; it was readmitted, 1870.
- In 1900 a powerful hurricane lashed Galveston, killing at least 8,000.
- Cotton and cattle were dominant until 1901, when the Spindletop gusher, near Beaumont, launched the petroleum and petrochemical industries.
- By 2000 the state's population ranked second in the United States.

The Alamo (a mission converted into a fortress) was the site of a 13-day siege in 1836.

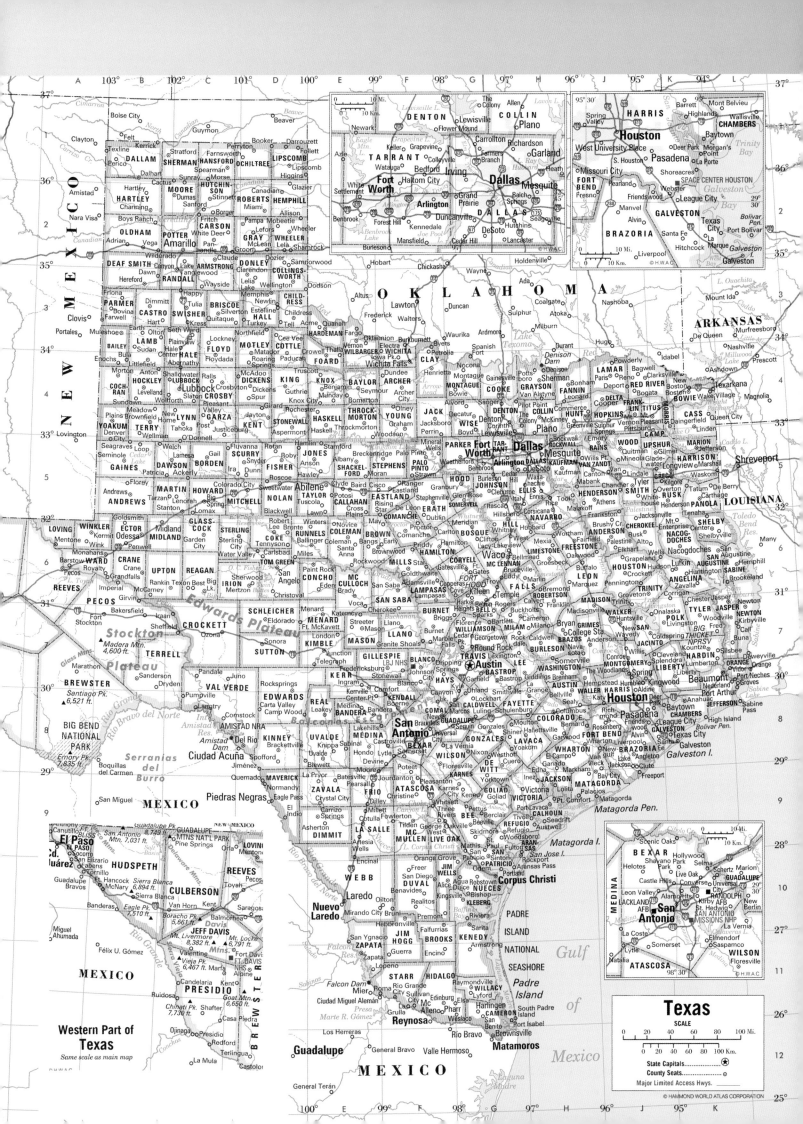

Texas

SCALE

| 0 | 20 | 40 | 60 | 80 | 100 Mi. |

| 0 | 20 | 40 | 60 | 80 | 100 Km. |

State Capitals.................★
County Seats...................⊛
Major Limited Access Hwys.

© HAMMOND WORLD ATLAS CORPORATION

Western Part of Texas
Same scale as main map

Texas

FACTS & FIGURES

GEOGRAPHY

Total area: 268,581 sq mi (ranked 2nd in size)

Acres forested: 17.1 million

CLIMATE:

Extremely varied; driest region is the Trans-Pecos; wettest is the northeast

STATE TREE

Pecan tree

AVERAGE TEMPERATURE

CITY	JUN	DEC
Austin	81.0	52.1
Dallas	80.9	46.7
Houston	81.3	53.7

FAMOUS TEXANS

- Lance Armstrong (b. 1971), cyclist
- James Bowie (1796–1836), pioneer and soldier
- Dwight D. Eisenhower (1890–1969), 34th U.S. president
- Howard Hughes (1905–76), aviator
- Lyndon B. Johnson (1908–73), 36th U.S. president
- Barbara Jordan (1936–96), U.S. congresswoman
- Chester Nimitz (1885–1966), World War II naval commander
- Sandra Day O'Connor (b. 1930), U.S. Supreme Court justice
- H. Ross Perot (b. 1930), businessman

Howard Hughes

ATTRACTIONS

Padre Island National Seashore

Big Bend National Park, *near El Paso*

Guadalupe Mountains National Park, *Salt Flat*

The Alamo; San Antonio Missions National Historical Park, *San Antonio*

Fort Davis

Cowgirl Hall of Fame; Kimball Art Museum, *Fort Worth*

Lyndon B. Johnson National Historical Park, *Johnson City;* Lyndon B. Johnson Library and Museum, *Austin*

Texas State Aquarium, *Corpus Christi*

George Bush Library, *College Station*

TOPOGRAPHY

- Gulf Coastal Plain in the south and southeast
- North Central Plains slope upward with some hills
- Great Plains extend over the Panhandle, are broken by low mountains
- The Trans-Pecos is the southern extension of the Rockies

Highest elevation: Guadalupe Peak, 8,749 ft

Lowest elevation: Gulf of Mexico, sea level

The Lyndon B. Johnson Space Center in Houston is home to NASA's Mission Control Center, which oversees all human spaceflights in the United States.

The Rio Grande has cut the deep Santa Elena Canyon through Big Bend National Park. Half of the canyon is in the United States; half is in Mexico.

Created by a dam in 1974, beautiful Lake McKenzie, in Silverton, Texas, draws hikers, boaters, fishermen, and archeologists interested in the area's rich prehistory.

CAPITAL CITY: **AUSTIN**

Austin is the capital of Texas and home to the University of Texas at Austin. The metro area has a population of 1.5 million.

Residents are known as "Austinites" and are part of a diverse and eclectic community that includes university professors and staff, government employees, white- and blue-collar workers, students, and musicians. Austin is home to major technology corporations, which has earned it the nickname "Silicon Hills." The city is also known as "The Live Music Capital of the World," because of its many resident musicians, performance venues, and popular music festivals.

In 2006, Austin was selected as the number-two "Best Big City" in *Money* magazine's survey of the best places to live. It has also been named the "Greenest City in America" for its concern with environmentalism.

Area: 251.5 sq mi

Population (2005): 690,252

Population density: 2,745 per sq mi

Per-capita income: $32,494

The state capital, which was briefly capital of the short-lived Republic of Texas, Austin is known for its liberalism, large, well-educated population, and dedication to music.

Texas longhorn cattle, bred for their lean beef, have adapted to the rugged Texas landscape. A steer's horns may measure 120 inches from tip to tip.

Texas

SPOTLIGHT CITY: **DALLAS**

The Dallas–Fort Worth–Arlington metro area has a population of 8 million. It is the nation's largest inland metropolitan area; it has no direct link to the sea.

Dallas was founded in 1841 and historically has been a center for cotton and oil. In modern times the city is known for computer and telecommunications innovations. Much of its success has come from the ambition and entrepreneurial abilities of its numerous business tycoons. By 1873, several railroads came through Dallas—some built as the result of political manipulation that influenced state legislators in the city's favor.

The skyline shows off a number of postmodernist buildings, with enough structures more than 700 feet high to make Dallas the 15th tallest city in the world.

In 1963, Dallas was the scene of President John F. Kennedy's assassination.

Area: 342.5 sq mi

Population (2005): 1,213,825

Population density: 3,544 per sq mi

Per-capita income: $35,502

The third largest city in Texas, Dallas sprawls across both banks of the Trinity River. The city is currently undergoing a rapid recovery after almost two decades of economic recession.

Rodeos, which have a long history in Spanish-influenced areas of the United States and Mexico, are popular events in Texas. Events like roping calves and riding bulls are now part of the organized sport of rodeo (Spanish for "round up," referring to the sport's origins in cattle herding). The first National Finals Rodeo was held in Dallas, Texas, in 1959.

SPOTLIGHT CITY: **HOUSTON**

Situated near the Gulf Coast, Houston was established in 1836, named after Republic of Texas hero Sam Houston.

The original port and railroad operations were already booming when oil was discovered in 1901, making Houston a center of the petrochemical industry. Since then, the economy has diversified, led by energy, technology, and aeronautics industries.

Texas Medical Center has the world's largest grouping of health-care and research enterprises. Rice University and the University of Houston are both leading research institutions.

The city is also home to NASA's Lyndon B. Johnson Space Center.

Houston is the nation's fourth largest city and the state's largest. Known for its dynamic cultural scene, Houston has fulltime resident companies in all the performing arts, and 7 million visitors annually visit the various institutions of the city's museum district.

Area: 579.4 sq mi

Population (2005): 2,016,582

Population density: 3,480 per sq mi

Per-capita income: $36,852

Founded in 1836, Houston is now the largest city in Texas and an economic, technological, and cultural hub of the United States.

The Houston Astrodome, opened in 1966, was the first indoor baseball stadium ever built.

UTAH

FACTS & FIGURES

Industry

Settled: *1847*

Origin of name: *From Navajo word meaning "upper" or "higher up"*

Capital: *Salt Lake City*

Population (2005): *2,469,585 (ranked 34th in size)*

Population density: *30.1 per sq mi*

ECONOMY

Chief industries: *Services, trade, manufacturing, government, transportation, utilities*

Chief manufactured goods: *Medical instruments, electronic components, food products, fabricated metals, transportation equipment, steel and copper*

Chief crops: *Hay, corn, wheat, barley, apples, potatoes, cherries, onions, peaches, pears*

Commercial fishing (2004): *$18.2 million*

Gross state product (2005): *$89.8 billion*

Employment (May 2006): *17.4% government; 19.3% trade/transportation/utilities; 10.1% manufacturing; 10.9% education/health; 13.2% professional/business services; 8.9% leisure/hospitality; 5.9% finance; 7.8% construction; 5.7% other services*

Per-capita income (2005): *$28,061*

STATE FLOWER

Sego lily

STATE BIRD

Seagull

THE BEEHIVE STATE

Utah is nicknamed for the bees that symbolized the hard-working early Mormon settlers, whose descendants make up more than two-thirds of this Mountain State's population. Most Utahans live in the north central region, near Salt Lake City, world headquarters of the Mormon Church. The nearby Great Salt Lake, Utah's best-known natural feature, is the largest saltwater lake in the Western Hemisphere. The Colorado River runs southwestward through Utah, which is on the western edge of the Rockies. The state is mountainous in the north and east, while the western third is mainly high desert, 4,000 feet above sea level. The climate is moderate in much of Utah, although the desert regions are hot and arid. The first Mormons developed extensive agricultural operations by irrigating parts of the desert. Since then, manufacturing has become the main industry. Utah experienced 43 percent population growth from 1990 to 2005 and had the highest birthrate and lowest median age of any state in the country.

A Brief History

- Ute, Gosiute, Southern Paiute, and Navajo peoples lived in the region at the time of first European contact.
- Spanish Franciscans visited the area, 1776; American fur traders followed.
- Permanent settlement began with the arrival of the Mormons, 1847, who irrigated and farmed the arid land, creating a prosperous economy.
- Organized in 1849, the Mormon state of Deseret asked admission to the Union; instead, Congress established Utah Territory, 1850, which included a portion of Deseret; Brigham Young was appointed governor.
- The Union Pacific and Central Pacific railroads were joined near Promontory Point, May 10, 1869, thereby creating the first American transcontinental railroad.
- Statehood was achieved, 1896, after a long controversy over the Mormons' economic isolationism and polygamy, which the church renounced in 1890.
- The 20th century brought expansion in mining, defense-related industries, and, more recently, information technologies.

In 1869 the first transcontinental railroad joined the Union Pacific and Central Pacific railroads.

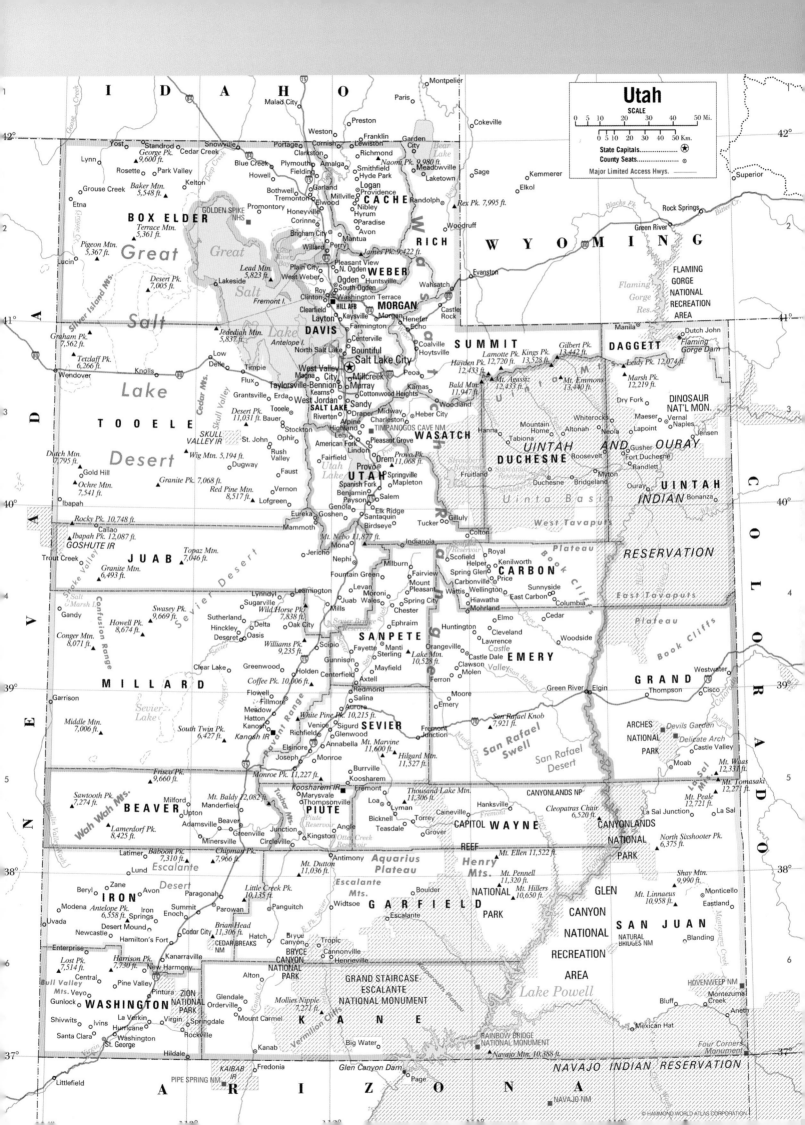

Utah

FACTS & FIGURES

GEOGRAPHY

Total area: *84,899 sq mi (ranked 13th in size)*

Acres forested: *15.7 million*

CLIMATE:

Arid; ranging from warm desert in southwest to alpine in northeast

STATE TREE

Blue spruce

AVERAGE TEMPERATURE

CITY	JUN	DEC
Milford	66.7	28.6
Salt Lake City	69.0	30.2

FAMOUS UTAHANS

- John Moses Browning (1855–1926), firearms designer
- Marriner Eccles (1890–1979), economist
- Philo Farnsworth (1906–71), inventor
- James Fletcher (1919–91), entomologist and botanist
- J. Willard Marriott (1900–85), entrepreneur
- Wallace Stegner (1909–93), writer
- Brigham Young (b. 1801, in Vermont– 1877), Mormon leader

Brigham Young

ATTRACTIONS

Temple Square, Mormon Church headquarters, *Salt Lake City*

Great Salt Lake, *northern Utah*

Zion National Park, *Springdale*

Canyonlands and Arches national parks, *near Moab*

Bryce Canyon, *Tropic*

Capitol Reef National Park, *near Torrey*

Dinosaur National Monument, *Jensen;* Rainbow Bridge National Monument, *Page;* Natural Bridges National Monument, *near Blanding*

Timpanogos Cave, *near American Fork*

Lake Powell, *on the Colorado River*

Flaming Gorge National Recreation Area, *near Manila*

TOPOGRAPHY

- *High Colorado plateau is cut by brilliantly colored canyons of the southeast*
- *Broad, flat, desertlike Great Basin of the west*
- *The Great Salt Lake and Bonneville Salt Flats to the northwest*
- *Middle Rockies in the northeast run east–west; valleys and plateaus of the Wasatch Front*

Highest elevation: King's Peak, 13,528 ft

Lowest elevation: Beaver Dam Wash, 2000 ft

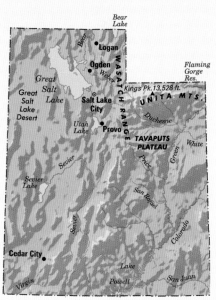

Newspaper Rock State Historic Monument, near Moab, is home to one of the largest collections of Native American petroglyphs (images engraved on stone) ever found.

CAPITAL CITY: **SALT LAKE CITY**

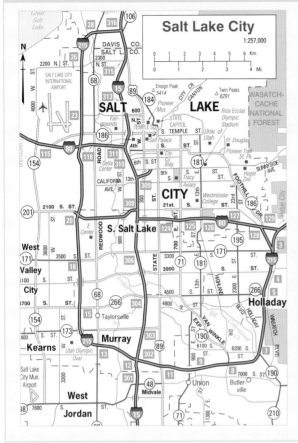

Salt Lake City

1:257,000

Salt Lake City is Utah's capital and largest city, with a metro area of 1 million. The city is in the Salt Lake Valley, an ancient lake bed. To the northwest is the Great Salt Lake; mountain ranges—with peaks around 11,000 feet—are to the east and west.

In the heart of Salt Lake City is Temple Square, with the temple of the Church of Jesus Christ of Latter-day Saints, or Mormon Church. The Mormons established the city in 1847, after seeking a place to practice their faith without being persecuted. Agriculture prospered thanks to their irrigation of the desert. By the time Utah entered the Union in 1896, mining and railroads had attracted new residents of various religions and ethnicities.

A thriving regional economy relies on trade, transportation, government, education, service companies, utilities, tourism, and outdoor recreation. Salt Lake City calls itself the "Crossroads of the West."

Area: 109.1 sq mi

Population (2005): 178,097

Population density: 1,666 per sq mi

Per-capita income: $27,629

Founded in 1847 by Brigham Young, leader of the Mormon Church, Salt Lake City was a boom town in the Old West and remains the most populous city in Utah today.

Named with a Hebrew word meaning "sanctuary," Zion National Park is both a geological and ecological preserve, with the richest plant diversity in Utah.

Utah

Great Salt Lake, named for its high salt content, is the remnant of an enormous lake that thousands of years ago covered most of Utah and parts of Idaho and Nevada.

Park City's Deer Valley is one of the premier ski resorts in the country. In 2002, it was one of the sites that hosted the Winter Olympics held in and around Salt Lake City.

Monument Valley lies on the southern border of Utah. While it is a popular tourist attraction, it is best known for the many movies and television shows that have been shot there.

The San Juan and Colorado rivers together created Glen Canyon, which is also the site of the second largest man-made lake in the United States, Lake Powell.

VERMONT

FACTS & FIGURES

Freedom and unity

Settled: *1764*

Origin of name: *From French* vert, *meaning green, and* mont, *meaning mountain*

Capital: *Montpelier*

Population (2005): *623,050 (ranked 49th in size)*

Population density: *67.4 per sq mi*

ECONOMY

Chief industries: *Manufacturing, tourism, agriculture, trade, finance, insurance, real estate, government*

Chief manufactured goods: *Machine tools, furniture, scales, books, computer components, specialty foods*

Chief crops: *Dairy products, apples, maple syrup, greenhouse/nursery, vegetables and small fruits*

Gross state product (2005): *$23.1 billion*

Employment (May 2006): *18% government; 19.4% trade/transportation/utilities; 11.9% manufacturing; 18% education/health; 7.3% professional/business services; 9.8% leisure/hospitality; 4.3% finance; 5.8% construction; 5.4% other services;*

Per-capita income (2005): *$33,327*

STATE FLOWER	STATE BIRD

Red clover	Hermit thrush

THE GREEN MOUNTAIN STATE

Vermont's nickname is from the French-Canadian name for the region in colonial times: *les Vert Monts,* or Green Mountains. Vermont is the most northwestern of the New England states, with Canada to the north. In the west, Lake Champlain and the Taconic Mountains divide the state from New York. Vermont's eastern border is the Connecticut River, with New Hampshire on the other side. The Green Mountain range runs north to south, the length of the state. Because of Vermont's elevation and inland location, its climate is cold, its winters offering some of the best skiing and snowboarding in the Northeast. The chief industries are manufacturing—especially machine tools and computer equipment—and tourism. Dairy dominates Vermont agriculture, and the state is known for its cheese and ice cream. It is also famous for maple syrup and is the national leader in maple sugar products. Other important crops include apples and greenhouse and nursery plants. Ranking 49th in population, Vermont is mainly rural, with no substantial metropolitan area.

A Brief History

- Inhabited for 10,000 years or more, the region attracted Abenaki and Mohican peoples before Europeans arrived.
- Samuel de Champlain explored the lake that now bears his name, 1609.
- The first European settlement was on Isle la Motte, in Lake Champlain, 1666.
- During the American Revolution, Ethan Allen and the Green Mountain Boys captured Fort Ticonderoga, 1775.
- Under a constitution that provided for public schools and abolished slavery, settlers declared a republic, 1777.
- Vermont joined the Union, 1791.
- Agriculture dominated in the 19th century; tourism and manufacturing expanded after World War II, though Vermont remained a mostly rural state; IBM became the largest private employer.

Named after the French explorer Samuel de Champlain, Lake Champlain, bordering New York and Canada in northwestern Vermont, had been used for centuries by various Native American tribes.

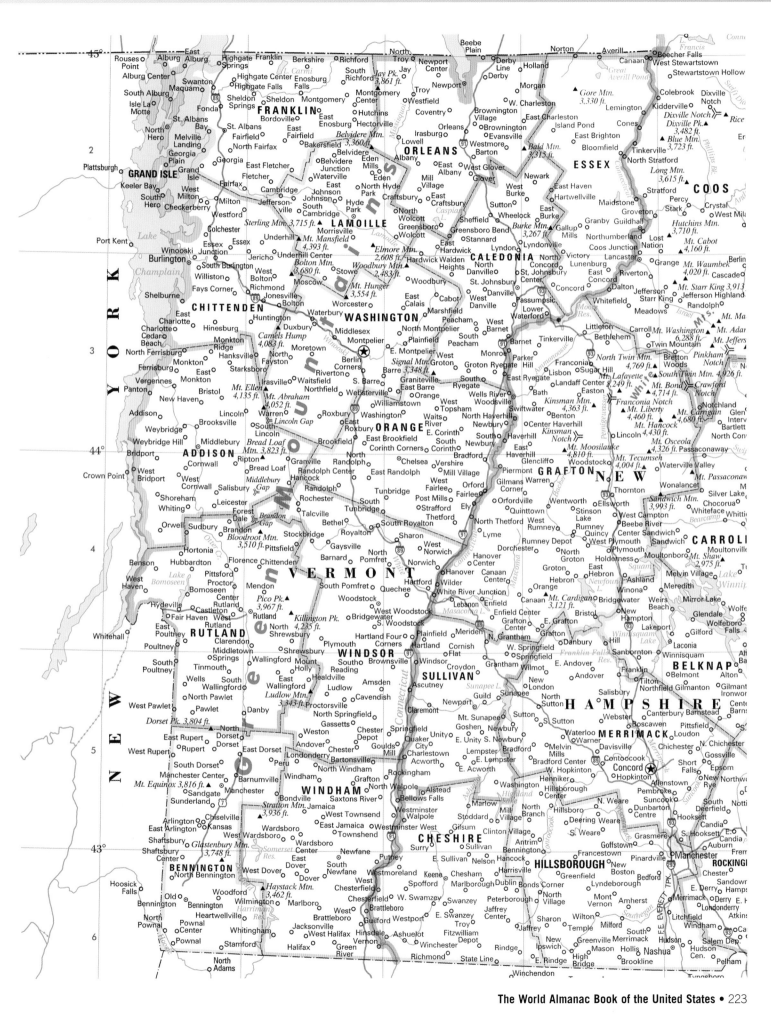

Vermont

FACTS & FIGURES

GEOGRAPHY

Total area: 9,614 sq mi
(ranked 45th in size)

Acres forested: 4.6 million

CLIMATE:

Temperate, with considerable temperature extremes; heavy snowfall in mountains

STATE TREE

Sugar maple

AVERAGE TEMPERATURE

CITY	JUN	DEC
Burlington	65.6	24.8

FAMOUS VERMONTERS

- Chester A. Arthur (1830–86), 21st U.S. president
- Calvin Coolidge (1872–1933), 30th U.S. president
- John Deere (1806–86), agricultural and construction manufacturer
- George Dewey (1837–1917), Navy admiral
- John Dewey (1859–1952), philosopher
- Stephen A. Douglas (1813–61), politician
- Dorothy Canfield Fisher (1879–1958), writer

Rudy Vallee

- James Fisk (1763–1844), U.S. senator
- James Jeffords (b. 1934), U.S. senator
- Rudy Vallee (1901–86), singer and actor

ATTRACTIONS

Shelburne Museum

Rock of Ages Quarry, *Graniteville*

Vermont Marble Exhibit, *Proctor*

Bennington Battle Monument

President Calvin Coolidge estate, *Plymouth*

Maple Grove Maple Museum, *St. Johnsbury*

Ben & Jerry's factory, *Waterbury*

TOPOGRAPHY

- Green Mts. north–south backbone 20–36 miles wide
- Average altitude of 1,000 ft

Highest elevation:
Mt. Mansfield, 4,393 ft

Lowest elevation:
Lake Champlain, 95 ft

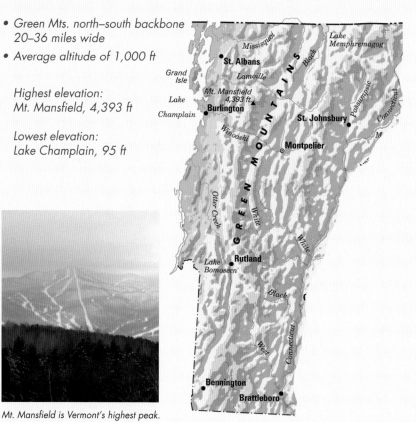

Mt. Mansfield is Vermont's highest peak.

CAPITAL CITY: **MONTPELIER**

Montpelier is the smallest of all the country's state capitals. Most of the town's businesses are still privately owned, with remarkably few franchises.

Vermont's glorious fall foliage draws visitors from all around the country. The peak of the foliage season typically occurs in late September through mid-October.

With annual snowfall averaging between 60 and 100 inches, Vermont is known for both downhill and cross-country skiing.

VIRGINIA

Sic Semper Tyrannis (Thus always to tyrants)

Settled: *1607*

Origin of name: *Named by Sir Walter Raleigh, in honor of Queen Elizabeth, the Virgin Queen of England*

Capital: *Richmond*

Population (2005): *7,567,465 (ranked 12th in size)*

Population density: *191.1 per sq mi*

ECONOMY

Chief industries: *Services, trade, government, manufacturing, tourism, agriculture*

Chief manufactured goods: *Food processing, transportation equipment, printing, textiles, electronic and electrical equipment, industrial machinery and equipment, lumber and wood products, chemicals, rubber and plastics, furniture*

Chief crops: *Tobacco, grain corn, soybeans, winter wheat, peanuts, lint and seed cotton*

Chief ports: *Hampton Roads, Richmond, Alexandria*

Commercial fishing (2004): *$160.3 million*

Gross state product (2005): *$352.7 billion*

Employment (May 2006): *18% government; 17.6% trade/transportation/utilities; 8% manufacturing; 10.9% education/health; 16.6% professional/business services; 9.1% leisure/hospitality; 5.2% finance; 7% construction; 7.3% other services*

Per-capita income (2005): *$38,390*

STATE FLOWER	STATE BIRD

American dogwood	Cardinal

OLD DOMINION

A South Atlantic State, Virginia occupies the middle of the eastern seaboard, with a broad, level coastal plain along the ocean. Tidal estuaries link the coast to the rivers, giving the region the name "Tidewater." Attracted by Virginia's mild climate, the first English settlers established colonies along the coast, eventually forming the "Colony and Dominion of Virginia," the origin of the nickname "Old Dominion." In the west, two main mountain ranges, the Alleghenies and the Blue Ridge, are cut by the Shenandoah River to form a valley of fertile agricultural land. Central Virginia is part of the Piedmont Plateau, an upland that widens from 40 miles in the north to 160 miles in the south. Manufacturing—of tobacco products, transportation equipment, textiles, and electronic and electrical equipment—is a mainstay. Agriculture, especially tobacco-growing, has traditionally been a leading industry, but tourism has surpassed it in economic importance.

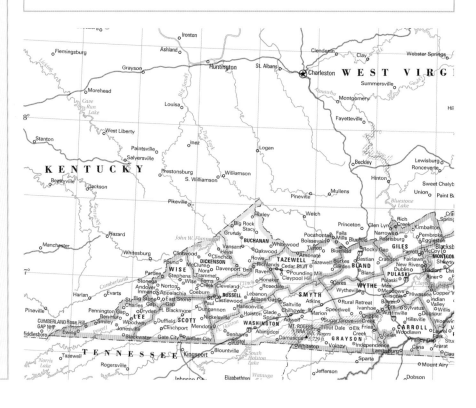

A Brief History

- Cherokee and Susquehanna peoples and the Algonquians of the Powhatan Confederacy occupied the region when Europeans arrived.
- Jamestown was founded by English settlers, 1607.
- Virginians were indispensable to the founding of the American republic; four of the first five U.S. presidents (Washington, Jefferson, Madison, and Monroe) were Virginians.
- The conclusive battle of the Revolutionary War took place at Yorktown, 1781.
- The state profited from tobacco, cotton, and the slave trade; in 1860, slaves made up nearly one-third of the population.
- Virginia seceded from the Union, 1861, and Richmond became the capital of the Confederacy, but western counties, loyal to the Union, split off to become West Virginia, 1863.
- The war ended with Lee's surrender to Grant at Appomattox, 1865; Virginia was readmitted to the Union, 1870.
- In the 20th century, expansion of federal civilian jobs and military facilities transformed the economy.

The home of Wilmer McLean, a Virginia militia major, was the site of General Robert E. Lee's surrender to General Ulysses S. Grant in April 1865, the year this photograph was taken.

Virginia has hundreds of miles of shoreline, most of which are along the Chesapeake Bay. Other popular beaches are on the Atlantic Ocean.

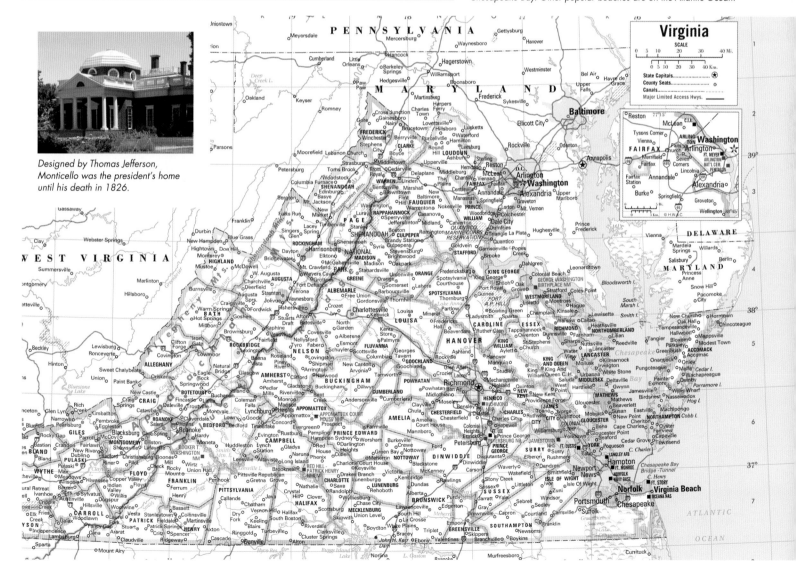

Designed by Thomas Jefferson, Monticello was the president's home until his death in 1826.

Virginia

FACTS & FIGURES

GEOGRAPHY

Total area: 42,774 sq mi (ranked 35th in size)

Acres forested: 16.1 million

CLIMATE:

Temperate and mild, with hot and humid summers

STATE TREE

Flowering dogwood

AVERAGE TEMPERATURE

CITY	JUN	DEC
Norfolk	74.5	44.2
Richmond	73.5	40.4

FAMOUS VIRGINIANS

- Richard E. Byrd (1888–1957), aviator and polar explorer
- Thomas Jefferson (1743–1826), 3rd U.S. president
- Robert E. Lee (1807–70), Confederate general
- James Madison (1751–1836), 4th U.S. president
- Edgar Allan Poe (1809–49), writer
- Walter Reed (1851–1902), U.S. Army physician
- Booker T. Washington (1856–1915), educator and writer
- George Washington (1732–99), 1st U.S. president
- Woodrow Wilson (1856–1924), 28th U.S. president

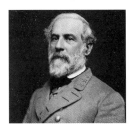

Robert E. Lee

ATTRACTIONS

Colonial Williamsburg; Busch Gardens, *Williamsburg*

Wolf Trap Farm, *near Falls Church*

Arlington National Cemetery

Mt. Vernon, home of George Washington, *near Alexandria;* Monticello, home of Jefferson, *Charlottesville*

Robert E. Lee's birthplace, *Stratford Hall*

Appomattox

Shenandoah National Park, *Waynesboro*

Blue Ridge Parkway, *near Roanoke*

Virginia Beach

TOPOGRAPHY

- Mountain and valley region in the west, including the Blue Ridge Mts.
- Rolling Piedmont Plateau
- Tidewater, or coastal plain, including the eastern shore

Highest elevation: Mt. Rogers, 5,729 ft

Lowest elevation: sea level

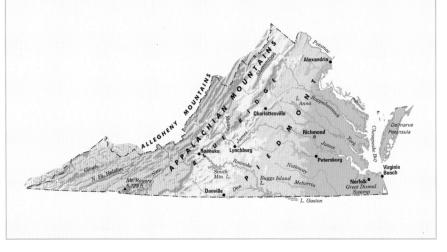

Colonial Williamsburg, an open-air, live history museum, allows visitors to experience life as it was in colonial Virginia. Once the colonial capital, Williamsburg has drawn 100 million visitors since 1932.

The Blue Ridge Mountains run through Shenandoah National Park, with Virginia's Piedmont to the east and the Shenandoah Valley to the west. Nearly 80,000 acres in the park are designated as wilderness.

CAPITAL CITY: **RICHMOND**

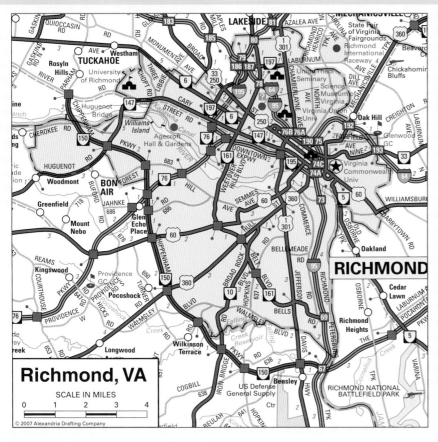

Richmond, VA

SCALE IN MILES

0 1 2 3 4

© 2007 Alexandria Drafting Company

The earliest English settlers, who arrived in 1607, were the first colonists to smoke the Native American plant tobacco, soon to be a leading colonial commodity. Richmond was founded in 1737 on the James River, which provided water power to operate mills and helped make the city a major manufacturing center.

Historical landmarks honor Richmond's colonial heritage and Civil War history, when the city was the capital of the Confederacy.

Richmond has a metro area of 1.2 million people. Few metro areas have more Fortune 500 company head-quarters than Richmond, with nine in the city. Leading industries include banking, government, and law, along with developing enterprises in biotech-nology and pharmaceuticals.

Richmond has a vibrant perform-ing arts community and an extensive municipal parks system that is one of the oldest in the country.

Area: 62.5 sq mi

Population (2005): 193,777

Population density: 3,292.6 per sq mi

Per-capita income: $34,802

Since its founding in 1737, Richmond has played a significant role in American history. It was the site of Patrick Henry's "Give me liberty or give me death" speech, urging Virginia to fight the British.

SPOTLIGHT CITY: **NORFOLK**

The seaport city of Norfolk is on Hampton Roads, a broad harbor at the mouth of Chesapeake Bay. Founded in 1682 and incorporated in 1736, Norfolk is the financial and cultural center of a region that includes nine cities and seven counties, with 1.6 million people.

Surrounded by bodies of water, Norfolk has had naval and shipbuilding installations since before the found-ing of the United States. It was the scene of important actions during the Revolutionary and Civil War periods. The famous ironclad CSS *Virginia*, rebuilt from the USS *Merrimack*,

was constructed in Norfolk during the Civil War. The Norfolk Naval Base, headquarters of the Atlantic fleet, is the largest in the world. Military shipbuild-ing and ship repair is a major industry.

Urban renewal, beginning in the 1970s, transformed a formerly obsolete and blighted industrial waterfront into parks, markets, and pavilions with riverfront views.

Area: 53.7 sq mi

Population (2005): 231,954

Population density: 4,319 per sq mi

Per-capita income: $31,811

Norfolk became an important port in the late 17th century, when warehouses were built by royal decree for the export of tobacco.

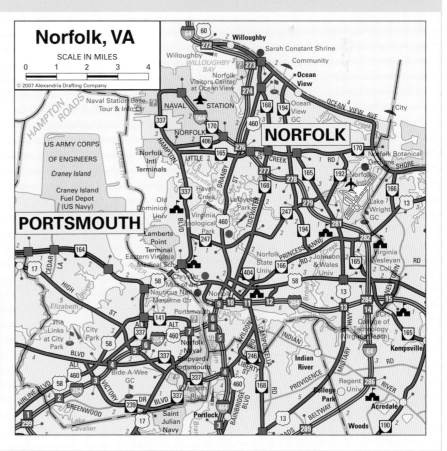

Norfolk, VA

SCALE IN MILES

0 1 2 3 4

© 2007 Alexandria Drafting Company

WASHINGTON

Alki (By and by)

Settled: *1811*

Origin of name: *Named for George Washington*

Capital: *Olympia*

Population (2005): *6,287,759 (ranked 14th in size)*

Population density: *94.5 per sq mi*

ECONOMY

Chief industries: *Advanced technology, aerospace, biotechnology, international trade, forestry, tourism, recycling, agriculture and food processing*

Chief manufactured goods: *Computer software, aircraft, pulp and paper, lumber and plywood, aluminum, processed fruits and vegetables, machinery, electronics*

Chief crops: *Apples, potatoes, hay, farm forest products*

Chief ports: *Seattle, Tacoma, Vancouver, Kelso-Longview*

Commercial fishing (2004): *$175.1 million*

Gross state product (2005): *$268.5 billion*

Employment (May 2006): *18.8% government; 18.8% trade/transportation/utilities; 9.8% manufacturing; 11.9% education/health; 11.6% professional/business services; 9.6% leisure/hospitality; 5.5% finance; 6.7% construction; 7.1% other services*

Per-capita income (2005): *$35,409*

STATE FLOWER	STATE BIRD

Coast rhododendron	Willow goldfinch

THE EVERGREEN STATE

The "Evergreen State" is an appropriate nickname for this heavily wooded state, a national leader in timber production, especially the evergreen Douglas fir. The state tree is the Western hemlock, also an evergreen. Bordering Canada, Washington is the most northwestern of the 48 contiguous states. Its mild climate benefits from the warm ocean currents that flow down the Pacific Coast. The state has four distinct topographical areas. In the west, the Olympic Mountains peninsula has the largest temperate rain forest in the country. Inland is a low region, with the inlets, islands, and major cities of Puget Sound. The Cascade Mountains, with peaks above 14,000 feet, divide the state, with the semiarid tableland of the Columbia Plateau to the east. West of the Cascades, rainfall is heavy. Manufacturing has surpassed even lumber, which once dominated the economy. Aircraft-building, advanced technology, aerospace, and biotechnology are major industries.

A Brief History

- At the time of European contact, Nez Perce, Spokane, Yakima, Cayuse, Okanogan, Walla Walla, and Colville peoples lived in the interior; Nooksak, Chinook, Nisqually, Clallam, Makah, Quinault, and Puyallup peoples lived along the coast.
- Spain's Bruno Hezeta sailed the coast, 1775.
- In 1792, British naval officer George Vancouver mapped Puget Sound and American Captain Robert Gray sailed up the Columbia River.
- Fur traders and missionaries arrived, 1800–50.
- Completion of a transcontinental rail link, 1883, aided immigration; Washington became a state, 1889.
- In the 20th century, cheap hydroelectric power spurred growth in the aluminum and aircraft industries; Microsoft, founded in 1975, became a computer software giant.
- Mt. St. Helens erupted, killing 57 people, 1980.

Though no known totem poles date from before the 18th century, the traditional indigenous art form is believed to be much older.

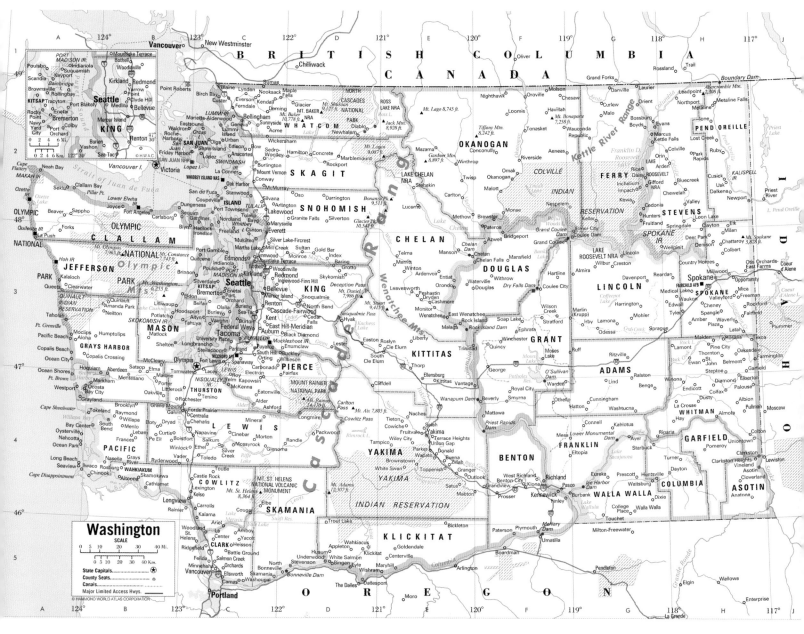

Washington

SCALE

0   5 10   20   30   40 Mi.

0   5 10 20   30   40 Km.

State Capitals..................................★
County Seats.................................⊙
Canals
Major Limited Access Hwys. ━━━

© HAMMOND WORLD ATLAS CORPORATION

Picturesque but deadly, Mount St. Helens is an active volcano, whose most famous explosion in 1980 removed 1,314 feet from the summit and killed 57 people.

Washington

FACTS & FIGURES

GEOGRAPHY

Total area: *71,300 sq mi (ranked 18th in size)*

Acres forested: *21.8 million*

CLIMATE:

Mild, dominated by the Pacific Ocean and protected by the Cascades

STATE TREE

Western hemlock

AVERAGE TEMPERATURE

CITY	JUN	DEC
Olympia	58.2	38.0
Seattle	61.1	41.3

FAMOUS WASHINGTONIANS

- Raymond Carver (1938–88), writer
- Bing Crosby (1907–77), singer
- William O. Douglas (1898–1980), U.S. Supreme Court justice
- Bill Gates (b. 1955), entrepreneur
- Jimi Hendrix (1942–70), musician
- Gary Larson (b. 1950), cartoonist
- Mary McCarthy (1912–89), writer
- Robert Motherwell (1915–91), painter
- Edward R. Murrow (1908–65), journalist
- Theodore Roethke (1908–63), poet

Bing Crosby

ATTRACTIONS

Waterfront; Seattle Center and Space Needle; Museum of Flight; Underground Tour, *Seattle*

North Cascades National Park, *near Seattle*

Mt. Rainier National Park, *near Tacoma*

Olympic National Park, *near Port Angeles*

Mt. St. Helens, *in Cascade Range*

Puget Sound

San Juan Islands

Grand Coulee Dam

Columbia River Gorge National Scenic Area

Riverfront Park, *Spokane*

TOPOGRAPHY

- Olympic Mts. on northwest peninsula
- Open land along coast to Columbia River
- Flat terrain of Puget Sound lowland
- Cascade Mts. region's high peaks to the east
- Columbia Basin in central portion

- Highlands to the northeast
- Mountains to the southeast

Highest elevation: Mt. Rainier, 14,410 ft

Lowest elevation: sea level

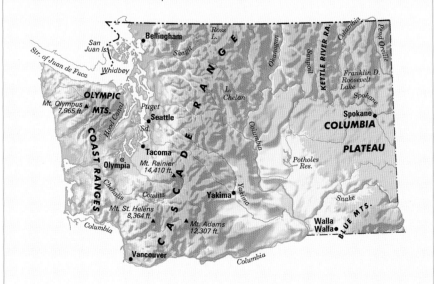

CAPITAL CITY: **OLYMPIA**

Olympia, Washington's capital, was built on a site first recorded by Peter Puget during his 1792 expedition.

SPOTLIGHT CITY: **SEATTLE**

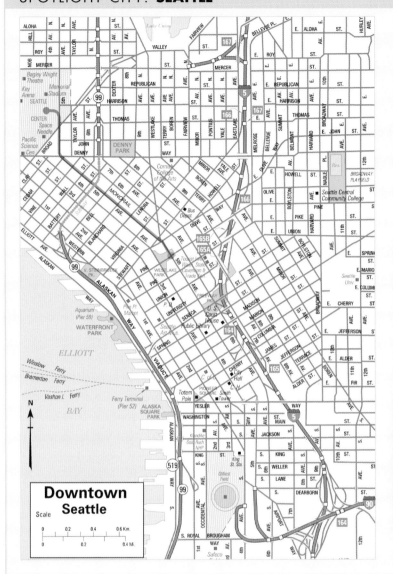

Downtown Seattle

Scale

0   0.2   0.4   0.6 Km.

0   0.2   0.4 Mi.

The 1851 founders of the settlement near Puget Sound that would become Seattle named the community New York. Later, the name was changed to honor local Native American chieftain Noah Sealth.

Seattle has a metro population of 3.3 million and is the center of the Greater Puget Sound region. Seattle has the highest proportion of college graduates of any American city. In 2005 it was ranked the nation's "most literate city."

Nicknames include "Emerald City," alluding to its many evergreens, and "Jet City," a reference to the Boeing Company, the aerospace and defense corporation that has operations there. Also headquartered in Seattle are five of the nation's largest companies, including Internet giant Amazon.com and coffee company Starbucks.

While Seattle is ranked high as a city favorable to business expansion, the city's real estate is among the most expensive in the country.

Area: 83.9 sq mi

Population (2005): 573,911

Population density: 6,840 per sq mi

Per-capita income: $41,634

The largest city in the Pacific Northwest, Seattle has grown from a frontier town in the mid-19th century to a booming center of technology, industry, and culture.

The current bridge crossing the mile-long span over Puget Sound replaced the first Tacoma Narrows Bridge, which famously collapsed in 1940 as the result of a disastrous and unforeseen mechanical failure.

More than 2 million people visit Deception Pass State Park every year, making it one of Washington's most popular parks.

WEST VIRGINIA

Montani Semper Liberi (Mountaineers are always free)

Settled: *1774*

Origin of name: *Named for western counties of Virginia that refused to secede*

Capital: *Charleston*

Population (2005): *1,816,856 (ranked 37th in size)*

Population density: *75.5 per sq mi*

ECONOMY

Chief industries: *Manufacturing, services, mining, tourism*

Chief manufactured goods: *Machinery, plastic and hardwood products, fabricated metals, chemicals, aluminum, automotive parts, steel*

Chief crops: *Apples, peaches, hay, tobacco, corn, wheat, oats*

Chief port: *Huntington*

Gross state product (2005): *$53.8 billion*

Employment (May 2006): *19.1% government; 18.5% trade/transportation/utilities; 8.1% manufacturing; 15.2% education/health; 7.8% professional/business services; 9.4% leisure/hospitality; 4% finance; 5.3% construction; 9% other services*

Per-capita income (2005): *$27,215*

STATE FLOWER	STATE BIRD

Rhododendron	Cardinal

THE MOUNTAIN STATE

A Southeast State, West Virginia is also called a Tidewater State because of its proximity to the tidal estuaries. West Virginia is mountainous, its average elevation of 1,500 feet making it the highest state east of the Mississippi. Because of its elevation, West Virginia's climate is much colder than the other Tidewater States. In the south-central region, the capital, Charleston, receives 41 inches of precipitation annually, including 31 inches of snow. The Ohio River forms the state's western border, flowing southwest. The Potomac River borders the northeast and flows into neighboring Maryland and Virginia. Much of West Virginia's settlement originated from Virginia, but the north and west look to Pennsylvania and Ohio, respectively. Tourism is important, but manufacturing is the principal industry, founded on mining, especially coal, in which West Virginia is a national leader. Important products include machinery, steel, fabricated metal products, automotive parts, and chemicals.

A Brief History

- Sparsely inhabited before European contact, the area was primarily Native American hunting grounds.
- British explorers Thomas Batts and Robert Fallam reached the New River, 1671.
- Coal, discovered in 1742, was mined extensively by the mid-19th century.
- White settlement led to conflicts, including a major battle in which frontiersmen defeated an Indian confederacy at Point Pleasant, 1774.
- The region joined the Union as part of Virginia, 1788.
- Virginia seceded, 1861.
- Delegates of western counties, meeting at Wheeling, repudiated the secession and created a new state, which was admitted to the Union in 1863.
- Eight-term U.S. senator Robert Byrd in 2006 became the longest-serving member in Senate history.

Despite its formation during the Civil War as a Union state, West Virginia has a monument dedicated to the Confederate fallen, reflecting torn sympathies.

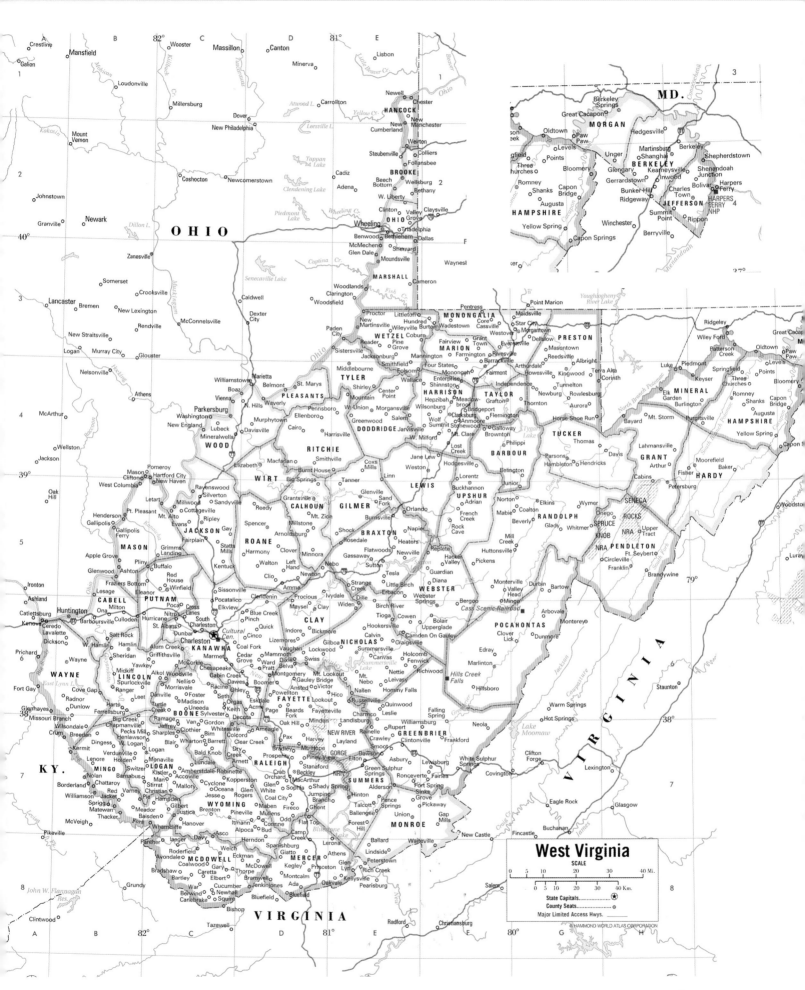

West Virginia

SCALE

0 5 10   20   30   40 Mi.

0 5 10   20   30   40 Km.

State Capitals......................✪
County Seats.......................○
Major Limited Access Hwys._____

© Hammond World Atlas Corporation

West Virginia

FACTS & FIGURES

GEOGRAPHY

Total area: 24,230 sq mi
(ranked 41st in size)

Acres forested: 12.1 million

CLIMATE:

Humid continental climate
except for marine modification
in the lower panhandle

STATE TREE

Sugar maple

AVERAGE TEMPERATURE

CITY	JUN	DEC
Charleston	69.9	37.5
Huntington	71.3	37.1

FAMOUS WEST VIRGINIANS

- Newton D. Baker
  (1871–1937), U.S.
  secretary of war
- Pearl Buck
  (1892–1973), writer
- Robert Byrd (b. 1917),
  U.S. senator
- Thomas "Stonewall"
  Jackson (1824–63),
  Confederate general
- Mary Lou Retton
  (b. 1968), gymnast
- Walter Reuther
  (1907–70), labor
  union leader

- Jerry West (b. 1938),
  basketball player
- Charles "Chuck" Yeager
  (b. 1937), test pilot

Thomas "Stonewall" Jackson

ATTRACTIONS

Harpers Ferry National Historic Park

Science and Cultural Center; Sternwheel Regatta,
Charleston

The Greenbrier, *White Sulphur Springs*

Berkeley Springs

New River Gorge, *Fayetteville*

Winter Place; Exhibition Coal Mine, *Beckley*

Monongahela National Forest

Fenton Glass, *Williamstown;* Viking Glass,
New Martinsville; Blenko Glass, *Milton*

Mountain State Forest Festival,
Allegheny Mts.

TOPOGRAPHY

- Ranging from hilly to mountainous
- Allegheny Plateau in the west,
  covering two-thirds of the state
- Mountains are the highest in the
  state, over 4,000 ft

Highest elevation:
Spruce Knob, 4,861 ft

Lowest elevation:
Potomac River, 240 ft

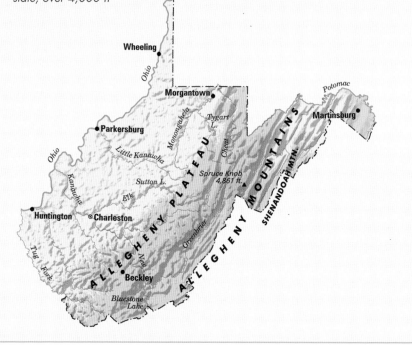

Built in 1976 out of recovered parts from older mills,
Glade Creek Grist Mill is a fully operable re-creation,
paying tribute to the hundreds of mills that operated
in West Virginia at the turn of the century.

The imposing Seneca Rocks are located in the
Spruce Knob–Seneca Rocks National Recreation
Area. Rising 900 feet above the Potomac River, the
crag is a popular destination for rock climbers.

Deep coal mines and far-reaching railroads brought employment to West Virginia in the late 19th century.
Coal mining still plays a major role in the state's economy.

CAPITAL CITY: **CHARLESTON**

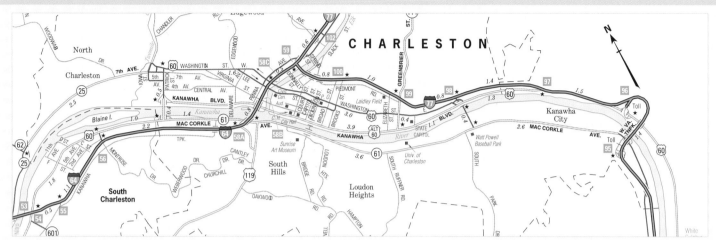

The capital of West Virginia, Charleston is at the confluence of the Elk and Kanawha rivers. It is the state's largest city, with a metropolitan population of 307,000. The earliest pioneers included Daniel Boone, who opened the region to settlement in the 1700s.

The first white community, begun in 1788, was Fort Lee, when the area was part of Virginia. Charleston was officially established in 1794, with seven houses and 35 residents. Salt mining was the first important industry. While drilling for salt in the early 1800s, miners struck natural gas, which eventually became a leading commodity, along with coal.

When Virginia seceded from the Union in 1861, the western counties resisted. In 1863, they were admitted as the 35th state, West Virginia. Charleston became the capital in 1877.

Among the city's leading attractions is the Clay Center for the Arts and Sciences.

Area: 32.7 sq mi

Population (2000): 53,421

Population density: 1,690.4 per sq mi

Per-capita income: $26,232

Now West Virginia's largest city, Charleston did not become the capital until 1877, 14 years after the formation of the state.

New River Gorge Bridge was the longest steel-arch bridge in the world when it was built in 1977, and, at a height of 876 feet, was the highest until the Millau Viaduct was built in France in 2004.

WISCONSIN

WISCONSIN

1848

Forward

Settled: *1670*

Origin of name: *From Indian name, believed to mean "grassy place" in Chippewa*

Capital: *Madison*

Population (2005): *5,536,201 (ranked 20th in size)*

Population density: *101.9 per sq mi*

ECONOMY

Chief industries: *Services, manufacturing, trade, government, agriculture, tourism*

Chief manufactured goods: *Food products, motor vehicles and equipment, paper products, medical instruments and supplies, printing, plastics*

Chief crops: *Corn, hay, soybeans, potatoes, cranberries, sweet corn, peas, oats, snap beans*

Chief ports: *Superior, Ashland, Milwaukee, Green Bay, Kewaunee, Port Washington, Manitowoc, Sheboygan, Marinette, Kenosha*

Commercial fishing (2004): *$3.1 million*

Gross state product (2005): *$217.5 billion*

Employment (May 2006): *14.7% government; 18.6% trade/transportation/utilities; 17.4% manufacturing; 13.9% education/health; 9.2% professional/business services; 9.3% leisure/hospitality; 5.5% finance; 4.8% construction; 6.5% other services*

Per-capita income (2005): *$33,565*

STATE FLOWER	STATE BIRD

Wood violet	American robin

THE BADGER STATE

This Great Lakes State has long shorelines on Lake Michigan and Lake Superior and a western border formed, for most of its length, by the Mississippi River. Wisconsin's forests and lakes have made tourism a major industry, although manufacturing is also important. A major industrial region extends south from Milwaukee, on Lake Michigan, toward Chicago. Wisconsin ranks among the top 20 states in production of food products, motor vehicles and equipment, and paper products. In the south, the rich soil attracted early settlement; more than half the state is still farmland, with dairy bringing in the most income. The state's climate is tempered by the waters of the Great Lakes, but Wisconsin has long, cold winters and short, warm summers. Milwaukee averages 46 inches of snow annually, while northern regions receive more. Nicknamed the "Badger State" after that aggressive animal, Wisconsin is also called "America's Dairyland," as well as the "Copper State" because of its rich copper deposits.

A Brief History

- At the time of European contact, Ojibwa, Menominee, Winnebago, Kickapoo, Sauk, Fox, and Potawatomi peoples inhabited the area.
- French explorer Jean Nicolet reached Green Bay, 1634; French missionaries and fur traders followed.
- The United States won the land after the American Revolution but did not wield control until forts were established at Green Bay and Prairie du Chien, 1816.
- Native Americans rebelled against the seizure of tribal lands in the Black Hawk War, 1832, but were defeated and relocated to reservations.
- Wisconsin became a territory, 1836, and a state, 1848.
- Some 96,000 soldiers served the Union cause during the Civil War.
- Many immigrants arrived from Germany, Poland, and Scandinavia.
- Wisconsin agriculture focused on dairy; Milwaukee became a manufacturing center.
- As governor, 1901–06, Robert La Follette pushed Progressive reforms such as direct primary voting.
- An era of "McCarthyism" ended when anti-Communist crusader Senator Joseph McCarthy (R–WI) was censured by the U.S. Senate, 1954.

Early settlers built their houses out of wood from the ample supply in the surrounding forests.

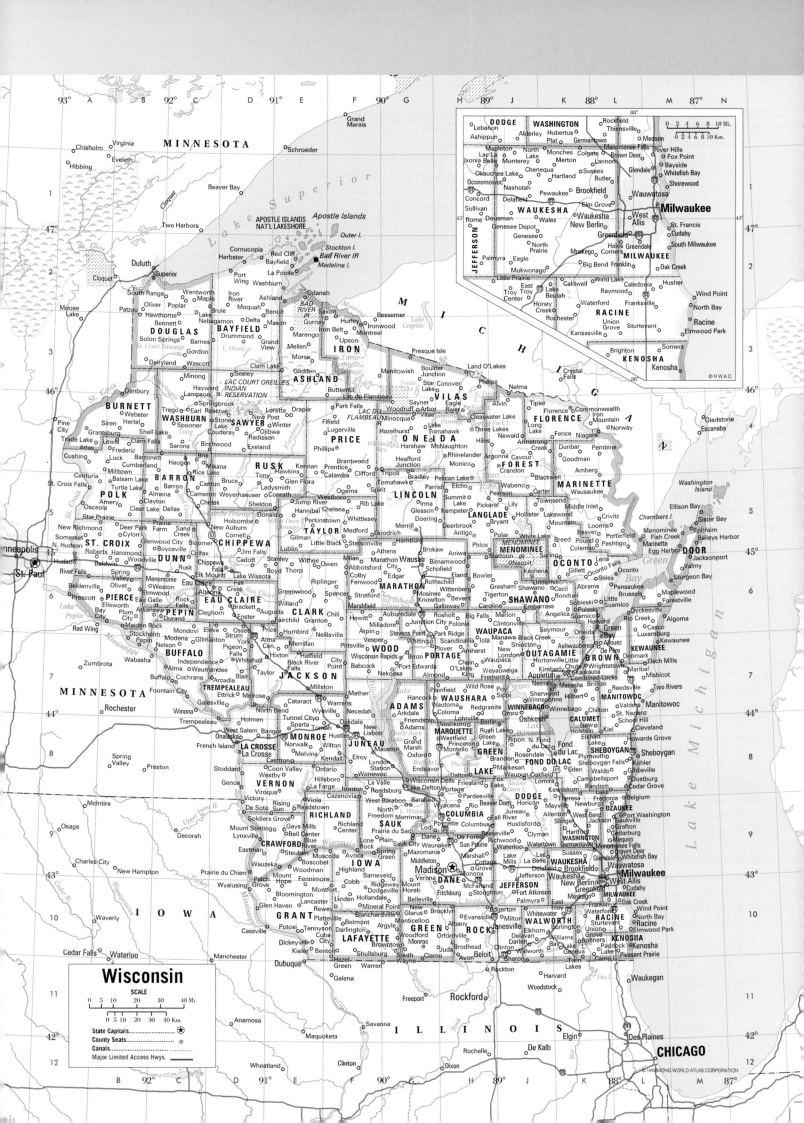

Wisconsin

FACTS & FIGURES

GEOGRAPHY

Total area: 65,498 sq mi
(ranked 23rd in size)

Acres forested: 16 million

CLIMATE:

Long, cold winters and short, warm summers tempered by the Great Lakes

STATE TREE

Sugar maple

AVERAGE TEMPERATURE

CITY	JUN	DEC
Madison	67.0	23.0
Milwaukee	66.3	26.2

FAMOUS WISCONSINITES

- Harry Houdini (1874–1926), magician and escape artist
- Robert La Follette (1855–1925), U.S. senator
- William H. Rehnquist (1924–2005) U.S. Supreme Court justice
- John Ringling (1866–1936), founder of the Ringling Brothers Circus
- Donald K. "Deke" Slayton (1924–93), astronaut
- Spencer Tracy (1900–67), actor
- Orson Welles (1915–85), actor, screenwriter, director
- Laura Ingalls Wilder (1867–1957), writer
- Thornton Wilder (1897–1975) playwright

Orson Welles

ATTRACTIONS

Old Wade House and Carriage Museum, *Greenbush*

Villa Louis, *Prairie du Chien*

Circus World Museum, *Baraboo*

Wisconsin Dells

Old World Wisconsin, *Eagle*

Chequamegon–Nicolet National Forest, *northern Wisconsin*

Lake Winnebago, *eastern Wisconsin*

House on the Rock, *Dodgeville*

Monona Terrace, *Madison*

TOPOGRAPHY

- Narrow Lake Superior lowland plain met by Northern Highland, which slopes gently to the sandy crescent Central Plain
- Western upland in the southwest
- Three broad parallel limestone ridges running north-south are separated by wide and shallow lowlands in the southeast

Highest elevation: Timms Hill, 1,951 ft

Lowest elevation: Lake Michigan, 579 ft

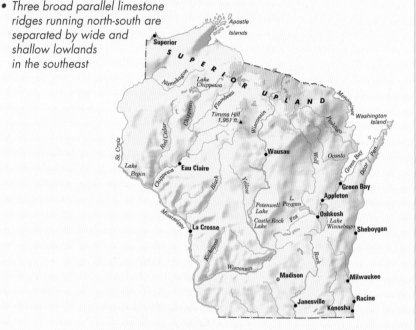

With almost 15,000 lakes, 33,000 miles of running water, and forests covering nearly half of the state, Wisconsin is known for its natural and pristine beauty.

This female cardinal, like the rest of Wisconsin's wildlife, is adapted to the cold, snowy winters, which average 45 inches of snow a year.

Since the 19th century, Wisconsin has been a primary producer of dairy products, particularly cheese. Today, 1.3 million dairy cows account for Wisconsin's national lead in cheese production.

CAPITAL CITY: **MADISON**

Madison was chosen to be the capital of Wisconsin Territory in 1836—even before the town was built. Boosters laid out a town and lobbied the legislature for the designation. They were successful in part because the planned city was in the midst of the important mining district.

Madison was named after recently deceased former president James Madison. The village of Madison was incorporated in 1846, and Wisconsin became a state two years later.

Madison is nicknamed the "City of Four Lakes" for the lakes in the Yahara River system. It is also known as "Mad City."

Madison is Wisconsin's second-largest city, after Milwaukee, with a metropolitan area of 543,000 people. The city is home to the University of Wisconsin–Madison, a major influence in the cultural life and economy. Government and the university are leading employers, with high tech, advertising, and health services growing in importance.

Area: 68.7 sq mi

Population (2005): 221,551

Population density: 3,225 per sq mi

Per-capita income: $37,447

Madison's downtown is located on the isthmus purchased in 1829 by its founder, James Duane Doty, although the city has since expanded beyond its historic boundaries.

SPOTLIGHT CITY: **MILWAUKEE**

In 1818, Quebec trader and land speculator Solomon Juneau was the first white settler of Juneautown, which in 1846 became part of Milwaukee. He served as the first mayor and founded the *Milwaukee Sentinel* newspaper, the city's oldest continuously running business.

Sited on the shore of Lake Michigan, the town attracted many immigrants, especially Germans. Through the 19th century and into the 20th, Milwaukee was known for its mighty manufacturing output and as the world's number-one beer-brewing city. Although industrial production waned in the late

20th century, by the end of the century the city had undergone massive renewal and revitalization. In addition to brewing enterprises, 13 Fortune 1000 corporations have their headquarters in Milwaukee and its suburbs.

Milwaukee is also the region's cultural center, with two symphony orchestras, an opera company, ballet, theaters, and museums.

Area: 96.1 sq mi

Population (2005): 578,887

Population density: 6,024 per sq mi

Per-capita income: $36,488

Milwaukee derives its name from an Algonquian Indian word meaning "good/beautiful land."

WYOMING

Equal rights

Settled: *1834*

Origin of name: *From Algonquian words for "large prairie place"*

Capital: *Cheyenne*

Population (2005): *509,294 (ranked 51st in size)*

Population density: *5.2 per sq mi*

ECONOMY

Chief industries: *Mineral extraction, oil, natural gas, tourism and recreation, agriculture*

Chief manufactured goods: *Refined petroleum, wood, stone, clay products, foods, electronic devices, sporting apparel, and aircraft*

Chief crops: *Wheat, beans, barley, oats, sugar beets, hay*

Gross state product (2005): *$27.4 billion*

Employment (May 2006): *24.7% government; 18.9% trade/transportation/utilities; 3.6% manufacturing; 8.2% education/health; 6.1% professional/business services; 11.7% leisure/hospitality; 4% finance; 8.2% construction; 5.3% other services*

Per-capita income (2005): *$36,778*

STATE FLOWER	STATE BIRD

Indian paintbrush	Western meadowlark

THE EQUALITY STATE

With only 5.2 people per square mile, Wyoming is the second least densely populated state after Alaska (1.1 per sq mi). Its neighbor Montana is third at 6.2. In the heart of the Mountain States, Wyoming was in the forefront of women's rights in 1869 when its territorial legislature gave women the right to vote—the origin of the state's nickname. The North Platte River cordons off the state's southeastern corner, a region of foothills that is part of the Great Plains. In the northwest are the Rockies, with some of the country's highest peaks. Yellowstone and Grand Teton national parks, which bring in over 2 million visitors each year, are in this region. Tourism is a major industry. Wheat and livestock are leading industries, but Wyoming's main business is mining. The state is the leading producer of coal west of the Mississippi, and a top producer of crude oil, natural gas, and uranium.

A Brief History

- Inhabited for at least 12,000 years, the region supported Shoshone, Crow, Cheyenne, Oglala Sioux, and Arapaho peoples when Europeans arrived.
- France's Vérendrye brothers were the first Europeans to see the region, 1742–43.
- John Colter, an American, traversed the Yellowstone area, 1807–08.
- Trappers and fur traders followed in the 1820s.

In the 19th century, settlers, hunters, and trappers devastated the bison herds that roamed through Wyoming. Today, a herd of a few thousand lives in Yellowstone National Park.

- Forts Laramie and Bridger became important stops on trails to the West Coast.
- Population grew after the Union Pacific crossed the state, 1867–68.
- Wyoming became a territory, 1868, and the first to extend full voting rights to women, 1869.
- Statehood was attained, 1890.
- Disputes between large landowners and small ranchers culminated in the Johnson County Cattle War, 1892; federal troops were called in to restore order.
- Nellie Tayloe Ross was the first woman governor to take office in the United States, 1925.
- Wyoming, the least populous state, has relied economically on the energy, tourism, and ranching industries in recent decades.

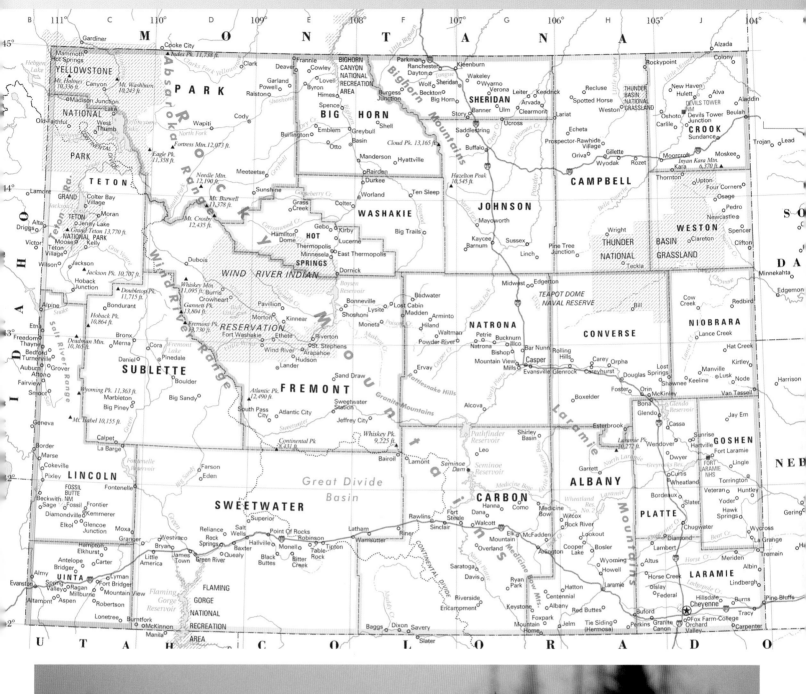

Yellowstone National Park's wildlife, as well as natural beauty, draws visitors. It is a refuge for many species, including bison, wolves, grizzly bears, and elk.

Wyoming

FACTS & FIGURES

GEOGRAPHY

Total area: *97,814 sq mi (ranked 10th in size)*

Acres forested: *11.0 million*

CLIMATE:

Semidesert conditions throughout; true desert in the Big Horn and Great Divide basins

STATE TREE

Plains
cottonwood

AVERAGE TEMPERATURE

CITY	JUN	DEC
Casper	62.7	23.8
Cheyenne	61.5	27.1

FAMOUS WYOMINGITES

- James Bridger (1804–81), explorer
- Patricia MacLachlan (b. 1938), writer
- Esther Hobart Morris (1814–1902), leader in woman's suffrage movement
- John Perry Barlow (b. 1947), lyricist and activist
- Jackson Pollock (1912–1956), artist
- E. Annie Proulx (b. 1925), writer
- Red Cloud (1822–1909), chief of the Oglala Sioux

Nellie Tayloe Ross

- Nellie Tayloe Ross (1876–1977), 1st woman to serve as governor of a U.S. state

ATTRACTIONS

Yellowstone National Park

Grand Teton National Park

National Elk Refuge, *Jackson*

Devils Tower National Monument, *Gillette*

Fort Laramie National Historic Site; Cheyenne Frontier Days, *Cheyenne*

Buffalo Bill Historical Center, *Cody*

Jackson Hole, *central Wyoming*

TOPOGRAPHY

- The eastern Great Plains rise to the foothills of the Rocky Mts.
- The Continental Divide crosses the state from the northwest to the southeast

Highest elevation: Gannett Peak, 13,804 ft

Lowest elevation: Belle Fourche River, 3,099 ft

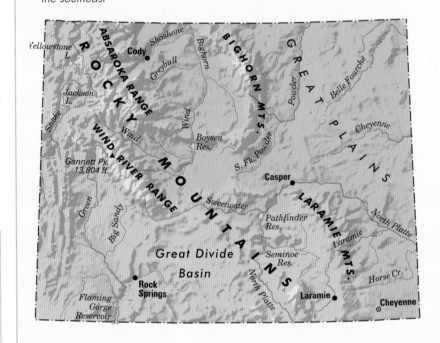

Rising 1,267 feet above the Belle Fourche River, the extraordinary geological formation called Devils Tower is the centerpiece of Devils Tower National Monument, dedicated by President Theodore Roosevelt in 1906.

CAPITAL CITY: **CHEYENNE**

Wyoming's capital and largest city, Cheyenne was laid out in 1867 by surveyors planning the route of the Union Pacific Railroad, then under construction. Soon after track was laid, 4,000 settlers arrived, and the town sprang up as if from the ground, earning the name, "Magic City, Queen of the Plains."

The surveyors named the town for the warlike Cheyenne, whose land it had been, and who harassed the railroad builders, though without success. The city became the territorial capital in 1868 and state capital in 1890 when Wyoming was admitted.

Stockyards that prepared cattle for transport by railroad were the major industry. Agriculture remains a key business, but the city's economy is also dependent on nearby Warren Air Force Base, part of the region's network of nuclear missile silos.

The Cheyenne Botanic Gardens are a city highlight, featuring a solar-powered and heated conservatory.

Area: 21.2 sq mi

Population (2005): 55, 731

Population density: 2,629 per sq mi

Per-capita income: $34,559

Planned as a stop on the Union Pacific Railroad, Cheyenne was a settlement whose population exploded almost overnight in 1867.

The Teton Range rises more than 7,000 feet above the valley of Jackson Hole, overlooking the glacial lakes of Grand Teton National Park.

WASHINGTON, D.C.

FACTS & FIGURES

Justitia omnibus (Justice for all)

Settled: *1790*

Origin of name: *Named for George Washington*

Population (2005): *550,521*
(ranked 50th in size)

Population density: *8,966.1 per sq mi*

ECONOMY

Chief industries: *Government, service, tourism*

Gross product (2005): *$82.8 billion*

Employment (May 2006): *33.3% government;
4.1% trade/transportation/utilities;
0.3% manufacturing; 13.7% education/health;
21.9% professional/business services;
8.4% leisure/hospitality; 4.4% finance;
1.9% construction; 12% other services*

Per-capita income (2005): *$54,985*

GEOGRAPHY

Total area: *68 sq mi*
(ranked 50th in size)

CLIMATE

Hot and humid summers, mild winters

TOPOGRAPHY

Low hills rise toward the north away from the Potomac River and slope to the south

Highest elevation: 410 ft
Lowest elevation: Potomac River, 1 ft

FLOWER

American Beauty rose

BIRD

Wood thrush

THE DISTRICT

The District of Columbia is a 61-square-mile zone on the east bank of the Potomac River, which contains the city of Washington, the United States capital. The District is surrounded on three sides by Maryland, with Virginia across the river. Washington was created as a "federal city" in 1790, its location between North and South the result of national compromise. It is coextensive—shares the same borders—with the federal District. Congress has ultimate control of the District, even though Washington has a mayor and city council. In the midst of governmental opulence and gleaming buildings, Washington struggles with poverty, unable to collect revenues from its main business: tax-exempt federal operations. Half the city's workers are employed by the government. Tourism, attracted by the many monuments and memorials, is the major industry. Another highlight is the Smithsonian Institution's museums, dedicated to art, history, and science.

A Brief History

- The Piscataway, an Algonquian-speaking people, were living in the region when Europeans arrived in the 17th century.
- Authorized by Congress, 1790, President George Washington chose the site for the district.
- The original 100-square-mile site was taken from the sovereignty of Maryland and Virginia. Virginia's portion was given back in 1846.
- President Washington chose Pierre Charles L'Enfant, a Frenchman, to plan the capital.
- Washington laid the cornerstone of the north wing of the Capitol building, 1793.
- President John Adams moved to the new national capital, 1800.
- The City of Washington was incorporated, 1802.
- British troops invaded, 1814, setting fire to the Capitol, the President's House (as the White House was then called), and other buildings.
- The 23rd Amendment granted residents the right to vote for president and vice president, 1961.
- In 1974, voters approved a congressionally drafted charter that gave them the right to elect their own mayor and city council.
- After a 34-year absence, Major League Baseball returned to the city in 2005.

Located at 1600 Pennsylvania Avenue, the White House has been home to every U.S. president since 1800.

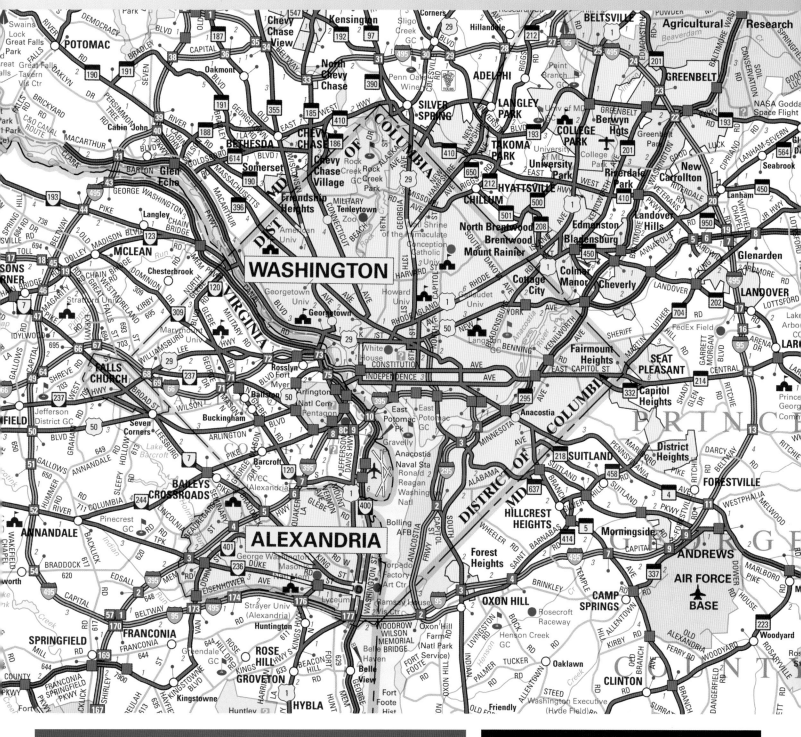

Located at the east end of the National Mall, the Capitol building houses both chambers of Congress, the Senate in the north wing and the House of Representatives in the south wing.

The statue of President Abraham Lincoln, by sculptor Daniel Chester French, was created for the Lincoln Memorial, dedicated in 1922.

Index

Index

Index

Photo Credits

The following abbreviations are used: SS–Shutterstock; ISP–IstockPhoto; IO–Index Open; JI–Jupiter Images; WI–Wikimedia; BS–BigStock Photo; SXC–Stock. xchng; LOC–Library of Congress; t–top; b–bottom; l–left; r–right; c–center

FRONT MATTER 3 SS/Steve Adamson **4** SS/Andrea LG Ferguson **6** IO/James Denk **7** JI **14l** SS/pmphoto **14tl** ISP/Richard Gunion **15b** SS/Geoffrey Kuchera **16l** SS/Pete Hoffman **16tr** ISP/Dennis Morris **17** ISP/Justin Horrocks

ALABAMA 18bl WI/Luukas **18bl** WI **18tr** JI **18br** LOC **20tl** WI/Gotty **20cl** LOC **20cr** SS/Gary W. Parker **20cr** WI/Clarkbhm **20br** WI **21tl** WI/J. Michael Dockery **21br** WI/John Morse **ALASKA 22bl** WI/David Monniaux **22bl** WI/Jimfbleak **24tl** WI/Walter Siegmund **24cl** WI/United Church of Canada collection **24tr** JI **24br** WI/National Geographic Magazine **25tr** WI **25tr** IO/Mistral Images **25br** IO **26** JI **27l** JI **27tr** SS/Laura Lohrman Moore **27cr** SS/Jason Watson **27br** SS/James K. Troxell **ARIZONA 28bl** ISP/Marcy Ugstad **28bl** WI/Mark Wagner **28tr** SS/Csongor Tari **28bc** JI **30tl** WI/Stan Shebs **30cl** LOC **30br** SS/Peter Kunasz **31bl** IO **32** SS/Csongor Tari **33tl** JI **33tr** IO/Amy and Chuck Wiley/Wales **33b** IO/Charlie Borland **ARKANSAS 34bl** WI/Bev Sykes **34bl** BS/Phillip Wilkerson **34tr** WI/Larry Donald, U.S. Army Corps of Engineers **34br** SS/Jonathan Brizendine **35b** BS/Loredana Bell **36tl** WI **36cl** WI/U.S. Army Signal Corps **36c** SS/Lori Martin **36cr** SS/Stephanie Coffman **36br** SS/Jon Michael Weidman **37tr** IO **37b** SS/Stephanie Coffman **CALIFORNIA 38bl** WI **38bl** SS **38tr** SS/Jenny Solomon **40tl** WI **40cl** WI **40br** SS/Jonathan Lenz **41tr** SS/Artifan **41cr** JI **41bl** JI **41br** SS/Cristi Bastian **42br** IO **43br** JI **43br** SS/Byron W.Moore **43bl** SS/David Pruter **44** IO **45l** IO **45tr** SS/Mike Brake **45br** IO **COLORADO 46bl** IO **46bl** Utah Division of Wildlife Resources **48tl** SS/prism_68 **48cl** LOC **48tr** SS/Kerrie Jones **48br** WI **49bl** IO **49tr** SS/Mike Norton **49cr** JI **50** SS/Mike Norton **51tl** SS/Kaleb Timberlake **51tr** SS/R Craig Pitman **51b** SS/Haemin Rapp **CONNECTICUT 52bl** ISP/John Teate **52bl** WI/Ken Thomas **52tr** IO **52br** LOC **53bl** SS/Jennifer Nickert **53br** SS/Julie Fine **54tl** WI **54cl** LOC **54c** SS/Bruce Grubbs **54cb** SS/Thea Reilkoff **54br** SS/Jennifer Nickert **55** SS/Laura Stone **55bl** SS/Arthur Connors **DELAWARE 56bl** WI **56bl** WI **56tr** SS/Sam Aronov **56br** LOC **58l** BS/Teresa Levite **58cl** LOC **58bl** WI/W. S. Stewart **58tr** BS/Capitol Photo Distribution **58br** WI **59tr** JI **59cl** BS/Teresa Levite **59cr** IO/VStock LLC **59b** SS/Teresa Levite **FLORIDA 60bl** WI **60bl** WI/Ryan Hagerty **60tr** SS/Frank Boellmann **60br** LOC **62tl** SS/Frank Boellmann **62cl** WI/SEWilco **62cr** ISP/Jonathan Lyons **62br** ISP/Cezary Gesikowski **63cl** IO/Richard Stockton **63cr** JI **63b** WI/Tom Schaefer **64cl** WI **64cr** SS/Stephen Pamment **64bl** SS/Kato Inowe **64br** SS/kristian sekulic **65tr** JI **65cr** WI **65bl** JI **GEORGIA 66bl** SS/United States Federal Government **66bl** SS/Robert Hambley **66tr** SS/Lawrence Cruciana **66br** WI/J. Williams **68tl** SS/Sebastien Windal **68cl** Courtesy of the Reagan Library **68cr** SS/Sebastien Windal **68cr** SS/Gennady Stetsenko **69tr** JI **69bl** SS/Brandon Holmes **70bl** WI/MG **70bl** SS/Sharon Workman **70tr** JI **HAWAII 70br** WI **71b** JI **72cl** WI **72cb** JI **72br** JI **73cr** IO **73b** JI **74l** JI **74tr** JI **74br** JI **75t** JI **75b** JI **IDAHO 76bl** SS/Leah-Anne Thompson **76bl** WI/NaturesPics Online **76tr** SS/Lane Lambert **76br** WI/Curtis, Edward S. **77tr** SS/Robynrg **78tl** U.S. Forest Service **78cl** WI/Alvin Langdon Coburn **78c** SS/Mike Norton **78c** WI **78cr** SS/Robynrg **78br** SS/Robynrg **79tr** SS/Lane V. Erickson

79b SS/Mike Norton **ILLINOIS 80bl** SS/Potapov Alexander **80bl** ISP/Bill Raboin **80tr** SS/Bryan Busovicki **80bc** WI **82tl** BS/Juergen Roth Photography **82cl** LOC/WI **82tc** SS/Mike Grindley **83t** WI/Fritz Geller-Grimm **83b** WI/Derek Collins **84bl** Morguefile/Click **84tr** WI **84br** WI **85r** SS/Bryan Busovicki **INDIANA 86bl** SS/Elaine Davis **86bl** SS/Eric Lawton **86br** WI **88tl** SS/cassiopeia **88cl** USASEARCH.GOV **88tc** WI/Derek Jensen **88c** SS/Thomas Barrat **88br** SS/Bryan Busovicki **89tr** SS/w shane dougherty **89bl** WI/Derek Jensen **IOWA 90bl** BS/Horst Petzold **90bl** BS/Stephen Muskie **92cl** LOC **92tr** SS/Steve Adamson **92br** WI **93tr** SS/Arlen E Breiholz **93cr** SS/Madeleine Openshaw **93bl** SS/Michael Rolands **KANSAS 94bl** BS/Jakub Cejpek **94bl** BS/Elemental Imaging **95br** WI/Edwin Olson **96tl** SS/Mike Norton **96cl** WI/Marion S. Trikosko **96br** ISP **97tl** WI/Hugh Mason **97c** SS/Mary Lane **97b** ISP/ecliptic blue **KENTUCKY 98bl** SS/Chris Hill **98bl** SS/Tom Hirtreiter **98tr** SS/Melissa Tuttle **99bl** LOC **99br** LOC **100tl** SXC/David Austin **100cl** LOC **100br** WI **101tr** SS/Benjamin F. Haith **101bl** SS/Anne Kitzman **101br** SS/David Davis **LOUISIANA 102bl** WI/Gunnar Ries **102bl** WI/Alan D. Wilson **102tr** SS/Kirk Peart Professional Imaging **102br** SS/Leon Ritter **103tr** ISP/Donald Gruener Creative Services **103b** SS/Larry Powell **104tl** SS/Michael Jason Shehan **104cl** LOC **104br** SS/David Huntley **105tr** SS/Lebraix LeDoux **105bl** SS/Natalia Bratslavsky **MAINE 106bl** SS/Winthrop Brookhouse **106bl** WI/Ian McEwen **106tr** IO/Jim Schwabel **106br** LOC **108tl** WI/Robert H. Mohlenbrock **108cl** LOC **108tc** SS/Chee-Onn Leong **108br** SS/Chee-Onn Leong **109tl** SS/Kevin Tavares **109b** SS/Kerry Muzzey **110** SS/Chee-Onn Leong **111t** SS/Michael Rickard **111b** IO/Jim Schwabel **MARYLAND 112bl** BS/Anthony Berenyi **112bl** BS/Kenneth Dill **112cr** SS/Anton Albert **113br** LOC **114tl** BS/Juergen Roth Photography **114cl** WI **114tr** SS/L. Kragt Bakker **114c** SS/Svetlana Larina **114cr** SS/C. Kurt Holter **115tr** SS/Svetlana Larina **115bl** SS **115br** SS/amygdala imagery **MASSACHUSETTS 116bl** BS/gregg williams **118cl** WI **118tr** SS/Chee-Onn Leong **118br** LOC **119tr** SS/Mike Liu **119tr** SS/PJARD Photography **119bl** SS/GemPhoto **MICHIGAN 120tr** SS/SNEHIT **120br** WI **122cl** LOC **122br** WI **123tr** IO/Jim Schwabel **123bl** SS **123br** SS/Julio Yeste **MINNESOTA 124br** WI/Vannerson, Julian **126cl** WI/Roger Higgins, World Telegram staff photographer **126br** SS/July Flower **127tr** WI/John Polo **127bl** IO/Charlie Borland **MISSISSIPPI 128tr** WI **128br** LOC **130cl** WI/Orland Fernandez, World Telegram staff photographer **130br** WI **130tl** SS/Christopher Lofty **131tr** ISP/Jon McIntosh **MISSOURI 132tr** SS/Gary L. Brewer **132bc** WI **133b** SS/Sharon D **134tl** JI **134br** IO **135tr** WI **135b** SS/Mark Shipley **MONTANA 136tr** IO/Wallace Garrison **136br** LOC **137b** SS **138cl** WI **138br** JI **139tr** SS/Jason Maehl **139b** SS/Glenn R. McGloughlin **140t** SS/Mike Norton **140b** SS/Jason Maehl **141** IO **NEBRASKA 143bl** SS/Weldon Schloneger **143br** LOC **144cl** LOC **144br** SS/Chad Bontrager **145tr** WI **145bl** SS/James "BO" Insogna **NEVADA 146tr** WI **146br** LOC **148cl** WI **148tr** ISP/Chee-Onn Leong **148br** WI **149tr** IO/Stewart Cohen **149br** JI **NEW HAMPSHIRE 150tr** SS/Andrea LG Ferguson **150br** LOC **152cl** WI **152br** WI **153tl** IO/photolibrary.com pty. ltd. **153tr** SS/Andrea LG Ferguson **153b** JI **NEW JERSEY 154tr** SS/Natalia Bratslavsky **154br** LOC **156cl** WI/George C. Cox **156tr** ISP/Andrew F Kazmierski **156br** SS/William Frederick Lawson **157t** IO/Rudi Von Briel **157bl** SS/Holger W. **NEW MEXICO 158tr** SS/george michael warnock **158br** IO **159b** WI **160cl** WI/Alfred Stieglitz **160br** SS/

george michael warnock **161tr** SS/Elemental Imaging **161bl** ISP/Jill Fromer **161br** SS/amygdala imagery **162t** SS/Jonathan Larsen **162b** WI **163t** SS/John Blanton **163b** SS/Gary L. Brewer **NEW YORK 164br** SS/Michael Coddington **165bl** SS/Michael Coddington **166cl** WI **166tr** IO/Barry Winiker **166br** LOC **167tr** SS/Stephanie Lupoli **167tr** WI/Matthew Trump **167br** WI **168tl** SS/Donald R. Swartz **168bl** WI **169tl** WI/Thomas Wieczorek **169bl** SS/Chad Palmer **169br** BS/Michael Shake **NORTH CAROLINA 170cr** JI **171bl** WI **171br** WI **172tl** WI **172cl** WI/Carl Van Vechten **172tr** ISP/David Raboin **172tr** JI **173tr** SS/Matej Krajcovic **173bl** JI **NORTH DAKOTA 176tl** WI/Henry hartley **176cl** WI **176tr** WI/MatthewUND **177tr** WI **177bl** ISP/Pastel Dakota Photo **OHIO 178br** WI **180tl** WI **180cl** WI **180br** IO/Charlie Borland **181tr** IO/Richard Stockton **181bl** WI **OKLAHOMA 182bl** SS/Danilo Ducak **182c** SS/Darlene Tompkins **183br** WI/Aaron Walden **184cl** WI **184br** SS/Darlene Tompkins **185tr** SS/Shane Wilson Link **185bl** SS/Phil Anthony **OREGON 186tr** IO/FogStock LLC **186br** ISP/picmax **187b** IO **188cl** WI **188br** WI **189tr** IO **189b** WI **PENNSYLVANIA 190bl** WI **191br** WI **192cl** WI **192br** WI **193tl** IO **193tl** WI **193tr** WI **193bl** SS/Michael Coddington **RHODE ISLAND 194tr** SS/Kelli Westfal **194br** WI **196cl** LOC **196cr** SS/Gary Detonnancourt **196br** SS/Galina Dreyzina **197tr** SS/Joy Brown **197cl** SS/Carolyn M Carpenter **197bl** JI **197br** SS/Donna Carlson **SOUTH CAROLINA 198tr** JI **198br** WI **199b** JI **200cl** LOC **200br** WI **201tr** SS/Lori Skelton **201bl** SS/Jason Tench **SOUTH DAKOTA 202tr** JI **202br** LOC **203b** SS/Elena Belinschi **204cl** WI **204br** IO/FogStock LLC **205t** IO/FogStock LLC **205b** SS/Winthrop Brookhouse **TENNESSEE 206cr** SS/Jeff Kinsey **207br** SS/Mary Terriberry **207bc** SS/Mark Scott **208cl** WI **208c** SS/Carolina K. Smith, M.D. **208cr** ISP/Steven Allan **208br** SS/Brian Dunne **209cr** IO/Charlie Borland **209bl** ISP/Roger Cotton **TEXAS 210tr** IO **210br** JI **212cl** LOC **212c** WI **212cr** IO/James Denk **212br** IO **213tr** SS/Bobby Deal/ RealDealPhoto **213b** ISP/Karen Harrison **214tr** IO/Richard Stockton **214b** ISP/Claude Dagenais **215tl** ISP/John Zellmer **215b** JI **UTAH 216tr** IO/FogStock LLC **216br** WI **218cl** LOC **218br** ISP/Jeremy Edwards **219** SS/Natalia Bratslavsky **219tr** SS/phdpsx **219b** IO/FogStock LLC **220t** SS/Rebecca Dickerson **220b** ISP/Rick Hyman **221t** IO/Peter Adams **221b** SS/Natalia Bratslavsky **VERMONT 222bl** WI **222tr** SS/Chee-Onn Leong **222br** ISP/Jan Tyler **224cl** LOC **224tr** ISP/Jan Tyler **224br** ISP/Eldon Griffin **225t** ISP/Jan Tyler **225b** ISP/Stephen Giordano **VIRGINIA 226tr** ISP/Glen Jones **227cl** SS/Richard Slack **227tr** SS/catnap **227c** WI **228cl** WI **228br** ISP/John Keith **228cr** SS/gary lynn moseley **229tr** JI **229bl** WI **WASHINGTON 230tr** SS/Paul Pickett **230br** SS/Joseph Calev **231b** JI **232cl** WI **232br** SS/Katrina Outland **233tr** JI **233bl** JI **233br** IO/Shmuel Thaler **234tr** ISP/Cheryl Triplett **234br** SS/Timothy R. Nichols **236cl** LOC **236c** ISP/Joanna Pecha **236cr** ISP/Eric Foltz **236br** SS/Glenda M. Powers **236cr** ISP/James Pauls **237b** ISP/Robert Pernell **WISCONSIN 238tr** SS/Michael Rolands **238cb** ISP/Timothy Hughes **240cl** WI **240c** SS/Sean/TheShaman **240cr** ISP/Bill Raboin **240br** SS/Travis Klein **241tr** SS/Suzanne Tucker **241bl** SS/Blaine Walulik **WYOMING 242tr** JI **242br** SS/Brian Sallee **243b** SS/Ferenc Cegledi **243cl** LOC **244tl** WI **244br** IO/FogStock LLC **245b** IO/Chris Rogers **245tr** SS/Jonathan Lenz **247bl** JI **247br** JI